CHRONOLOGICAL HISTORY OF THE ROBINSON FAMILY AND THEIR DESCENDANTS

CHRONOLOGICAL HISTORY OF THE ROBINSON FAMILY AND THEIR DESCENDANTS

Abt 1780 - 2014

King & Queen County, Virginia

Researched By:
Robert Lorenzo Lockley

Copyright © 2014 by Robert Lorenzo Lockley.

Library of Congress Control Number:		2014920598
ISBN:	Hardcover	978-1-5035-1807-0
	Softcover	978-1-5035-1809-4
	eBook	978-1-5035-1808-7

All rights reserved. No part of this book may be reproduced or transmitted in any form or by any means, electronic or mechanical, including photocopying, recording, or by any information storage and retrieval system, without permission in writing from the copyright owner.

Any people depicted in stock imagery provided by Thinkstock are models, and such images are being used for illustrative purposes only.
Certain stock imagery © Thinkstock.

Print information available on the last page.

Rev. date: 03/26/2015

To order additional copies of this book, contact:
Xlibris
1-888-795-4274
www.Xlibris.com
Orders@Xlibris.com
677537

CONTENTS

Preface 9

Chapter 1

    Gabriel Robinson 69

Chapter 2

    Kitty Carter 71

Chapter 3

    John Robinson 72

    Melvina Robinson 118

        Thomas Lockley 144

        Earl Lockley 145

        Iverson Lockley 146

        Elmore Lockley 147

        Philip Mckenley Lockley 148

    Dabney Robinson 149

    Dunbar Robinson 152

        Lorenzo Robinson 187

        Ethel Lucy Napper 193

Chapter 4

    Polly Robinson 1803 – 1881 207

Chapter 5

- Lorenzo Dow Robinson 237
- Archibald Robinson 284
- Virginia Robinson 289
  - Robert Oceola Lockley 292
  - Robert Lorenzo Lockley 299
  - Reginald Elwood Lockley 328
  - Harold Preston Lockley 334
- Edith Alyce Lockley 339
- Lorenza C. Lockley 344

Chapter 6

- Rosetta Robinson 348
- Rosie Jane Jordan 396
- George Moses Davenport 400
- John Davenport.. 402

Chapter 7

- Margarett Robinson 407

Chapter 8

- George Robinson 413

Bibliography.. 419

Appendix... 421

Dedication

This work is dedicated with gratitude, to the memory of those great, inspiring and perceptive ancestors who enriched our Lives by paving a path for us to follow.

PREFACE

Background Information to the reader

The information in this book was gathered from information in the census records, order books, wills, Vital Statics and deeds all available at the Virginia Library, Richmond, Va. and the King & Queen County, Va. Court, which provided the basis for this book about a family that lived in King & Queen County, Virginia at a time when being a person of Color came with many restrictions.

According to the 1830 United States Census Grace Mitchell the matriarch of this family was a free woman of color, head of a free family of 11 that included 5 slaves. Although no date of birth is given for her, she would have been born in the late 1700's. This Virginia Family of mixed Ancestry who, through law, luck and enormous hard work and enterprise, escaped the awful fate of so many other like themselves. Slavery has to have been in the history of this family at some point. When did Grace Mitchell become free? The King & Queen County, Va. Personal Property List shows that she was billed I Tithe tax for herself in 1813.

Government in the eighteenth-century Virginia, where this story begins, was modeled on the English system. Each county had a sheriff and a county court with its "gentlemen justices," who sat as judges and had other administrative and legal duties. Under Virginia Law during this period unwed mothers were subjected to a heavy fine and the child was taken from her if she could not prove that she could support the child. This also applied to families who could not support their children. These children were "indentured" to someone willing to care for, train and, in some cases, educate them until they became adults. The period of indenture varied, some to age 18 and others to age 31. If a mother could not pay the fine involved, she, too, was bond out as a servant for several years, with the money from the sale of her indenture applied toward the fine she owed. These indentures were usually to a White Master.

As the result of the Denmark Vesey revolt in 1822 and the Nate Turner rebellion in 1831 all southern states passed and enforced more repressive laws against blacks. In 1830, the Virginia General Assembly passed a variety of laws curtailing free Negroes' the right to assembly, forbade preaching by slaves, free Negroes, or mulattoes at religious meetings. It was forbidden for free people of color to hold any religious meetings during the day or evening. The penalty for violating this was a public whipping of 39 lashes.

This Book contains chapters on the heirs of Grace Mitchell, some family documents included as appendices. I hope that the information in this book answers questions that relatives may have about our family. If not it should provide a foundation for future research.

This Family was true "free persons of color". There is no record of slavery being a part of their lives except as an inconvenience. Although depicted in the press of that time as being debased, lazy individuals, burdens to society. Although discriminated against, and restricted by law, they survived.

This is the story of one family that survived in spite of these restrictions.

CHRONOLOGICAL HISTORY OF THE ROBINSON FAMILY

For a family historian, writing a chronological history of a family from a county with many missing or otherwise scattered records affords a challenge as exciting as it is daunting. When I traveled the county roads during my many trips to the King & Queen County, Court House, I always felt that there didn't seem to be much change in the county physically from its appearance during years past. After leaving route 33 heading to the Court House, there were no stores or gas stations, nothing but farms and woodland for mile after mile.

The Matriarch of the Robinson family (Grace Mitchell) first appears in the 1830 United States Federal Census as a free colored female, head of a household that consists of:

1830 United States Federal Census	
Name:	Grace Mitchell
Home in 1830 (City, County, State):	King and Queen, Virginia
Free Colored Persons - Males - 10 thru 23:	2
Free Colored Persons - Males - 24 thru 35:	1
Free Colored Persons - Females - 10 thru 23:	2
Free Colored Persons - Females - 55 thru 99:	1
Slaves - Males - Under 10:	3
Slaves - Males - 36 thru 54:	2
Total Slaves:	5
Total Free Colored Persons:	6
Total - All Persons (Free White, Slaves, Free Colored):	11

The 1840 Federal Census consists of the following:

1840 United States Federal Census	
Name:	**Grace Mitchell**
Home in 1840 (City, County, State):	King and Queen, Virginia
Free Colored Persons - Females - 10 thru 23:	1
Free Colored Persons - Females - 55 thru 99:	1
Slaves - Males - 10 thru 23:	1
Slaves - Males - 55 thru 99:	1
Slaves - Females - 10 thru 23:	1
Slaves - Females - 55 thru 99:	1
Persons Employed in Agriculture:	4
Total Free Colored Persons:	2
Total Slaves:	4
Total All Persons - Free White, Free Colored, Slaves:	6

Free blacks, who had been allowed to own slaves before 1832, were prohibited after 1835 from acquiring any more slaves, except spouses, children, or those gained "by descent.' After 1857 free blacks were prohibited from acquiring family members as well. Because most slave holding free blacks involved the purchase of family members in order to assure their protection (and their eventual freedom), this last restriction was considered particularly oppressive.

The Federal Census for the 1830 & 1840 years were among those that only listed the names of Heads of Households. Other documents were necessary to identify the children of Grace Mitchell. One such document was a list of Free Negroes and Mulattoes, 1833 King & Queen County, found in the County Commissioner of Accounts Records.

This document listed Grace Mitchell as a land owner with the following children: Lorenzo Robinson, John R. Robinson, Dew Robinson, George Robinson, Peggy Robinson and Rose Robinson.

> **A List of Free Negroes and Mulattoes, 1833**
> **King and Queen County**
>
> *A List of Free Negroes and mulattoes in the County of King and Queen this year 1833, their names, ages, place of abode, particular trades, occupations, etc.*
>
> The list was found in the Commissioner of Accounts records for King and Queen County and is transcribed here by VLH Davis. While presented in the record in columnar form, each name will be followed with the identifying information conforming to the categories previously listed. The double underline approximates the underlining that seems to designate family groupings, or individuals not a part of a family group. While the writing is uniform and precise, it is very difficult to read. Interested researchers should consult the original for verification.
>
> **Bob Mitchell**; male; Daniel Watts land; Farmer
> **Kitt Lockley**; male; John Carlton (miller); Farmer
> **Polly Lockley**; female; wife of said Kitt and with him; Spinner
> Grace Mitchell; female; Own land; Farming
> John R. Robinson; male; Ditcher
> Lorenzo, Dew; male; sons of Grace Mitchell and with her; Farming
> Geo. Robinson; male; ditto
> Peggy Robinson; female; daughters of Grace Mitchell
> **Rose Robinson**; female; and with her
> Sam Kauffman; male; George Cardwells land; Farmer
> Lucy Kauffman; female; wife of said Sam and with him; Spinner
> George Kauffman; male; son of said Sam & Lucy and with Kitt Lockley
> Euclid, James, John; male; children of said Sam and Lucy
> **Parks & Polly**; female; and with them
> Jenny Sea; female; Beverly Waltons Estate; Spinner
> Margaret, Ann; female; children of said Jenny and with her
> John, Walker, Is.; male; ditto
> **William**; male; son of Jenny and living with Ransom Harris, Jr
> Jemy Day; male; Beverly Waltons Estate; Ditcher
> **Betty Day**; female; wife of said Jemy and with him; Spinner
> Caty Carter; female; Isaac Waltons; Spinner
> Polly, Grace, Hetty; female; children of said Caty and with her
> **John, Nat, William**; male; ditto
> Patty Freeman; female; with Ann Fleet; Spinner
> Jinand; male; son of said Patty and living with Wm B. Fleet
> Daniel, Telemaishus & Loraxo; male; children of said Patty
> Polly; female; and living with her
> Sally Kidd; female; New Church; Farming
> John Kidd; male; son of Sally and with her; Farming
> William Kidd; male; ditto
> Polly Kidd; female; Paul Phillips land; Wood cutting
> Maria, Sarah, Polly, Elizabeth; female; children of Polly
> **James**; male; and living with her
> Elizabeth Kidd; female; on Henry Wares Land (Very old)
> **Humphrey Kidd**; male; George Morris Land; Farming
> Peter Meggs; male; about Centerville; Ditcher, etc.
> Mariah Hickman; female; Vincent Harts Estate; Spinner
> Mary; female; children of said Maria
> **Tom, James**; male; and with her
> **Hannah Williams**; female; Frank Kidds
>
> This is the first record showing any children of Grace Mitchell by name

By 1847 Grace Mitchell was deceased. On May 10, 1847 a suite is filed against Benjamin Hart, deceased to resolve a land transaction in Grace Mitchell deceased against the heirs of Benjamin Hart deceased. The suit was filed by the following heirs of Grace Mitchell: John Robinson, Lorenzo Robinson, George Robinson, Gabriel Robinson, Margaret Robinson, Rosetta Robinson, Polly Robinson and Kitty Robinson.

Suit by the Heirs of Grace Mitchell, Deceased against the Heirs of Benjamin Hart, deceased for land purchased by Grace Mitchell on the 12th of July 1842. Suite dated May 10, 1849. Page 290. Chancery Order Book. King & Queen County, Va. 1831-58

From these documents and events the identity of the children and heirs of Grace Mitchell was established, although I was unable to determine why her children had the Robertson surname in the 1850 Federal Census and the Robinson Surname in all subsequent records, attempts to answer those questions are ongoing.

Another complication was caused by the Laws of Virginia during this period. Slaves could not legally marry, and even free Negroes and Mulattoes often found it almost impossible to get married in legally recognized ceremonies, as the marriage laws of Virginia were not held to apply. Because of this many white licensed ministers were not willing to perform marriage ceremonies for Negroes. Most Negroes, slave or free, married by having their own ceremonies or agreements, whether casual or elaborate.

With social, legal, and economic practices stacked against them, most free Negroes remained impoverished. Considering the paltry sums that even skilled women earned for their work, it is not surprising that among free people, women of color were at the bottom of the economic hierarchy. In Grace Mitchell's case, however, financial frugality and business acumen defied the rule.

In August 1993 Barbara Beigun Kaplan, PhD, wrote a book titled Land and Heritage in the Virginia Tidewater, a History of King & Queen County. In this book she identified Grace Mitchell as one of the few black women to own property in this period, she owned 485 Acres of land between 1839 and 1844. This property was eventually sold to Lorenzo and John Robinson, who divided it among their own heirs.

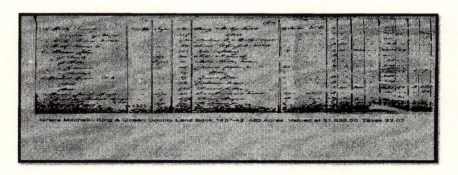

Kinship Report for Grace Mitchell

Name:	Birth Date:	Relationship:
Mitchell, Grace	Abt. 1780	Self
Robinson, John	1800	Son
Robinson, Lorenzo D.	1810	Son
Robinson, Gabriel	1798	Son
Robinson, George	1828	Son
Robinson, Polly	1803	Daughter
Robinson, Rosetta	1815	Daughter
Robinson, Kitty		Daughter
Robinson, Margaret	1820	Daughter
Robinson, Charley	1871	Grandson
Robinson, Archibald	1837	Grandson
Robinson, Cornelius	1849	Grandson
Robinson, Clarence	1858	Grandson
Kauffman, Jeremia	1834	Grandson
Kauffman, James	1829	Grandson
Kauffman, Richard	1851	Grandson
Kauffman, John	1823	Grandson
Robinson, Lewis J.	1860	Grandson
Robinson, Joseph	1854	Grandson
Robinson, William	1865	Grandson
Robinson, Moses	1872	Grandson
Robinson, Dunbar	1834	Grandson
Robinson, Dabney	1835	Grandson
Robinson, John Jr.	1842	Grandson
Robinson, James	1851	Grandson
Harris, Calvert	1841	Grandson

Bluefoot, Isiah	1857	Grandson
Robinson, Margarett	1841	Granddaughter
Robinson, Lucy J.	1880	Granddaughter
Robinson, Martha H.	14 Mar 1874	Granddaughter
Robinson, Maria S.	11 Nov 1872	Granddaughter
Robinson, Letha J	1878	Granddaughter
Robinson, Lecter	1873	Granddaughter
Gilmore, Fanny Ellen	1843	Granddaughter
Robinson, Lucy	1843	Granddaughter
Robinson, Lilly O.	1871	Granddaughter
Robinson, Mary A.	1864	Granddaughter
Robinson, Roberta	1869	Granddaughter
Robinson, Rebecca	1877	Granddaughter
Robinson, Sarah T.	1868	Granddaughter
Kauffman, Henrietta	1836	Granddaughter
Robinson, Virginia	1880	Granddaughter
Robinson, Matilda A.	1854	Granddaughter
Robinson, Mary E.	1864	Granddaughter
Robinson, Melvina	1849	Granddaughter
Robinson, Pinky	1840	Granddaughter
Bluefoot, Polly Ann	07 Apr 1853	Granddaughter
Robinson, Leah	1875	Granddaughter
Jordan, Priscilla	1852	Granddaughter
Jordan, Sarah J.	1849	Granddaughter
Robinson, Catherine	1843	Granddaughter
Jordan, Lucy	1845	Granddaughter
Jordan, Maria Irena	1851	Granddaughter
Kauffman, Catherine	1842	Granddaughter

Kauffman, Grace	1845	Granddaughter
Kauffman, Martha Ellen	1839	Granddaughter
Kauffman, Phillis Ann	1849	Granddaughter
Kauffman, Mary Francis	1832	Granddaughter
Gilmore, Sarah Jane	1849	Granddaughter
Robinson, Georgiana	1867	Granddaughter
Robinson, Jane	1848	Granddaughter
Gilmore, Harriett T	1847	Granddaughter
Gilmore, Lucy Ann	1845	Granddaughter
Harris, Margarett	1842	Granddaughter
Harris, Quitta	1847	Granddaughter
Robinson, Elizabeth	1847	Granddaughter
Robinson, Fannie E.	1866	Granddaughter
Robinson, Emeline	1838	Granddaughter
Lee, William	1867	Great grandson
Lockley, Christopher C.	1877	Great grandson
Lee, James		Great grandson
Lee, John R.	1868	Great grandson
Lockley, James Beverly	12 May 1875	Great grandson
Lockley, Knox	1883	Great grandson
Lockley, Columbus	07 Sep 1878	Great grandson
Lockley, Jack	1868	Great grandson
Robinson, Lorenzo	1868	Great grandson
Robinson, Robert S.	1912	Great grandson
Robinson, Richard	1900	Great grandson
Robinson, Stanley	1908	Great grandson
Robinson, Sam	1907	Great grandson
Kauffman, Robert	1860	Great grandson

Kauffman, William T.	1853	Great grandson
Robinson, Isaiah P.	1865	Great grandson
Kauffman, Robert	1860	Great grandson
Lockley, Lorenzo C.	1909	Great grandson
Robinson, John Thomas	1873	Great grandson
Robinson, John Caleb	02 Dec 1873	Great grandson
Robinson, Joseph	1910	Great grandson
Robinson, Brown	1915	Great grandson
Robinson, George T.	1902	Great grandson
Robinson, James A.	1870	Great grandson
Robinson, John	1901	Great grandson
Robinson, James E.	1909	Great grandson
Robinson, Alfred G.	1888	Great grandson
Lockley, Thomas	1870	Great grandson
Robinson, Jr Moses	1905	Great grandson
Lockley, Robert	1875	Great grandson
Lockley, Robert Oceola	12 Aug 1905	Great grandson
Mardin, Russell	1908	Great grandson
Robinson, Alfred G.	1888	Great grandson
Mardin, Everett	1906	Great grandson
Robinson, Joshua Dunbar	1879	Great grandson
Kauffman, John E.	1855	Great grandson
West, Harvey Holder	Jan 1882	Great grandson
Warner, Lorenzo	13 Nov 1913	Great grandson
Collins, William Archie	1878	Great grandson
Jordan, Samuel Isiah	22 Feb 1891	Great grandson
Kauffman, Elias	1862	Great grandson
Harris, Bernard U.	14 Mar 1917	Great grandson

West, Howard T.	Mar 1896	Great grandson
Jordan, Ethan Allen	14 May 1896	Great grandson
West, Edward W.	Jul 1898	Great grandson
Henderson, Henry		Great grandson
Jordan, George Franklin	Feb 1883	Great grandson
Jordan, John Kelly	18 Feb 1885	Great grandson
Jordan, James Elijah	1880	Great grandson
Jordan, James Albert	1871	Great grandson
Warner, Granville	29 Oct 1909	Great grandson
Collins, Elias	1869	Great grandson
Robinson, Nathan P.	1876	Great grandson
Williams, James A.	1873	Great grandson
Collins, George Mason	1876	Great grandson
Kauffman, Jeremia Jr.	1866	Great grandson
Jordan, William Thomas	15 May 1882	Great grandson
Kauffman, James H.	1859	Great grandson
Kauffman, Jeremia Jr.	1866	Great grandson
Robinson, William	1907	Great grandson
Warner, Clifford	01 Jan 1911	Great grandson
Warner, Charles	1918	Great grandson
Collins, Llewelyn		Great grandson
West, Laura	Aug 1879	Great granddaughter
West, Matcade	1870	Great granddaughter
Williams, Polly	1872	Great granddaughter
West, Josephine	Nov 1878	Great granddaughter
Williams, Catherine A.	1870	Great granddaughter
West, Gertrude	Mar 1895	Great granddaughter
Robinson, Josephine	1917	Great granddaughter

Robinson, Marian	1901	Great granddaughter
Robinson, Margaret	1882	Great granddaughter
Robinson, Margaret	1882	Great granddaughter
Robinson, Virginia	1898	Great granddaughter
Robinson, Tressie J.	1896	Great granddaughter
Robinson, Victoria	1866	Great granddaughter
Robinson, Othena	1906	Great granddaughter
Robinson, Luvanna	1838	Great granddaughter
Warner, Helen	09 Dec 1910	Great granddaughter
Robinson, Julie A.	1836	Great granddaughter
Robinson, Julia	1913	Great granddaughter
Robinson, Julie A.	1836	Great granddaughter
Robinson, Lida W.	1898	Great granddaughter
Robinson, Leburta	1896	Great granddaughter
Robinson, Ketuia	1857	Great granddaughter
Robinson, Helen	1904	Great granddaughter
Kauffman, Elvira	1865	Great granddaughter
Kauffman, Esperilla	1856	Great granddaughter
Kauffman, Elvira	1865	Great granddaughter
Kauffman, Elizabeth J.	1859	Great granddaughter
Kauffman, Elizabeth J.	1959	Great granddaughter
Kauffman, Esterrilla	1856	Great granddaughter
Kauffman, Matilda Ellen	1868	Great granddaughter
Kauffman, Miriam A.	1853	Great granddaughter
Kauffman, Matilda Ellen	1868	Great granddaughter
Kauffman, Mary F.	1847	Great granddaughter
Kauffman, Mary F.	1848	Great granddaughter
Jordan, Rosie Jane	10 Jan 1878	Great granddaughter

Collins, Martha J.	1871	Great granddaughter
Collins, Mary Alice	1869	Great granddaughter
Collins, Leander		Great granddaughter
Collins, Atta	1867	Great granddaughter
Collins, Ida		Great granddaughter
Collins, Mary E.	1876	Great granddaughter
Holmes, Mabel	1896	Great granddaughter
Jordan, Lucy	1878	Great granddaughter
Gatewood, Mary E.	1874	Great granddaughter
Collins, Sarah C.	1876	Great granddaughter
Collins, Sarah Louise	1884	Great granddaughter
Robinson, Ann Eliza	1867	Great granddaughter
Robinson, Annie May	1903	Great granddaughter
Mardin, Mary C.	1903	Great granddaughter
Lockley, Milly	1874	Great granddaughter
Lockley-White-Bell, Edith Alyce	1907	Great granddaughter
Robinson, Emma	1883	Great granddaughter
Robinson, Harriet	1879	Great granddaughter
Robinson, Harriet	1879	Great granddaughter
Robinson, Fatima	1868	Great granddaughter
Robinson, Fannie E.	1885	Great granddaughter
Robinson, Fannie E.	1885	Great granddaughter
Lockley, Goalder	1876	Great granddaughter
Kauffman, Pinky	1869	Great granddaughter
Kauffman, Pinky	1869	Great granddaughter
Kauffman, Pinky	1862	Great granddaughter
Kauffman, Mirian	1853	Great granddaughter
Kauffman, Pinkie E.	1862	Great granddaughter

Kauffman, Sarah J.	1850	Great granddaughter
Lee, Nancy		Great granddaughter
Lee, Rose	1869	Great granddaughter
Lee, Mary A.	1865	Great granddaughter
Lee, Daisy		Great granddaughter
Lee, Lillian		Great granddaughter
Jordan, Herbert Nathaniel	03 Jun 1928	2nd great grandson
McDonald, Robert	1911	2nd great grandson
Jordan, Henry Clay	31 Jul 1923	2nd great grandson
Jordan, Herbert Lee		2nd great grandson
Jordan, James Thomas	24 Feb 1926	2nd great grandson
Jordan, Larry		2nd great grandson
Lockley, Warner	1923	2nd great grandson
Jordan, John Hollis	08 Mar 1917	2nd great grandson
Jordan, John Mark	04 Jul 1920	2nd great grandson
Patterson, James H.	1910	2nd great grandson
Patterson, James H.	1910	2nd great grandson
Jordan, Burnett Allen	01 Nov 1921	2nd great grandson
Patterson, John A.	1908	2nd great grandson
Jordan, Doxie Alfonza	27 Jul 1932	2nd great grandson
McDonald, Robert	1911	2nd great grandson
Jordan, George Wilbur	18 Mar 1921	2nd great grandson
Patterson, Albert M.	1925	2nd great grandson
Patterson, Albert M.	1925	2nd great grandson
Lockley, Walnut	1920	2nd great grandson
Lockley, Philip McKenley	16 Jan 1917	2nd great grandson
Lockley, Clarence	1894	2nd great grandson
Jordan, William Robert	14 Sep 1914	2nd great grandson

Lockley, Reginald Elwood	29 Aug 1933	2nd great grandson
Lockley, Earl	03 Dec 1911	2nd great grandson
Lockley, Harold Preston	18 Aug 1937	2nd great grandson
Lockley, James B. Jr.	1919	2nd great grandson
Lockley, Elmore	30 Apr 1918	2nd great grandson
Lockley, John	1895	2nd great grandson
Jordan, Rexford	28 Mar 1917	2nd great grandson
Jordan, Robert Nathan	04 Jan 1926	2nd great grandson
Jordan, Morvitz Sinclair	14 Mar 1930	2nd great grandson
Jordan, Oliver Wendell	1908	2nd great grandson
Jordan, Roscoe Samuel	15 Jun 1916	2nd great grandson
Lockley, Robert Lewis	10 Dec 1910	2nd great grandson
Jordan, William Preston	22 May 1914	2nd great grandson
Lockley, Sr Iverson	22 Jul 1930	2nd great grandson
Lockley, Robert Lorenzo	19 Nov 1931	2nd great grandson
Patterson, John A.	1908	2nd great grandson
Robinson, Clarence	1905	2nd great grandson
Davenport, John Thomas	1870	2nd great grandson
Jordan, Thomas A.	06 Sep 1918	2nd great grandson
Robinson, Chancellor D.	1904	2nd great grandson
Patterson, William	1919	2nd great grandson
Davenport, Robert L.T.	31 Mar 1910	2nd great grandson
Patterson, William	1919	2nd great grandson
Davenport, George Moses	10 Sep 1913	2nd great grandson
Robinson, Wilbur	1899	2nd great grandson
Brown, James E.	1931	2nd great grandson
Robinson, Willie	1909	2nd great grandson
Robinson, Orrin Blide	1916	2nd great grandson

Robinson, Jr John C.	1913	2nd great grandson
Davenport, Elijah	25 Jun 1917	2nd great grandson
Brown, Roger	1938	2nd great grandson
Dungey, Thomas R.	1905	2nd great grandson
Jordan, Austin Douglas	13 Sep 1913	2nd great grandson
Green, Russell	1924	2nd great grandson
Green, Moses	1935	2nd great grandson
Dungey, Wilbore O.	1910	2nd great grandson
Dungey, Rudyard K.	1916	2nd great grandson
Dungey, Herbert W.	1914	2nd great grandson
Dungey, Lwellen C.	1908	2nd great grandson
Dungey, Louell L.	1912	2nd great grandson
Patterson, Prisallie P.	1921	2nd great granddaughter
Lockley, Ollin	1925	2nd great granddaughter
Lockley, Olima	1917	2nd great granddaughter
Patterson, Ethel	1912	2nd great granddaughter
Lockley, Pearl Virginia	10 Apr 1921	2nd great granddaughter
Robinson, Edith Madeline	1901	2nd great granddaughter
Lockley, Martha	1907	2nd great granddaughter
Lockley, Landonia	1908	2nd great granddaughter
Lockley, Nora	1899	2nd great granddaughter
T. Jordan, Thelma	05 Apr 1915	2nd great granddaughter
Lockley, Nancy Mary	26 Aug 1929	2nd great granddaughter
Lockley, Thersa	1918	2nd great granddaughter
Robinson, Ethel Irene	15 Mar 1912	2nd great granddaughter
Robinson, Eva Ladocia	1906	2nd great granddaughter
Patterson, Sarah	1914	2nd great granddaughter
Robinson, Anna Bessie	1908	2nd great granddaughter

Patterson, Sarah	1914	2nd great granddaughter
Robinson, Cora L.	1915	2nd great granddaughter
Robinson, Margaret D.	1902	2nd great granddaughter
Robinson, Maud	1903	2nd great granddaughter
Lockley, Phillis	1919	2nd great granddaughter
Patterson, Prisallie P.	1921	2nd great granddaughter
Lockley, Ruth	09 Jul 1925	2nd great granddaughter
Robinson, Gladys M.	1916	2nd great granddaughter
Patterson, Ethel	1912	2nd great granddaughter
Davenport, Pearl Jane	26 Jan 1908	2nd great granddaughter
Dungey, Garnett E.	1919	2nd great granddaughter
Dungey, Mary U.	1907	2nd great granddaughter
Davenport, Luvenia Ann	16 Jun 1902	2nd great granddaughter
Davenport, Mary Frances	18 Aug 1916	2nd great granddaughter
Davenport, Missouri Olivia	08 Aug 1921	2nd great granddaughter
Jordan, Bertha Edna	24 Apr 1931	2nd great granddaughter
Jordan, Catherine	12 Nov 1915	2nd great granddaughter
Jordan, Catherine	1919	2nd great granddaughter
Dungey, Thelma G.	1903	2nd great granddaughter
Green, Edna	1937	2nd great granddaughter
Green, Evelyn	1933	2nd great granddaughter
Brown, Lillian	1923	2nd great granddaughter
Collins, Ada		2nd great granddaughter
Collins, Lilly		2nd great granddaughter
Brown, Constance	1934	2nd great granddaughter
Brown, Elenora M.	1925	2nd great granddaughter
Brown, Lelia	1924	2nd great granddaughter
Davenport, Helen M.	Apr 1901	2nd great granddaughter

Davenport, Hyburnies N.	05 Nov 1906	2nd great granddaughter
Davenport, Lillian E.	20 May 1919	2nd great granddaughter
Davenport, Ella Bertha	21 Jun 1903	2nd great granddaughter
Davenport, Etha Irene	07 Jan 1912	2nd great granddaughter
Davenport, Hattie B.	21 Aug 1904	2nd great granddaughter
Jordan, Cressa Erlene		2nd great granddaughter
Lockley, Alice Lillian	10 Aug 1932	2nd great granddaughter
Lockley, Anna B.	1905	2nd great granddaughter
Lockley, Catherine	1911	2nd great granddaughter
Jordan, Viola	1921	2nd great granddaughter
Kidd, Lizzie	1916	2nd great granddaughter
Lockley, Aburtia	1909	2nd great granddaughter
Lockley, Emmalyn	1928	2nd great granddaughter
Lockley, Ethel	1914	2nd great granddaughter
Lockley, Eva	1909	2nd great granddaughter
Lockley, Celia	1911	2nd great granddaughter
Lockley, Eliza	1898	2nd great granddaughter
Lockley, Ellen	1912	2nd great granddaughter
Jordan, Fannie Vernell	16 Dec 1923	2nd great granddaughter
Jordan, Florentine Melanie	24 Jun 1909	2nd great granddaughter
Jordan, Ida B.	Oct 1913	2nd great granddaughter
Jordan, Dorothy Nadine	05 Jan 1920	2nd great granddaughter
Jordan, Elizabeth Maurice	05 Feb 1936	2nd great granddaughter
Jordan, Evelyn Ruth	14 Jul 1924	2nd great granddaughter
Jordan, Ruth Esther	11 Apr 1913	2nd great granddaughter
Jordan, Sarah Beatrice	13 Jul 1918	2nd great granddaughter
Brown, Bertha	1928	2nd great granddaughter
Jordan, Lillian Juanita	16 Jan 1923	2nd great granddaughter

Name	Date	Relationship
Jordan, Mary Celestine	01 Jan 1939	2nd great granddaughter
Jordan, Olivia Elizabeth	18 Jan 1928	2nd great granddaughter
Jordan, Jr John H.	01 Jul 1946	3rd great grandson
Jordan, Jr Morvitz S.	05 Feb 1950	3rd great grandson
Reed, Walter Perry	02 Mar 1939	3rd great grandson
Jordan, Jr Doxie A.	27 Jun 1969	3rd great grandson
Jordan, Keith	31 Jan 1953	3rd great grandson
Peterson, Warren L.	22 Mar 1938	3rd great grandson
Peterson, Russell	14 Sep 1940	3rd great grandson
Jordan, Keith Vincent	09 Jul 1960	3rd great grandson
Jordan, Larry	30 Sep 1955	3rd great grandson
Jordan, George W.	16 Oct 1963	3rd great grandson
Jordan, Carl		3rd great grandson
Jordan, Daymon		3rd great grandson
Smith, James Robert	13 Aug 1958	3rd great grandson
Jordan, Bryant Clifton	16 Nov 1959	3rd great grandson
Jordan, Deotis	27 Jul 1974	3rd great grandson
Jordan, Franklin N.	22 Nov 1939	3rd great grandson
Jordan, Garry Maxwell		3rd great grandson
Jordan, Eric N.	08 Jul 1950	3rd great grandson
Richardson, Kyle	02 Apr 1966	3rd great grandson
Palmes, Walter	1928	3rd great grandson
Napper, Wilbur James	22 Sep 1935	3rd great grandson
Peterson, Daniel E.	08 Oct 1936	3rd great grandson
Lewis, Don Kenrick	28 Jul 1951	3rd great grandson
Napper, Issac B. II	02 Apr 1934	3rd great grandson
Lockley, Jr Iverson	03 Dec 1958	3rd great grandson
Lockley, Robert Lorenzo Jr.	22 Jan 1960	3rd great grandson

Lockley, Elmore Jr.	08 Nov 1953	3rd great grandson
Lockley, Harold Preston Jr.	18 Jan 1962	3rd great grandson
Jordan, W. Franklin	03 Feb 1941	3rd great grandson
Jordan, Montez		3rd great grandson
Peterson, Robert T.	24 Apr 1948	3rd great grandson
Jordan, Lawrence D.	07 Jul 1953	3rd great grandson
Jordan, Leon G.	08 May 1951	3rd great grandson
Jordan, Preston Garest	15 Jul 1943	3rd great grandson
Jordan, Thomas		3rd great grandson
Jordan, Vincent		3rd great grandson
Jordan, Robert M.	03 Sep 1952	3rd great grandson
Jordan, Samuel T.	15 Feb 1942	3rd great grandson
Thornton, Thomas M.	02 Jul 1945	3rd great grandson
Baylor, Gordon	02 Jul 1951	3rd great grandson
Davenport, James	05 Mar 1943	3rd great grandson
Davenport, John	02 May 1937	3rd great grandson
Thornton, Edward S.	20 Nov 1969	3rd great grandson
Dickens, Derrick A.	19 Aug 1964	3rd great grandson
Thornton, Brian Ethan	25 Oct 1974	3rd great grandson
Davenport, Philbert	26 Aug 1952	3rd great grandson
Davenport, Robert L.T.	31 Mar 1910	3rd great grandson
Baylor, Timothy	23 May 1954	3rd great grandson
Ward, Juan G.	20 Nov 1968	3rd great grandson
Wormley, Allen	28 Jul 1939	3rd great grandson
White, Verdell	05 Nov 1949	3rd great grandson
Brokenborough, Toney	02 Oct 1953	3rd great grandson
Thornton, William B.	07 Jan 1939	3rd great grandson
Davenport, George Moses	10 Sep 1913	3rd great grandson

Ward, Joseph T.	22 Aug 1963	3rd great grandson
Ward, Duane M.	14 Jul 1966	3rd great grandson
Terry, Michael		3rd great grandson
Helm, Cappie	1955	3rd great grandson
Guest, Jerome	11 Sep 1942	3rd great grandson
Guest, George	19 Sep 1941	3rd great grandson
Thornton, John R.	30 Jan 1937	3rd great grandson
Taylor, Jr Nathaniel	28 Apr 1957	3rd great grandson
Smith, Thomas Edward	15 Aug 1960	3rd great grandson
Taylor, William	19 Mar 1959	3rd great grandson
Guest, Cecil	27 Sep 1946	3rd great grandson
Jordan, Anthony	11 Nov 1966	3rd great grandson
Taylor, Welford	19 Mar 1959	3rd great grandson
Smith, Lucy Ellen	10 Sep 1963	3rd great granddaughter
Ward, Rene	24 Aug 1965	3rd great granddaughter
Wormley, Joan	27 Feb 1941	3rd great granddaughter
Smith, Mary Ann	05 Sep 1959	3rd great granddaughter
Napper, Ethel Lucy	24 Feb 1930	3rd great granddaughter
Napper, Edith Irene	19 Jun 1931	3rd great granddaughter
Lockley, Zelda	23 Oct 1949	3rd great granddaughter
Lockley, Robin Laverne	24 May 1956	3rd great granddaughter
Smith, Linda Ruth	20 Jan 1968	3rd great granddaughter
Napper, Anna	1932	3rd great granddaughter
Morrow, Charosangina L.	24 Nov 1963	3rd great granddaughter
Smith, Alice May	31 Aug 1961	3rd great granddaughter
Taylor, Marilyn	06 Aug 1960	3rd great granddaughter
Peterson, Margaret	02 Feb 1945	3rd great granddaughter
Peterson, Gwendolyn D.	29 Apr 1951	3rd great granddaughter

Thornton, Carol Maxann	28 Dec 1941	3rd great granddaughter
Reed, Rosetta	30 Mar 1931	3rd great granddaughter
Thornton, Thelma J.	02 Jan 1938	3rd great granddaughter
Roye, Joyce	04 Jul 1947	3rd great granddaughter
Ward, Aleta M.	03 Dec 1957	3rd great granddaughter
Saugling, Sandra	1969	3rd great granddaughter
Taylor, Cheryl	30 Apr 1958	3rd great granddaughter
Peterson, Ellen J.	03 Dec 1933	3rd great granddaughter
Peterson, Edna E.	05 Sep 1942	3rd great granddaughter
Reed, Mary	29 Nov 1936	3rd great granddaughter
Guest, Deborah	28 May 1948	3rd great granddaughter
Guest, Diane	03 May 1950	3rd great granddaughter
Jordan, A. Cassell	14 Jun 1953	3rd great granddaughter
Davenport, Shirley	06 Dec 1940	3rd great granddaughter
Glover, Regenia Elizabeth	29 Aug 1961	3rd great granddaughter
Glover, Rhonda Elaine	13 Aug 1964	3rd great granddaughter
Jordan, Avery Miles	08 Dec 1963	3rd great granddaughter
Jordan, Barbara	15 Jul 1945	3rd great granddaughter
Jordan, Barbara O.	26 May 1945	3rd great granddaughter
Jordan, Alberetta		3rd great granddaughter
Jordan, Arlena		3rd great granddaughter
Jordan, Arlette	18 Dec 1951	3rd great granddaughter
Davenport, Pearl Jane	26 Jan 1908	3rd great granddaughter
Baylor, Ruthie B.	08 Aug 1949	3rd great granddaughter
Bright, Linda Pearl	09 Sep 1958	3rd great granddaughter
Davenport, Cheryl	10 Dec 1953	3rd great granddaughter
Baylor, Joan B.	13 Jul 1950	3rd great granddaughter
Baylor, Kathy	18 Mar 1961	3rd great granddaughter

Baylor, Linda	07 Jul 1952	3rd great granddaughter
Davenport, Lillian E.	20 May 1919	3rd great granddaughter
Davenport, Luvenia Ann	16 Jun 1902	3rd great granddaughter
Davenport, Missouri Olivia	08 Aug 1921	3rd great granddaughter
Davenport, Cynthia	25 Jul 1957	3rd great granddaughter
Davenport, Ella Bertha	21 Jun 1903	3rd great granddaughter
Davenport, Etha Irene	07 Jan 1912	3rd great granddaughter
Lewis, Donna W.	02 Feb 1949	3rd great granddaughter
Lockley, Ashley Clarice	24 Dec 1986	3rd great granddaughter
Lockley, Deloise	20 Jan 1940	3rd great granddaughter
Jordan, Silvia	08 Apr 1952	3rd great granddaughter
Jordan, Stephanie A.	11 Feb 1962	3rd great granddaughter
Jordan, Wanda		3rd great granddaughter
Lockley, Jacqueline	13 Oct 1948	3rd great granddaughter
Lockley, Monice Anita	30 Nov 1960	3rd great granddaughter
Lockley, Queen	04 Aug 1942	3rd great granddaughter
Lockley, Diane	27 Jul 1947	3rd great granddaughter
Lockley, Elmyrth	08 Mar 1948	3rd great granddaughter
Lockley, Iasha Dee	21 Nov 1981	3rd great granddaughter
Jordan, Rowena K.	14 Mar 1958	3rd great granddaughter
Jordan, Dorothy Lee	27 Sep 1952	3rd great granddaughter
Jordan, Eva P.	10 Jan 1944	3rd great granddaughter
Jordan, Glynis L.	31 Jan 1957	3rd great granddaughter
Jordan, Brenda		3rd great granddaughter
Jordan, Cynthia R.	11 Jan 1945	3rd great granddaughter
Jordan, Deborah A.	08 Apr 1955	3rd great granddaughter
Jordan, Laverne	12 Nov 1942	3rd great granddaughter
Jordan, Morvika D.	27 Aug 1970	3rd great granddaughter

Jordan, Regena	07 Jul 1953	3rd great granddaughter
Jordan, Joyce A.	13 Oct 1942	3rd great granddaughter
Jordan, Julia Pauline	05 Nov 1944	3rd great granddaughter
Jordan, Lasandra C.	16 Jul 1948	3rd great granddaughter
Mathews, Jr Oliver Lee	13 May 1967	4th great grandson
M. Hall, Manolo	28 Dec 2011	4th great grandson
Lockley, William James	25 Jan 1971	4th great grandson
Mathews, Kenneth	07 Aug 1969	4th great grandson
Miller, Ryan Andrew	19 May 1979	4th great grandson
Miller, Parrish Daneon	09 Jan 1983	4th great grandson
Miller, Earl Lee-Andrew III	17 Aug 1981	4th great grandson
Lockley, Demitruis Anthony	23 Dec 1972	4th great grandson
Lockley, David Elmore	07 Jul 1985	4th great grandson
Lockley, Clarance	11 Sep 1964	4th great grandson
Lockley, Harold Nyree	16 Sep 1985	4th great grandson
Young, Arron Lockley	15 Oct 1986	4th great grandson
Lockley, Robert Lorenzo III	12 Oct 1988	4th great grandson
Lockley, Nathaniel	23 Dec 1962	4th great grandson
Napper, Carl		4th great grandson
Smith, Richard Edward	06 Jul 1983	4th great grandson
Smith, Bryan Nicholas	19 Oct 1997	4th great grandson
Smith, Jr James Robert	09 Apr 1982	4th great grandson
Smith, Royal	23 Mar 1966	4th great grandson
Taliferro, Martin Jr	11 Jan 1978	4th great grandson
Taliferro, Adam	20 Dec 1981	4th great grandson
Stewart, Isaac Evans	22 Mar 1982	4th great grandson
Napper, Jr Wilbur James	23 Jun 1958	4th great grandson
Napper, John	21 May 1966	4th great grandson

Napper, Issac III	09 Jan 1969	4th great grandson
Peterson, Daniel	08 Aug 1974	4th great grandson
Scott, Jr Richard	08 Jul 1968	4th great grandson
Reed, Walter Perry	02 Mar 1939	4th great grandson
Peterson, William	07 Nov 1980	4th great grandson
Johnson, Dow Lorenzo	09 Mar 1951	4th great grandson
Davenport, Wayne	16 Sep 1958	4th great grandson
Guest, Cecil	27 Sep 1946	4th great grandson
Davenport, John Patrick	10 Dec 1956	4th great grandson
Johnson, Dartaniel Henry	25 Jan 1953	4th great grandson
Guest, George	19 Sep 1941	4th great grandson
Guest, Jerome	11 Sep 1942	4th great grandson
Davis, Waymon William	30 Jun 1999	4th great grandson
Johnson, Derward John	01 Feb 1952	4th great grandson
Blaine, Jonathan K.R.	13 Aug 1974	4th great grandson
Arline, Jr Kent E.	10 Sep 1967	4th great grandson
Glover, Andre Matthew	08 Mar 1988	4th great grandson
Dickens, Maxwell Anthony	25 Jun 1998	4th great grandson
Davenport, James	05 Mar 1943	4th great grandson
Blaine, Rahn A.	27 Dec 1975	4th great grandson
Dickens, Lauren Michell	13 Feb 2001	4th great granddaughter
Peterson, Nia M.	14 Apr 1980	4th great granddaughter
Lockley, Vanessa	01 Jul 1968	4th great granddaughter
Peterson, Bernadette	15 Feb 1978	4th great granddaughter
Peterson, Monique D.	18 Dec 1978	4th great granddaughter
Peterson, Jeanette	16 Jun 1971	4th great granddaughter
Peterson, Shani Danielle	22 Dec 1982	4th great granddaughter
Smith, Deanna Nancy	30 Aug 1984	4th great granddaughter

Davis, Danielle N.	09 Sep 1997	4th great granddaughter
Stewart, Rachel Christina	10 Dec 1978	4th great granddaughter
Stephens, Genine Lauren	23 Jan 1984	4th great granddaughter
Davis, Jaleesa Tachelle	18 May 1988	4th great granddaughter
Reed, Mary	29 Nov 1936	4th great granddaughter
Davis, Mariah Jade	03 Sep 1995	4th great granddaughter
Davis, Jessica Teleesa	20 Jan 1993	4th great granddaughter
Reed, Rosetta	30 Mar 1931	4th great granddaughter
Lockley, Marcella Evette	31 Dec 1971	4th great granddaughter
Lockley, Lorraine	19 Sep 1963	4th great granddaughter
Johnson, Donzeila Olivia	27 Jun 1957	4th great granddaughter
Hill, Iasha Dee Lockley	21 Nov 1981	4th great granddaughter
Johnson, Dellaphine Marie	20 Apr 1948	4th great granddaughter
Johnson, Denise	15 Jul 1955	4th great granddaughter
Lockley, Ava Ashley	17 Oct 1984	4th great granddaughter
Lockley, Angela	31 Dec 1960	4th great granddaughter
King, Britney Nicole	12 Aug 1990	4th great granddaughter
Johnson, Donzella	13 Jul 1954	4th great granddaughter
Lockley, Cynthia Renee	05 Mar 1970	4th great granddaughter
Johnson, Doreen Patricia	28 Nov 1949	4th great granddaughter
Lucas, Chrytal A.	01 Jan 1967	4th great granddaughter
Glover, Sharonda Antonette	11 Feb 1984	4th great granddaughter
Napper, Bonita	31 Jul 1958	4th great granddaughter
Napper, Claire		4th great granddaughter
Napper, Diane		4th great granddaughter
Napper, Dedoriad Lithiah	24 Apr 1947	4th great granddaughter
Miller, Tiffany Annette	27 Jun 1980	4th great granddaughter
Mathews, Sabrina	19 Jul 1984	4th great granddaughter

Hall, Cheyanne	20 Nov 2010	4th great granddaughter
Guest, Diane	03 May 1950	4th great granddaughter
Miller, Tarrah A'Lauri	15 May 1987	4th great granddaughter
Guest, Deborah	28 May 1948	4th great granddaughter
Patterson-Mcfadden, Sharron		4th great grandchild
Lockley, Tajay		5th great grandson
Lockley, James Kenneth	04 Feb 1984	5th great grandson
Lockley, Terance Phillip	21 Jun 1990	5th great grandson
Mathews, Oliver	15 Sep 1993	5th great grandson
Lockley, William Anthony	01 Jul 1991	5th great grandson
Lockley, James		5th great grandson
Johnson, Christopher David		5th great grandson
Johnson, Cass Avery	02 Sep 1967	5th great grandson
King, Marcus Edward	24 Feb 1972	5th great grandson
Lockley, Alan Devon	27 Jul 1989	5th great grandson
King, Shawn James	03 Mar 1973	5th great grandson
Mathews, Phillip		5th great grandson
Spearman, Michael S.	10 Nov 1990	5th great grandson
Spearman, Jonathan S.	16 Nov 1991	5th great grandson
Steward, Victor		5th great grandson
Witcher, Julius R.	21 Dec 2007	5th great grandson
Witcher, Amaini	24 Aug 2005	5th great grandson
Norde, Jonathan	13 Feb 1983	5th great grandson
Miller, Elijah	23 Sep 2009	5th great grandson
McFadden, Gregory		5th great grandson
Miller, Ryan Andrew Jr.	28 Aug 2001	5th great grandson
Napper, John	13 Feb 1983	5th great grandson
Napper, Issac IV		5th great grandson

Hawkins, Travis	16 Apr 2008	5th great grandson
Hipp, Carlton	14 Apr 1971	5th great grandson
Davenport, Wayne	16 Sep 1958	5th great grandson
Davenport, Joshua	1986	5th great grandson
Davenport, John Patrick	10 Dec 1956	5th great grandson
Davenport, Daniel	1988	5th great grandson
Davenport, Caleb	1984	5th great grandson
Dandridge, Gary Tamara	15 Mar 1974	5th great grandson
Barnby, Edward Lee	1964	5th great grandson
Bingham, Jr Gerald	16 Aug	5th great grandson
Dandridge, Cyrus Lamont	22 Aug 1972	5th great grandson
Napper, Cheasea		5th great granddaughter
Miller, Leanna Cynthia	12 Jun 2013	5th great granddaughter
McFadden, Shelby		5th great granddaughter
Miller, Isla	03 Aug 2013	5th great granddaughter
Miller, Celia Margaret Patricia	11 Jan 2007	5th great granddaughter
Miller, Ariana Adrean	14 Dec 2002	5th great granddaughter
Davenport, Laura	1986	5th great granddaughter
Stone, Bonita		5th great granddaughter
Chambliss, Ashley		5th great granddaughter
Johnson, Carvin	20 Jan 1968	5th great granddaughter
Taylor, Jaceelyn Juliet	10 Oct 2010	5th great granddaughter
Spearman, Crystal	26 Mar 1981	5th great granddaughter
Roberson, Bethlehem		5th great granddaughter
Roberson, Agnes		5th great granddaughter
Sealy, Rosita Junita	22 Jul 2001	5th great granddaughter
Roberson, Ruth		5th great granddaughter
Lockley, Jacqueline Evett	17 Jun 1985	5th great granddaughter

Hipp, Dedorid L.	03 Dec 1974	5th great granddaughter
Lockley, Marcella Mertine	20 Jun 1988	5th great granddaughter
Hawkins, Serena Karalee	08 Sep 2008	5th great granddaughter
Hawkins, Serenity Kaitlin	01 Sep 2004	5th great granddaughter
Johnson, Aanisa		5th great granddaughter
Johnson, Carma M.	24 May 1969	5th great granddaughter
Johnson, Charmine	04 Sep 1966	5th great granddaughter
King, Holly		5th great granddaughter
Johnson, Candice	1988	5th great granddaughter
King, Jeneene Marie	26 Jul 1979	5th great granddaughter
Lockley, Tiffany Nicloe	27 May 1987	5th great granddaughter
Mathews, Sabree	20 Jul 2003	5th great granddaughter
Fisher, Nicole Noel	31 Dec 1979	5th great granddaughter
Mays, Sheanise	15 Feb 1993	5th great granddaughter
Davenport, Micah	1990	5th great granddaughter
McFadden, Gabrielle		5th great granddaughter
Mathews, Kenya	23 Nov 1991	5th great granddaughter
Hawkins, Seralina Kamara	01 Dec 2012	5th great granddaughter
Lockley, Vanassa Renee	29 Jun 1984	5th great granddaughter
Malachi, Jacina	15 Jul 1985	5th great granddaughter
Mathews, Dora	04 Jul 1996	5th great granddaughter
Malachi, Lejean	04 Sep 1982	5th great granddaughter
Edmounds, Herbert	23 Sep 1991	6th great grandson
Herbert, Gerald Lamont	07 Jul 2001	6th great grandson
Mathews, Daquine	01 Apr 2004	6th great grandson
Mathews, Damade	18 Mar 2002	6th great grandson
King, Jordan Amir	30 Aug 2000	6th great grandson
Jones, Demarcus	27 Nov 1996	6th great grandson

King, Leilah James	04 Feb 2008	6th great grandson
Johnson, D.J.		6th great grandson
Davenport, Joshua	1986	6th great grandson
Dandridge, O'Ryan Tamara	09 Mar 2013	6th great grandson
Barnby, James		6th great grandson
Davenport, Caleb	1984	6th great grandson
Spearman, Keenan	30 Aug 2005	6th great grandson
Davenport, Daniel	1988	6th great grandson
Spearman, Ashley	19 Oct 1998	6th great granddaughter
King, Shayla Jenae	24 Feb 2004	6th great granddaughter
Neal, Khadejah	14 Nov 1997	6th great granddaughter
Austin, Manya	26 Jul 2001	6th great granddaughter
Lockley, Marissa Renee	21 Mar 2008	6th great granddaughter
Mack, Lori	10 Mar 1988	6th great granddaughter
Malachi, Cianni	29 Sep 2004	6th great granddaughter
Mack, Lisa	30 Sep 1982	6th great granddaughter
Richardson, Angel	04 Jul 2001	6th great granddaughter
Mack, Leah	21 Jan 1990	6th great granddaughter
Davenport, Micah	1990	6th great granddaughter
Edmounds, Crisona	27 Jul 1997	6th great granddaughter
Hambrick, Taylor Marie	24 Jun 2011	6th great granddaughter
Davenport, Laura	1986	6th great granddaughter
Barnby, Stacia		6th great granddaughter
Campbell, Nadjea	05 Aug 1997	6th great granddaughter
Dandridge, Malani	12 Jun 2010	6th great granddaughter
Harris, Serenity	10 Jun 2004	6th great granddaughter
Johnson, Courtney		6th great granddaughter
Johnson, Kalise		6th great granddaughter

Johnson, Khalia		6th great granddaughter
Johnson, Aja	10 Apr 1997	6th great granddaughter
Hawkins, Amber		6th great granddaughter
Hayes, Keira	15 Feb 2007	6th great granddaughter
Holloway, Madison	17 Jun 2004	6th great granddaughter
Conway, Abdullah	11 Jan 2004	7th great grandson
Conway, Damir	05 Jan 2009	7th great grandson
Sido, Raaiyah	31 May 2011	7th great granddaughter
Conway, Rugaiyyah	24 Apr 2002	7th great granddaughter
Banton, Rahyyah	05 Jun 2006	7th great granddaughter
Davenport, John Patrick	10 Dec 1956	2nd great grand nephew of great granddaughter
Davenport, Caleb	1984	3rd great grand nephew of great granddaughter
Davenport, Daniel	1988	3rd great grand nephew of great granddaughter
Davenport, Joshua	1986	3rd great grand nephew of great granddaughter
Davenport, Laura	1986	3rd great grand niece of great granddaughter
Davenport, Micah	1990	3rd great grand niece of great granddaughter
Hudgins, Maria E.	1836	Aunt of great grandson
Kauffman, James H.	1859	Brother of great grandson
Kauffman, John E.	1855	Brother of great grandson
Kauffman, William T.	1853	Brother of great grandson
Kauffman, James H.	1859	Brother of nephew of wife of son
Kauffman, John E.	1855	Brother of nephew of wife of son

Kauffman, William T.	1853	Brother of nephew of wife of son
Betsy	1822	Daughter-in-law
Harris, Mary	1818	Daughter-in-law
Hudgins, Martha	1840	Daughter-in-law
Judith	1831	Daughter-in-law
Key, Jane	1803	Daughter-in-law
Davenport, Robert L.T.	31 Mar 1910	Grand nephew of great granddaughter
Thornton, John R.	30 Jan 1937	Grand nephew of husband of great granddaughter
Thornton, Thomas M.	02 Jul 1945	Grand nephew of husband of great granddaughter
Thornton, William B.	07 Jan 1939	Grand nephew of husband of great granddaughter
Robinson, Clarence	1905	Grand nephew of wife of son
Robinson, Jr John C.	1913	Grand nephew of wife of son
Robinson, Willie	1909	Grand nephew of wife of son
Davenport, Lillian E.	20 May 1919	Grand niece of great granddaughter
Davenport, Missouri Olivia	08 Aug 1921	Grand niece of great granddaughter
Thornton, Carol Maxann	28 Dec 1941	Grand niece of husband of great granddaughter
Thornton, Thelma J.	02 Jan 1938	Grand niece of husband of great granddaughter

Robinson, Maud	1903	Grand niece of wife of son
Barton, Boyce Sr.	15 Dec 1899	Husband of 2nd great granddaughter
Baylor, Lloyd	22 Apr 1922	Husband of 2nd great granddaughter
Bright, Thomas	09 Sep 1914	Husband of 2nd great granddaughter
Campbell, Oliver	1903	Husband of 2nd great granddaughter
Ford, Frederick K.		Husband of 2nd great granddaughter
Guest, Benjamin	27 Nov 1916	Husband of 2nd great granddaughter
Harris, Major		Husband of 2nd great granddaughter
Helm, Moses		Husband of 2nd great granddaughter
Lewis, George	06 Feb 1925	Husband of 2nd great granddaughter
Lockley, Earl	03 Dec 1911	Husband of 2nd great granddaughter
Mathis, Luther		Husband of 2nd great granddaughter
Mullen, Edward		Husband of 2nd great granddaughter
Napper, Sr Issac B.	10 Mar 1911	Husband of 2nd great granddaughter
Palmes, Walter	1890	Husband of 2nd great granddaughter
Peterson, Daniel		Husband of 2nd great granddaughter

Reed, Perry W.	Oct 1895	Husband of 2nd great granddaughter
Richardson, Walter	1903	Husband of 2nd great granddaughter
Roye, Raymond	17 Jul 1914	Husband of 2nd great granddaughter
S. Thornton, Sr Edward	14 Sep 1931	Husband of 2nd great granddaughter
Smith, Robert Edward	08 Sep 1935	Husband of 2nd great granddaughter
Taylor, Nathaniel	31 Oct 1929	Husband of 2nd great granddaughter
Terry, Alfred		Husband of 2nd great granddaughter
Thornton, Jehu W.		Husband of 2nd great granddaughter
Ward, Jr Thomas Milton	11 Nov 1934	Husband of 2nd great granddaughter
White, Albert Clinton	14 Sep 1909	Husband of 2nd great granddaughter
Wilson, Frank		Husband of 2nd great granddaughter
Wormley, Roger	05 Dec 1910	Husband of 2nd great granddaughter
Arline, Sr Kent E.		Husband of 3rd great granddaughter
Bailey, Rickey A.		Husband of 3rd great granddaughter
Barton, Boyce Sr.	15 Dec 1899	Husband of 3rd great granddaughter
Blaine, Jonathan A.		Husband of 3rd great granddaughter

Cross, James | | Husband of 3rd great granddaughter
Davis, William Jr. | | Husband of 3rd great granddaughter
Franklin, Walter M. | 29 Aug 1945 | Husband of 3rd great granddaughter
Gaskins, George | | Husband of 3rd great granddaughter
Green, William H. | | Husband of 3rd great granddaughter
Guest, Benjamin | 27 Nov 1916 | Husband of 3rd great granddaughter
Hall, Kevin | 09 Nov 1985 | Husband of 3rd great granddaughter
Hart, James | 11 Nov 1936 | Husband of 3rd great granddaughter
Johnson, John Henry | 03 Sep 1903 | Husband of 3rd great granddaughter
Kent, Ulysses | | Husband of 3rd great granddaughter
Lucas, Jr Robert E. | 14 May 1931 | Husband of 3rd great granddaughter
Mathew, Sr Oliver Lee | 27 Sep 1943 | Husband of 3rd great granddaughter
Miller, Earl Lee Andrew Jr | 25 Feb 1953 | Husband of 3rd great granddaughter
Reed, Perry W. | Oct 1895 | Husband of 3rd great granddaughter
Robinson, Wayne E. | 14 Aug 1949 | Husband of 3rd great granddaughter
Scott, Richard | | Husband of 3rd great granddaughter

Smith, Jr William C.	02 Feb 1943	Husband of 3rd great granddaughter
Stewart, Edward	17 Jun 1951	Husband of 3rd great granddaughter
Taliferro, Sr Martin	18 Mar 1947	Husband of 3rd great granddaughter
Thomas, James S.	19 Jun 1931	Husband of 3rd great granddaughter
Walker, Walter R.		Husband of 3rd great granddaughter
Unknown		Husband of 4th great grandchild
Bingham, Gerald		Husband of 4th great granddaughter
Dandridge, William		Husband of 4th great granddaughter
Fisher, Richard		Husband of 4th great granddaughter
Hawkins, Charles	13 Jun 1980	Husband of 4th great granddaughter
Hipp, Billy	24 Apr 1947	Husband of 4th great granddaughter
Holster, Shawn		Husband of 4th great granddaughter
Ivy, Dennis		Husband of 4th great granddaughter
King, Jr James		Husband of 4th great granddaughter
Malachi, James		Husband of 4th great granddaughter
Mays, Eugene	24 Dec 1960	Husband of 4th great granddaughter

Meade, Carlton   Husband of 4th great granddaughter

Parker, James   Husband of 4th great granddaughter

Reed, Brian   Husband of 4th great granddaughter

Roberson, Paul   Husband of 4th great granddaughter

Spearman, Ralph   Husband of 4th great granddaughter

Swingler, Malik   Husband of 4th great granddaughter

Taylor, Jayson   Husband of 4th great granddaughter

Witcher, Timothy   Husband of 4th great granddaughter

Word, Alan   08 Mar 1966 Husband of 4th great granddaughter

Austin, Gary   Husband of 5th great granddaughter

Cantell, Richard   Husband of 5th great granddaughter

Davis, Rasael   Husband of 5th great granddaughter

Edmounds, Herbert   Husband of 5th great granddaughter

Hailey, Frank   Husband of 5th great granddaughter

Haywood, James   Husband of 5th great granddaughter

Holloway, Chancey   Husband of 5th great granddaughter

Johnson, John		Husband of 5th great granddaughter
Mack, Lance		Husband of 5th great granddaughter
Conway, James		Husband of 6th great granddaughter
Reed, Perry W.	Oct 1895	Husband of grand niece of great granddaughter
Bird, Thomas	1840	Husband of granddaughter
Bluefoot, Philip	1826	Husband of granddaughter
Collins, Leonidas	1841	Husband of granddaughter
Collins, William B.	1840	Husband of granddaughter
Gatewood, Philip		Husband of granddaughter
Gordon, Daniel		Husband of granddaughter
Harris, Joseph Huck	1855	Husband of granddaughter
Henderson, George W.	1830	Husband of granddaughter
Henderson, George W.	1830	Husband of granddaughter
Jordan, John Robert	01 Feb 1853	Husband of granddaughter
Kauffman, Jeremia	1834	Husband of granddaughter
Lee, Leroy	1844	Husband of granddaughter

Lee, Livi	1846	Husband of granddaughter
Lockley, Robert	1842	Husband of granddaughter
Lockley, Robert Henry	15 Dec 1877	Husband of granddaughter
Lockley, Wiley	1847	Husband of granddaughter
Mardin		Husband of granddaughter
Unknown		Husband of granddaughter
Warner, Frederick	1873	Husband of granddaughter
West, Andrew	Aug 1849	Husband of granddaughter
Williams, Robert Logan	1847	Husband of granddaughter
Bell, Edward		Husband of great granddaughter
Bordley		Husband of great granddaughter
Brown, James L.	1882	Husband of great granddaughter
Campbell, James		Husband of great granddaughter
Davenport, Jackson	1846	Husband of great granddaughter
Davenport, John Thomas	1870	Husband of great granddaughter
Dungey, Thomas M.	1876	Husband of great granddaughter

Green, Doney	1882	Husband of great granddaughter
Kademy, O.		Husband of great granddaughter
Kademy, O.		Husband of great granddaughter
Kidd, James L.	1896	Husband of great granddaughter
Lockley, Benjamin	1852	Husband of great granddaughter
McDonald, O.		Husband of great granddaughter
McDonald, O.		Husband of great granddaughter
Miller, Armstead	15 Nov 1873	Husband of great granddaughter
Patterson, John H.	1877	Husband of great granddaughter
Patterson, John H.	1877	Husband of great granddaughter
Robinson, William		Husband of great granddaughter
Simpson		Husband of great granddaughter
Simpson		Husband of great granddaughter
White, William		Husband of great granddaughter
Thornton, Jehu W.		Husband of niece of husband of great granddaughter
Davenport, Jackson	1846	Husband of sister of great granddaughter

Lockley, Benjamin	1852	Husband of sister of great granddaughter
Mays, Eugene	24 Dec 1960	Husband of step granddaughter of 2nd great granddaughter
Davenport, John Thomas	1870	Husband of step granddaughter of daughter
Barton, Boyce Sr.	15 Dec 1899	Husband of step great granddaughter of daughter
Baylor, Lloyd	22 Apr 1922	Husband of step great granddaughter of daughter
Guest, Benjamin	27 Nov 1916	Husband of step great granddaughter of daughter
Helm, Moses		Husband of step great granddaughter of daughter
Lewis, George	06 Feb 1925	Husband of step great granddaughter of daughter
Taylor, Nathaniel	31 Oct 1929	Husband of step great granddaughter of daughter
Terry, Alfred		Husband of step great granddaughter of daughter
Thornton, Jehu W.		Husband of step great granddaughter of daughter

Wilson, Frank		Husband of step great granddaughter of daughter
Wormley, Roger	05 Dec 1910	Husband of step great granddaughter of daughter
Thornton, Jehu W.		Husband of wife of 2nd great grandson
Bluefoot, Philip	1826	Husband of wife of grandson
Hudgins, Mary E.	1835	Mother of great grandson
Kauffman, Elias	1862	Nephew of husband of granddaughter
Henderson, Henry		Nephew of wife of grandson
Kauffman, Elias	1862	Nephew of wife of grandson
Kauffman, Elias	1862	Nephew of wife of son
Kauffman, James H.	1859	Nephew of wife of son
Kauffman, John E.	1855	Nephew of wife of son
Kauffman, William T.	1853	Nephew of wife of son
Robinson, John Caleb	02 Dec 1873	Nephew of wife of son
Robinson, Nathan P.	1876	Nephew of wife of son
Hudgins, Maria E.	1836	Sister-in-law of grandson
Hudgins, Maria E.	1836	Sister-in-law of son
Hudgins, Mary E.	1835	Sister-in-law of son
Bluefoot, James	1822	Son-in-law
Gatewood, James		Son-in-law
Gilmore, Alexander	1799	Son-in-law
Harris, Benjamin A.		Son-in-law
Jordan, George	1814	Son-in-law

Kauffman, George	Abt. 1784	Son-in-law
Baylor, Joan B.	13 Jul 1950	Step 2nd great granddaughter of daughter
Baylor, Kathy	18 Mar 1961	Step 2nd great granddaughter of daughter
Baylor, Linda	07 Jul 1952	Step 2nd great granddaughter of daughter
Baylor, Ruthie B.	08 Aug 1949	Step 2nd great granddaughter of daughter
Davenport, Cheryl	10 Dec 1953	Step 2nd great granddaughter of daughter
Davenport, Cynthia	25 Jul 1957	Step 2nd great granddaughter of daughter
Guest, Deborah	28 May 1948	Step 2nd great granddaughter of daughter
Guest, Diane	03 May 1950	Step 2nd great granddaughter of daughter
Jordan, Alberetta		Step 2nd great granddaughter of daughter
Jordan, Arlena		Step 2nd great granddaughter of daughter
Jordan, Arlette	18 Dec 1951	Step 2nd great granddaughter of daughter

Jordan, Barbara	15 Jul 1945	Step 2nd great granddaughter of daughter
Jordan, Brenda		Step 2nd great granddaughter of daughter
Jordan, Dorothy Lee	27 Sep 1952	Step 2nd great granddaughter of daughter
Jordan, Eva P.	10 Jan 1944	Step 2nd great granddaughter of daughter
Jordan, Joyce A.	13 Oct 1942	Step 2nd great granddaughter of daughter
Jordan, Julia Pauline	05 Nov 1944	Step 2nd great granddaughter of daughter
Jordan, Laverne	12 Nov 1942	Step 2nd great granddaughter of daughter
Jordan, Regena	07 Jul 1953	Step 2nd great granddaughter of daughter
Jordan, Silvia	08 Apr 1952	Step 2nd great granddaughter of daughter
Lewis, Donna W.	02 Feb 1949	Step 2nd great granddaughter of daughter
Taylor, Cheryl	30 Apr 1958	Step 2nd great granddaughter of daughter

Taylor, Marilyn	06 Aug 1960	Step 2nd great granddaughter of daughter
Thornton, Carol Maxann	28 Dec 1941	Step 2nd great granddaughter of daughter
Thornton, Thelma J.	02 Jan 1938	Step 2nd great granddaughter of daughter
Wormley, Joan	27 Feb 1941	Step 2nd great granddaughter of daughter
Baylor, Gordon	02 Jul 1951	Step 2nd great grandson of daughter
Baylor, Timothy	23 May 1954	Step 2nd great grandson of daughter
Brokenborough, Toney	02 Oct 1953	Step 2nd great grandson of daughter
Davenport, James	05 Mar 1943	Step 2nd great grandson of daughter
Davenport, Philbert	26 Aug 1952	Step 2nd great grandson of daughter
Guest, Cecil	27 Sep 1946	Step 2nd great grandson of daughter
Guest, George	19 Sep 1941	Step 2nd great grandson of daughter
Guest, Jerome	11 Sep 1942	Step 2nd great grandson of daughter
Helm, Cappie	1955	Step 2nd great grandson of daughter
Jordan, Anthony	11 Nov 1966	Step 2nd great grandson of daughter

Jordan, Carl		Step 2nd great grandson of daughter
Jordan, Daymon		Step 2nd great grandson of daughter
Jordan, Deotis	27 Jul 1974	Step 2nd great grandson of daughter
Jordan, Franklin N.	22 Nov 1939	Step 2nd great grandson of daughter
Jordan, Garry Maxwell		Step 2nd great grandson of daughter
Jordan, George W.	16 Oct 1963	Step 2nd great grandson of daughter
Jordan, Jr Doxie A.	27 Jun 1969	Step 2nd great grandson of daughter
Jordan, Keith	31 Jan 1953	Step 2nd great grandson of daughter
Jordan, Larry	30 Sep 1955	Step 2nd great grandson of daughter
Jordan, Lawrence D.	07 Jul 1953	Step 2nd great grandson of daughter
Jordan, Preston Garest	15 Jul 1943	Step 2nd great grandson of daughter
Jordan, Samuel T.	15 Feb 1942	Step 2nd great grandson of daughter
Jordan, Thomas		Step 2nd great grandson of daughter
Jordan, W. Franklin	03 Feb 1941	Step 2nd great grandson of daughter
Lewis, Don Kenrick	28 Jul 1951	Step 2nd great grandson of daughter
Taylor, Jr Nathaniel	28 Apr 1957	Step 2nd great grandson of daughter

Taylor, Welford	19 Mar 1959	Step 2nd great grandson of daughter
Taylor, William	19 Mar 1959	Step 2nd great grandson of daughter
Terry, Michael		Step 2nd great grandson of daughter
Thornton, John R.	30 Jan 1937	Step 2nd great grandson of daughter
Thornton, Thomas M.	02 Jul 1945	Step 2nd great grandson of daughter
Thornton, William B.	07 Jan 1939	Step 2nd great grandson of daughter
Wormley, Allen	28 Jul 1939	Step 2nd great grandson of daughter
Davenport, John Patrick	10 Dec 1956	Step 3rd great grandson of daughter
Davenport, Wayne	16 Sep 1958	Step 3rd great grandson of daughter
Davenport, Laura	1986	Step 4th great granddaughter of daughter
Davenport, Micah	1990	Step 4th great granddaughter of daughter
Davenport, Caleb	1984	Step 4th great grandson of daughter
Davenport, Daniel	1988	Step 4th great grandson of daughter
Davenport, Joshua	1986	Step 4th great grandson of daughter
Lockley, Angela	31 Dec 1960	Step granddaughter of 2nd great granddaughter

Jordan, Rosie Jane	10 Jan 1878	Step granddaughter of daughter
Jordan, Ethan Allen	14 May 1896	Step grandson of daughter
Jordan, George Franklin	Feb 1883	Step grandson of daughter
Jordan, John Kelly	18 Feb 1885	Step grandson of daughter
Jordan, Samuel Isiah	22 Feb 1891	Step grandson of daughter
Mays, Sheanise	15 Feb 1993	Step great granddaughter of 2nd great granddaughter
Davenport, Ella Bertha	21 Jun 1903	Step great granddaughter of daughter
Davenport, Etha Irene	07 Jan 1912	Step great granddaughter of daughter
Davenport, Hattie B.	21 Aug 1904	Step great granddaughter of daughter
Davenport, Helen M.	Apr 1901	Step great granddaughter of daughter
Davenport, Hyburnies N.	05 Nov 1906	Step great granddaughter of daughter
Davenport, Luvenia Ann	16 Jun 1902	Step great granddaughter of daughter
Davenport, Mary Frances	18 Aug 1916	Step great granddaughter of daughter
Davenport, Missouri Olivia	08 Aug 1921	Step great granddaughter of daughter
Jordan, Catherine	12 Nov 1915	Step great granddaughter of daughter
Jordan, Cressa Erlene		Step great granddaughter of daughter
Jordan, Elizabeth Maurice	05 Feb 1936	Step great granddaughter of daughter
Jordan, Fannie Vernell	16 Dec 1923	Step great granddaughter of daughter

Jordan, Florentine Melanie	24 Jun 1909	Step great granddaughter of daughter
Jordan, Ida B.	Oct 1913	Step great granddaughter of daughter
Jordan, Lillian Juanita	16 Jan 1923	Step great granddaughter of daughter
Jordan, Olivia Elizabeth	18 Jan 1928	Step great granddaughter of daughter
T. Jordan, Thelma	05 Apr 1915	Step great granddaughter of daughter
Davenport, George Moses	10 Sep 1913	Step great grandson of daughter
Davenport, Robert L.T.	31 Mar 1910	Step great grandson of daughter
Jordan, Austin Douglas	13 Sep 1913	Step great grandson of daughter
Jordan, Burnett Allen	01 Nov 1921	Step great grandson of daughter
Jordan, Doxie Alfonza	27 Jul 1932	Step great grandson of daughter
Jordan, Henry Clay	31 Jul 1923	Step great grandson of daughter
Jordan, Herbert Lee		Step great grandson of daughter
Jordan, John Hollis	08 Mar 1917	Step great grandson of daughter
Jordan, John Mark	04 Jul 1920	Step great grandson of daughter
Jordan, Roscoe Samuel	15 Jun 1916	Step great grandson of daughter
Jordan, Thomas A.	06 Sep 1918	Step great grandson of daughter

Jordan, William Preston	22 May 1914	Step great grandson of daughter
Thornton, Carol Maxann	28 Dec 1941	Stepdaughter of 2nd great grandson
Thornton, Thelma J.	02 Jan 1938	Stepdaughter of 2nd great grandson
Robinson, Fatima	1868	Stepdaughter of granddaughter
Robinson, Ketuia	1867	Stepdaughter of granddaughter
Robinson, Victoria	1866	Stepdaughter of granddaughter
Robinson, Dolly Lee	26 Jun 1930	Stepdaughter of great grandson
Thornton, John R.	30 Jan 1937	Stepson of 2nd great grandson
Thornton, Thomas M.	02 Jul 1945	Stepson of 2nd great grandson
Thornton, William B.	07 Jan 1939	Stepson of 2nd great grandson
Jordan, John Robert	01 Feb 1853	Stepson of daughter
Henderson, Henry		Stepson of granddaughter
Kauffman, James H.	1859	Stepson of grandson
Kauffman, John E.	1855	Stepson of grandson
Kauffman, William T.	1853	Stepson of grandson
Bias, Arletha		Wife of 2nd great grand nephew of great granddaughter
Petty, Wanda	01 Jan 1955	Wife of 2nd great grand nephew of great granddaughter

Adkins, Aleatha	14 Nov 1924	Wife of 2nd great grandson
Ball, Sadie	17 Sep 1920	Wife of 2nd great grandson
Campbell, Lizzie	1875	Wife of 2nd great grandson
Cancel, Ruiz Coello Raquel	03 Dec 1944	Wife of 2nd great grandson
Christian, Russell	02 Jul 1915	Wife of 2nd great grandson
Dickens, Joan		Wife of 2nd great grandson
Edwards, Francis	31 Dec 1928	Wife of 2nd great grandson
Ellis, Patricia	12 Jan 1937	Wife of 2nd great grandson
Fitchett, Virginia	07 Sep 1919	Wife of 2nd great grandson
Foster, Mertine Virginia	31 May 1921	Wife of 2nd great grandson
Garnett, Elizabeth		Wife of 2nd great grandson
Garnett, Julia A.	29 Aug 1919	Wife of 2nd great grandson
Gilmore, Yvonne	05 Feb 1939	Wife of 2nd great grandson
Glover, Annabelle	16 Jan 1941	Wife of 2nd great grandson
Haskins, Priscilla	1917	Wife of 2nd great grandson
Holmes, Barbara		Wife of 2nd great grandson

Hunter, Catherine	1923	Wife of 2nd great grandson
Ila		Wife of 2nd great grandson
Jocelyn		Wife of 2nd great grandson
Johnson, Gladys	26 Jul 1918	Wife of 2nd great grandson
Josephine		Wife of 2nd great grandson
Lacy, Constancy	08 Jul 1923	Wife of 2nd great grandson
Lee, Emma	1918	Wife of 2nd great grandson
Lenora		Wife of 2nd great grandson
Minor, Lily Bell	16 Apr 1916	Wife of 2nd great grandson
Morrow, Elizabeth Cherry		Wife of 2nd great grandson
Norton, Maxine	08 Nov 1937	Wife of 2nd great grandson
Payne, Charletta	06 May 1929	Wife of 2nd great grandson
Poindexter, Julia Elizabeth		Wife of 2nd great grandson
Rice, Flora Ruth	17 Apr 1935	Wife of 2nd great grandson
Robinson, Dolly Lee	26 Jun 1930	Wife of 2nd great grandson
Satterwhite, Gladys Marie	19 Nov 1942	Wife of 2nd great grandson

Saugling, Carolyn		Wife of 2nd great grandson
Stewart, Doshie	08 Aug 1919	Wife of 2nd great grandson
Stewart, Flossie	25 Aug 1933	Wife of 2nd great grandson
Sutherlin, Rosa Etta	02 Feb 1917	Wife of 2nd great grandson
Williams, Ludie Hilda	31 Dec 1921	Wife of 2nd great grandson
Atkins, Brenda	12 Oct 1947	Wife of 3rd great grandson
Bruce, Rosalind	22 May 1962	Wife of 3rd great grandson
Davis, Elizabeth	06 Jan 1944	Wife of 3rd great grandson
Dossanta, Olivia	20 Mar 1930	Wife of 3rd great grandson
Feggans, Francine		Wife of 3rd great grandson
Fitchett, Virginia	07 Sep 1919	Wife of 3rd great grandson
Giddings, Janine		Wife of 3rd great grandson
Jeffery, Meridel	05 Mar 1947	Wife of 3rd great grandson
Jones, Marlene Alethia	1958	Wife of 3rd great grandson
Lewis, Marion		Wife of 3rd great grandson
Libcomb, Karaleen		Wife of 3rd great grandson
Michelle		Wife of 3rd great grandson
Price, Priscilla	10 Jun 1941	Wife of 3rd great grandson
Reddick, Sherrie	02 Sep 1959	Wife of 3rd great grandson
Severa	01 Jan 1944	Wife of 3rd great grandson
Stephens, Annette	21 Oct 1956	Wife of 3rd great grandson
Unknown		Wife of 3rd great grandson
Unknown		Wife of 3rd great grandson
Whyte, Sheryl Robin	16 Nov 1963	Wife of 3rd great grandson
Bias, Arletha		Wife of 4th great grandson

Brown, Linda		Wife of 4th great grandson
Brown, Rachel		Wife of 4th great grandson
Chambliss, Lesa		Wife of 4th great grandson
Channel, Gale Stevens		Wife of 4th great grandson
Christiana		Wife of 4th great grandson
Hamilton, Enina		Wife of 4th great grandson
Holcomb, Dara		Wife of 4th great grandson
Johnson, Rhonda		Wife of 4th great grandson
Martin, Yolanda		Wife of 4th great grandson
Minerva		Wife of 4th great grandson
Nigeria		Wife of 4th great grandson
Petty, Wanda	01 Jan 1955	Wife of 4th great grandson
Plaza, Paula	Apr 1986	Wife of 4th great grandson
Sealy, Debra Ann	23 Dec 1955	Wife of 4th great grandson
Sierra, Adrean		Wife of 4th great grandson
Stone, Linda		Wife of 4th great grandson
Watson, Lindsey		Wife of 4th great grandson
Bias, Arletha		Wife of 5th great grandson
Harris, Charnelle		Wife of 5th great grandson
Hawkins, Patrice		Wife of 5th great grandson
Jones, Shala		Wife of 5th great grandson
Margarte		Wife of 5th great grandson
Petty, Wanda	01 Jan 1955	Wife of 5th great grandson
Treacie		Wife of 5th great grandson
Wooden, Tracie		Wife of 5th great grandson
Fitchett, Virginia	07 Sep 1919	Wife of grand nephew of great granddaughter
Anna	1874	Wife of grandson
Dungy, Atlanta	1855	Wife of grandson

E, Mary	1835	Wife of grandson
Etta	1869	Wife of grandson
Fanny	1873	Wife of grandson
Hampton, Gertrude	1894	Wife of grandson
Hampton, Gertrude	1895	Wife of grandson
Hodgess, Marion	1836	Wife of grandson
Hudgins, Maria E.	1836	Wife of grandson
Hudgins, Mary E.	1835	Wife of grandson
J, Margarette	1841	Wife of grandson
Jones, Lucy		Wife of grandson
Jones, Lucy A.	1822	Wife of grandson
Jordan, Sarah J.	1849	Wife of grandson
Morris, Useba	1852	Wife of grandson
Robinson, Pinky	1840	Wife of grandson
Williams, Mary Ann	1852	Wife of grandson
Allen, Maude	1891	Wife of great grandson
Baker, Lucy B.	1871	Wife of great grandson
Banks, Bessie Ann	1889	Wife of great grandson
Beckwith, Bessie	07 May 1918	Wife of great grandson
Collins, Bertha Jackson		Wife of great grandson
Collins, Sarah	1893	Wife of great grandson
Fields, Mary E.W	1875	Wife of great grandson
Holmes, Ruth		Wife of great grandson
Kauffman, Pinkey Jane	1885	Wife of great grandson
Key, Emma	1887	Wife of great grandson
Kidd, Rebecca	1890	Wife of great grandson
Kidd, Rebecca	1890	Wife of great grandson
Miles, Elizabeth	22 Oct 1891	Wife of great grandson

Morris, Eva S.	1894	Wife of great grandson
Nannie	1875	Wife of great grandson
Robinson, Texana	1872	Wife of great grandson
Rowe, Carie Bernice	1880	Wife of great grandson
Sutherlin, Francis	15 Jan 1868	Wife of great grandson
T, Sarah	1880	Wife of great grandson
Williams, Marion Clarice	11 Aug 1913	Wife of great grandson
E, Mary	1835	Wife of husband of granddaughter
Campbell, Lizzie	1875	Wife of husband of great granddaughter
Fields, Mary E.W	1875	Wife of nephew of wife of son
Nannie	1875	Wife of nephew of wife of son
Jones, Marlene Alethia	1958	Wife of step 2nd great grandson of daughter
Price, Priscilla	10 Jun 1941	Wife of step 2nd great grandson of daughter
Bias, Arletha		Wife of step 3rd great grandson of daughter
Petty, Wanda	01 Jan 1955	Wife of step 3rd great grandson of daughter
Ball, Sadie	17 Sep 1920	Wife of step great grandson of daughter
Edwards, Francis	31 Dec 1928	Wife of step great grandson of daughter
Fitchett, Virginia	07 Sep 1919	Wife of step great grandson of daughter
Garnett, Julia A.	29 Aug 1919	Wife of step great grandson of daughter

Ila		Wife of step great grandson of daughter
Jocelyn		Wife of step great grandson of daughter
Johnson, Gladys	26 Jul 1918	Wife of step great grandson of daughter
Lacy, Constancy	08 Jul 1923	Wife of step great grandson of daughter
Lenora		Wife of step great grandson of daughter
Minor, Lily Bell	16 Apr 1916	Wife of step great grandson of daughter
Payne, Charletta	06 May 1929	Wife of step great grandson of daughter
Stewart, Flossie	25 Aug 1933	Wife of step great grandson of daughter
Williams, Ludie Hilda	31 Dec 1921	Wife of step great grandson of daughter

CHAPTER 1

GABRIEL ROBINSON 1798 – NOV 1873

The U.S. Federal Census Non-Population Schedules, 1850-1880 showed that as of August 11, 1850 Gabriel Robinson was living on a small farm in Middlesex County, Virginia. By 1860 the size of his farm was 32 Acres. He was living on his farm with Jane Key who he married on September 2, 1840. Although he and Jane had no children, they often shared their home with in-laws until his death in November 1873.

1860 Agriculture Schedule

County/State	Middlesex County, VA
District	
Page	
NARA M#	
Owner/Agent/Mgr	Gabriel Robinson
Row #	

Year ending June 1, 1860

Description	Col	Value	
Name of Owner, Agent or Manager of the Farm	1	Gabriel Robinson	
Total Acres Improved	2	20	Acres
Total Acres Unimproved	3	12	Acres
Cash Value of Farm	4	$350	
Farm Implements & machinery value	5	$10	
Horses (no. of)	6	1	
Asses and Mules	7		
Milch Cows	8		
Working Oxen	9	1	
Other Cattle	10		
Sheep	11		
Swine	12	4	
Value of Livestock	13	$50	
Wheat	14		Bu
Rye	15		Bu
Indian Corn	16		Bu
Oats	17		Bu
Rice	18		Lbs
Tobacco	19		Lbs
Ginned cotton (400# bales)	20		bales
Wool	21		Lbs

Description	Col	Value	
Peas & Beans	22		Bu
Irish Potatoes	23	50	Bu
Sweet Potatoes	24	50	Bu
Barley	25		Bu
Buckwheat	26		Bu
Value of Orchard Products	27	$100	
Wine	28		Gals
Market Gardens Produce Value	29	$	
Butter	30	100	Lbs
Cheese	31		Lbs
Hay	32		Tons
Clover seed	33		Bu
Other Grass seeds	34		Bu
Hops	35		Lbs
Dew rotted Hemp	36		Tons
Water rotted Hemp	37		Tons
Other prepared Hemp	38		Tons
Flax	39		Lbs
Flaxseed	40		Bu
Silk Cocoons	41		Lbs
Maple Sugar	42		Lbs
Cane Sugar (1000 # hhds)	43		Hhds
Molasses	44		Gals
Beeswax	45		Lbs
Honey	46		Lbs
Value of Homemade Manufactures	47	$95	
Value of Animals slaughtered	48	$300	

CHAPTER 2
KITTY CARTER

Order Book Document (290) dated May 10, 1849. This document was prepared by the children of Grace Mitchell then deceased. This was an attempt to claim property owned by Grace Mitchell. All females listed in the document are shown with the names of their husbands with the exception of Kitty Carter. All males are listed with the surname Robinson. The researcher could find no information on Kitty Carter.

CHAPTER 3
JOHN ROBINSON 1800 – 10/15/1855

John Robinson is listed in the 1840 Census, as a free person of color, head of a household which consisted of 5 free person of color, and one Slave. The 1850 Census shows the name Jack Robertson however those that followed, shows John as the head of a household with the Robinson Surname. For unknown reasons John and his brother Lorenzo were both listed as Robertson in the 1850 census? Before 1850 and after 1850 they were always Robinson.

John raised his family on a small farm in St Stephens Parish, of King - Queen, Co VA, at the time of his death October 15, 1855 his real estate was listed as 50 Acres.

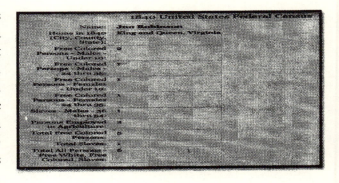

HON. JOHN E. DeHARDIT, JUDGE　　　　　　　　　　　　　　　　　　　　　CAREY C. HALL, CLERK
GLOUCESTER, VIRGINIA

CLERK'S OFFICE OF THE CIRCUIT COURT
King and Queen County
KING AND QUEEN C. H., VIRGINIA

From the 1862 Land Book, King and Queen County, Virginia. The following are named as those among whom the lands of JOHN ROBINSON are divided:

Dunbar Robinson
Lucy Robinson *
Elizabeth Robinson
Cornelius Robinson
Joseph Robinson
Jane Robinson
Dabney Robinson
John Robinson
The wife of John Collins*

The presumption is that these are the children of John Robinson, although the Land Book does not specifically say so.

*Women could not hold land in their own name at this time unless they were unmarried - land of a married woman was always listed in the name of the husband.

This material could not be photostated as the old book is too fragile.

Llewellyn Collins, Mary E. Dungey, Sarah L. Jordan and Leander Collins, children of Lucy Collins, dec'd a daughter of John Robinson are each entitled to one half of one sixth of one sixth of the whole.

Ada Collins and Lilly Collins, children of Elias Collins dec'd, a son of Lucy Collins dec'd a daughter of John Robinson dec'd are each entitled to one half of one sixth of one sixth of the whole.

Lilly Robinson, Mary E. Robinson, Margaret Kademy, Julia Patterson, Street Robinson, Harriet Robinson and Ketura Robinson, children of Dabney Robinson dec'd, son of John Robinson dec'd are each entitled to one ninth of one sixth of the whole.

Alfred Robinson, a son of Dabney Robinson was entitled to one ninth of one sixth of the property, but departed this life, leaving a widow Lomie Robinson, but no issue. This interest, subject to the dower interest of the said Lomie Robinson, will have to be divided among the surviving children of Dabney Robinson, to wit: lilly Robinson, Mary F. Robinson, Margaret Kademy, Julia Patterson, Street Robinson, Harriet Robinson, Keturah Robinson and Fannie Robinson.

Lilly Collins, one of the children of Elias Collins is an infant.

SECOND: John Robinson died sized and possessed of fifty (50) acres of land bounded on the west by the road from Truhart to Jerusalem Church, on the northeast by the road from said last mentioned road to Kerrs Mill, and also by the lands of William Littlepage.

THIRD: The said tract of land is not susceptible of partition in kind among the parties entitled thereto, in any of the modes prescribed by law, and it would be to the interest of all the parties to have the same sold and the proceeds divided.

FOURTH: The attention of your commissioner has been called to the fact that Dunbar Robinson, a son of John Robinson, whode interest in the land herein mentioned was conveyed to J. L. Cox by the children of said Dunbar Robinson, left a widow, Gertrude Robinson, who is not a party to the deed, nor is she a party to this suit. It is true that the dower of said Gertrude Robinson in the real estate of Dunbar Robinson has been assigned to her, yet out of abundant precaution your commissioner reports the fact to Court.

The depositions of Sarah L. Jordan and others, taken before me M.F. Bagby, as commissioner in cancery for the Court of King & Queen, in the State of Virginia, at King & Queen C.H., Va. On Tuesday, March 12, 1918, pursuant to the notice herewith returned, to be read as evidence on be-half of the complainants in a chancery suit now pending in the Circuit Court of King & Queen County, under the style of Cox et als., Complaints. Vs Jordan et als.', defts. Presc, R.B. Norman one of the complaints and Sarah L. Jordan and Elijah Jordan, her husband.

Sarah L. Jordan, a witness of lawful age, being first duly sworn, deposes and says, as follows in answer to questions by the commissioner.

Ques. 1. Please give your name, and residence.

Ans. Sarah L. Jordan, and I reside near Little Plymouth in King & Queen county.

Ques. 2. Are you one of the heirs at law of John Robinson, deceased, and if yes, will you please tell me how you are descended from John Robinson.

Ans. I am a daughter of Lucy Collins who was a daughter of John Robinson.

Ques. 3. Please give me the names of the children of Lucy Collins, and the names of the children of any of her children who have died.

Ans. Llewellyn Collins, Mary E. Dungey, Sarah L. Jordan, Leander Collins, are the children of Lucy Collins who are living. Ada and Lilly Collins are the children of Elias Collins who was a son of Lucy Collins, and who has died. Ida Bordley, is another daughter of Lucy Collins, but she has conveyed her interest in the land in this suit.

Ques. 4. Can you give me the names of the children of Dabney Robinson, who was a son of John Robinson and who has departed this life.

Ans. Lila Robinson, Keturah Robinson, Harriet Robinson, Mary Robinson, Margaret Kadeny, Fannie McDonald, Street Robinson, Julie Paterson, Alfred Robinson, The last named Alfred Robinson, having departed this life, leaving no issue. But Leaving a widow, Lomie Robinson.

Ques. 5. Any of the parties whom you have named as descendants of

Descendants of John Robinson

Generation 1

1. **John[1] Robinson** was born in 1800 in King & Queen County, Va. He died on 15 Oct 1855 in King & Queen, Virginia. He married **Mary Harris**. She was born in 1818 in King & Queen County, Va.

John Robinson and Mary Harris had the following children:

- 2. i. Dunbar[2] Robinson was born in 1834 in King & Queen County, Va. He married (1) Margarette J in 1863 in King & Queen County, Va. She was born in 1841 in King & Queen County, Va. He married (2) Gertrude Hampton, daughter of Thomas Hampton and Josephine on 15 Dec 1909 in King & Queen County, Va. She was born in 1894 in King & Queen County, Va.

- 3. ii. Dabney Robinson was born in 1835 in King & Queen County, Va. He married Mary E. She was born in 1835. He married (2) Sarah J. Jordan, daughter of George Jordan and Margaret Robinson on 26 Dec 1875 in King & Queen County, Va. She was born in 1849 in King & Queen County, Va.

- iii. Emeline Robinson was born in 1838 in King & Queen County, Va..

- iv. John Robinson Jr. was born in 1842 in King & Queen County, Va..

- 4. v. Lucy Robinson was born in 1843 in King & Queen County, Virginia. She married Leonidas Collins, son of Riley Collins and Lucy on 20 May 1866 in King & Queen County, Virginia. He was born in 1841 in King & Queen County, Virginia.

	vi.	Elizabeth Robinson was born in 1847 in King & Queen County, Virginia. She married George W. Henderson, son of Peter Henderson and Elizabeth Tuppence on 21 Dec 1871 in King & Queen County, Virginia. He was born in 1830 in King & Queen County, Virginia.
5.	vii.	Jane Robinson was born in 1848 in King & Queen County, Va.. She died on 27 Feb 1875 in King & Queen County, Va.. She married Leroy Lee. He was born in 1844 in King & Queen County, Va..
	viii.	Cornelius Robinson was born in 1849 in King & Queen County, Va.. He married Mary Ann Williams, daughter of Richard Williams and Ann Gilmore on 27 Feb 1878 in King & Queen County, Va.. She was born in 1852 in King & Queen County, Va..
6.	ix.	Melvina Robinson was born in 1849 in Gloucester County, Va.. She died in Apr 1878 in Gloucester County, Va.. She married Robert Lockley, son of Daniel Lockley and Milly Redmon on 29 Jun 1869 in Gloucester County, Va.. He was born in 1842 in Gloucester County, Va.
	x.	JAMES ROBINSON was born in 1851 in King & Queen County, Va.. He married Useba Morris, daughter of William Morris and Mary on 24 Dec 1874 in Middlesex County Va.. She was born in 1852 in Middlesex County, Va..
	xi.	JOSEPH ROBINSON was born in 1854 in King & Queen County, Va..

Generation 2

2. **Dunbar**[2] **Robinson** (John[1]) was born in 1834 in King & Queen County, Va.. He married (1) **Margarette J** in 1863 in King & Queen County, Va.. She was born in 1841 in King & Queen County, Va.. He married (3) **Gertrude Hampton**, daughter of Thomas Hampton and Josephine on 15 Dec 1909 in King & Queen County, Va.. She was born in 1894 in King & Queen County, Va..

Dunbar Robinson and Margarette J had the following children:

    i.   Isaiah P.[3] Robinson was born in 1865 in King & Queen County, Va.. He married Lucy B. Baker, daughter of Benjamin Baker and Rebecca on 28 May 1895 in Richmond, Virginia. She was born in 1871 in Richmond, Va..

    ii.   Ann Eliza Robinson was born in 1867 in King & Queen County, Va..

7.   iii.   Lorenzo Robinson was born in 1868 in King & Queen County, Va.. He married Texana Robinson, daughter of Albert Robinson and Sophia in 1898 in Philadelphia, Pa.. She was born in 1872 in Louisa, Virginia, USA.

    iv.   James A. Robinson was born in 1870 in King & Queen County, Va..

    v.   John Thomas Robinson was born in 1873 in King & Queen County, Va.. He married Sarah T in 1902 in Pennsylvania. She was born in 1880 in Virginia.

    vi.   Joshua Dunbar Robinson was born in 1879 in King & Queen County, Va.. He married Carie Bernice Rowe, daughter of James Rowe and Sarah on 31 Oct 1907 in King & Queen County, Va.. She was born in 1880 in King & Queen County, Va..

    vii.   Emma Robinson was born in 1883 in King & Queen County, Va..

viii.   Luvanna Robinson was born in 1888 in King & Queen County, Va..

3. Dabney[2] Robinson (John[1]) was born in 1835 in King & Queen County, Va.. He married Mary E. She was born in 1835. He married (2) Sarah J. Jordan, daughter of George Jordan and Margaret Robinson on 26 Dec 1875 in King & Queen County, Va.. She was born in 1849 in King & Queen County, Va..

Notes for Dabney Robinson:

The 1875 Marriage to Sarah Jordan was performed by his uncle Lorenzo Robinson

Dabney Robinson and Mary E had the following children:

- i.   Victoria[3] Robinson was born in 1866.
- ii. Ketuia Robinson was born in 1867.
- iii. Fatima Robinson was born in 1868.

Notes for Sarah J. Jordan:

Sarah J. Jordan took the sirname of her step father. Her father was Alexander Gilmore the first husband of her mother.

Dabney Robinson and Sarah J. Jordan had the following children:

- iv.   Harriet Robinson was born in 1879.
- v.   Margaret Robinson was born in 1882. She married O. Kademy.
- 8. vi. Fannie E. Robinson was born in 1885. She married O. McDonald.
- 9. vii. Julie A. Robinson was born in 1886. She married John H. Patterson. He was born in 1877.

viii. ALFRED G. ROBINSON was born in 1888. He married LOMIE.

4. LUCY² ROBINSON (John¹) was born in 1843 in King & Queen County, Virginia. She married Leonidas Collins, son of Riley Collins and Lucy on 20 May 1866 in King & Queen County, Virginia. He was born in 1841 in King & Queen County, Virginia.

Leonidas Collins and Lucy Robinson had the following children:

      i. LLEWELYN³ COLLINS.

10.   ii. MARY E. COLLINS was born in 1876 in King & Queen County, Va.. She married THOMAS DUNGEY. He was born in 1876 in King & Queen County, Va..

      iii. SARAH LOUISE COLLINS was born in 1884 in King & Queen County, Va.. She married James Elijah Jordan, son of John Robert Jordan and Polly Ann Bluefoot on 04 Jun 1909 in King & Queen County, Va.. He was born in 1880 in King & Queen County, Va.. He died on 25 Dec 1944 in Little Plymouth, Va..

      iv. LEANDER COLLINS.

11.   v. ELIAS COLLINS was born in 1869.

      vi. IDA COLLINS. She married BORDLEY.

      vii. ATTA COLLINS was born in 1867.

5. JANE² ROBINSON (John¹) was born in 1848 in King & Queen County, Va.. She died on 27 Feb 1875 in King & Queen County, Va.. She married LEROY LEE. He was born in 1844 in King & Queen County, Va..

Leroy Lee and Jane Robinson had the following children:

      i. ROSE³ LEE was born in 1869.

      ii. WILLIAM LEE was born in 1867.

iii. MARY A. LEE was born in 1865.

iv. JOHN R. LEE was born in 1868.

v. NANCY LEE.

6. MELVINA² ROBINSON (John¹) was born in 1849 in Gloucester County, Va.. She died in Apr 1878 in Gloucester County, Va.. She married Robert Lockley, son of Daniel Lockley and Milly Redmon on 29 Jun 1869 in Gloucester County, Va.. He was born in 1842 in Gloucester County, Va..

Robert Lockley and Melvina Robinson had the following children:

12. i. THOMAS³ LOCKLEY was born in 1870 in Gloucester County, Va.. He married (1) FRANCIS SUTHERLIN, daughter of John Sutherlin and Eliza Lockley on 29 Dec 1892 in Middlesex County, Virginia. She was born on 15 Jan 1868 in Middlesex County, Virginia. He married (2) BESSIE ANN BANKS, daughter of Lewis Banks and Nancy Lomax on 14 Nov 1909 in Middlesex County Va.. She was born in 1889 in Middlesex County, Virginia.

ii. MILLY LOCKLEY was born in 1874 in Gloucester County, Va..

iii. ROBERT LOCKLEY was born in 1875 in Gloucester County, Va..

iv. JACK LOCKLEY was born in 1868 in Gloucester County, Va.. He died on 15 Jun 1873 in Gloucester County, Va..

v. GOALDER LOCKLEY was born in 1876 in Gloucester County, Va.. She died in Nov 1876 in Gloucester County, Va..

Generation 3

7. **Lorenzo³ Robinson** (Dunbar², John¹) was born in 1868 in King & Queen County, Va.. He married Texana Robinson, daughter of Albert Robinson and Sophia in 1898 in Philadelphia, Pa.. She was born in 1872 in Louisa, Virginia, USA.

Lorenzo Robinson and Texana Robinson had the following children:

	i.	Wilbur⁴ Robinson was born in 1899 in Philadelphia, Pa.. He died on 03 Feb 1901 in Philadelphia, Pa..
	ii.	Edith Madeline Robinson was born in 1901 in Philadelphia, Pa..
	iii.	Margaret D. Robinson was born in 1902 in Philadelphia, Pa.. She married Luther Mathis.
	iv.	Chancellor D. Robinson was born in 1904 in Philadelphia, Pa.. He died on 21 Apr 1905 in Philadelphia, Pa..
	v.	Eva Ladocia Robinson was born in 1906 in Philadelphia, Pa.. She married Frederick K. Ford.
	vi.	Anna Bessie Robinson was born in 1908 in Philadelphia, Pa..
13.	vii.	Ethel Irene Robinson was born on 15 Mar 1912 in Philadelphia, Pa.. She died in Apr 1957 in Philadelphia, Pa.. She married Sr Issac B. Napper. He was born on 10 Mar 1911 in Philadelphia, Pa.. He died on 01 Mar 1943 in Philadelphia, Pa.. She married Edward Mullen.
14.	viii.	Cora L. Robinson was born in 1915 in Philadelphia, Pa.. She married Daniel Peterson.

8. **Fannie E³. Robinson** (Dabney², John¹) was born in 1885. She married **O. McDonald**.

O. McDonald and Fannie E. Robinson had the following child:

    i.   ROBERT[4] MCDONALD was born in 1911.

9. **JULIE A.**[3] **ROBINSON** (Dabney[2], John[1]) was born in 1886. She married **JOHN H. PATTERSON**. He was born in 1877.

John H. Patterson and Julie A. Robinson had the following children:

    i.   JOHN A.[4] PATTERSON was born in 1908.
    ii.   JAMES H. PATTERSON was born in 1910.
    iii.   ETHEL PATTERSON was born in 1912.
    iv.   SARAH PATTERSON was born in 1914.
    v.   WILLIAM PATTERSON was born in 1919.

10. **MARY E.**[3] **COLLINS** (Lucy[2] Robinson, John[1] Robinson) was born in 1876 in King & Queen County, Va.. She married **THOMAS DUNGEY**. He was born in 1876 in King & Queen County, Va..

Thomas Dungey and Mary E. Collins had the following children:

    i.   THELMA G.[4] DUNGEY was born in 1903.
    ii.   THOMAS R. DUNGEY was born in 1905.
    iii.   MARY U. DUNGEY was born in 1907.
    iv.   LWELLEN C. DUNGEY was born in 1908.
    v.   WILBORE O. DUNGEY was born in 1910.
    vi.   LOUELL L. DUNGEY was born in 1912.
    vii.   HERBERT W. DUNGEY was born in 1914.
    viii.   RUDYARD K. DUNGEY was born in 1916.
    ix.   GARNETT E. DUNGEY was born in 1919.

11. **Elias**[3] **Collins** (Lucy[2] Robinson, John[1] Robinson) was born in 1869.

   Elias Collins had the following children:

   i. Ada[4] Collins.

   ii. Lilly Collins.

12. **Thomas**[3] **Lockley** (Melvina[2] Robinson, John[1] Robinson) was born in 1870 in Gloucester County, Va.. He married (1) **Francis Sutherlin**, daughter of John Sutherlin and Eliza Lockley on 29 Dec 1892 in Middlesex County, Virginia. She was born on 15 Jan 1868 in Middlesex County, Virginia. He married (2) **Bessie Ann Banks**, daughter of Lewis Banks and Nancy Lomax on 14 Nov 1909 in Middlesex County Va.. She was born in 1889 in Middlesex County, Virginia.

   Thomas Lockley and Francis Sutherlin had the following children:

   i. Clarence[4] Lockley was born in 1894.

   ii. John Lockley was born in 1895. He married Josephine.

   iii. Eliza Lockley was born in 1898.

   iv. Nora Lockley was born in 1899.

   Thomas Lockley and Bessie Ann Banks had the following children:

   v. Robert Lewis Lockley was born on 10 Dec 1910 in Middlesex County, Virginia. He died on 26 Sep 1961 in Middlesex County, Va.. He married Emma Lee, daughter of Andrew Lee and Mollie Holmes-Lee on 16 Feb 1942 in Middlesex County Va.. She was born in 1918 in Middlesex County, Virginia.

15.   vi.   EARL LOCKLEY was born on 03 Dec 1911 in Middlesex County, Va.. He died on 02 Feb 1973. He married ELIZABETH GARNETT. He married (2) THELMA T. JORDAN, daughter of John Kelly Jordan and Eva S. Morris in 1955. She was born on 05 Apr 1915 in Middlesex County, Va.. She died on 20 Mar 2000 in Middlesex County, Va..

16.   vii.   PHILIP MCKENLEY LOCKLEY was born on 16 Jan 1917 in Middlesex County, Va.. He died on 15 Sep 1990 in Philadelphia, Pa.. He married Mertine Virginia Foster, daughter of James Foster and Otelia Kidd on 30 Sep 1939 in Middlesex County Va.. She was born on 31 May 1921 in Middlesex County, Virginia. She died in Jul 1977.

17.   viii.   ELMORE LOCKLEY was born on 30 Apr 1918 in Middlesex County, Va.. He died on 22 May 1984. He married RUSSELL CHRISTIAN. She was born on 02 Jul 1915.

18.   ix.   PEARL VIRGINIA LOCKLEY was born on 10 Apr 1921 in Middlesex County, Va.. She died on 13 Oct 1999. She married THOMAS BRIGHT. He was born on 09 Sep 1914. He died on 04 Apr 1921.

      x.   RUTH LOCKLEY was born on 09 Jul 1925 in Middlesex County, Va.. She died on 07 Jun 2005 in Brooklyn, N.Y.. She married MAJOR HARRIS.

19.   xi.   NANCY MARY LOCKLEY was born on 26 Aug 1929 in Middlesex County, Va.. She married Robert Edward Smith, son of Ernest Augusta Smith and Mattie Susan Fleet on 12 Aug 1957 in Middlesex County Va.. He was born on 08 Sep 1935 in Peary, Va. He died on 19 May 1979.

20.   xii.   SR IVERSON LOCKLEY was born on 22 Jul 1930 in Middlesex County, Va.. He married Flora Ruth Rice on 03 Dec 1957 in Boston, Mass. She was born on 17 Apr 1935 in Memphis, Tennessee.

xiii. ALICE LILLIAN LOCKLEY was born on 10 Aug 1932 in Middlesex County, Va..

Generation 4

13. ETHEL IRENE[4] ROBINSON (Lorenzo[3], Dunbar[2], John[1]) was born on 15 Mar 1912 in Philadelphia, Pa.. She died in Apr 1957 in Philadelphia, Pa.. She married **SR ISSAC B. NAPPER**. He was born on 10 Mar 1911 in Philadelphia, Pa.. He died on 01 Mar 1943 in Philadelphia, Pa.. She married **EDWARD MULLEN**.

Sr Issac B. Napper and Ethel Irene Robinson had the following children:

21. i. ISSAC B.[5] NAPPER II was born on 02 Apr 1934 in Philadelphia, Pa.. He married OLIVIA DOSSANTA. She was born on 20 Mar 1930 in South Wales, England. She died on 07 Feb 2008 in Philadelphia, Pa..

22. ii. ETHEL LUCY NAPPER was born on 24 Feb 1930 in Philadelphia, Pa.. She married John Henry Johnson on 03 Sep 1946 in De;ware. He was born on 03 Sep 1903 in Greensboro, North Carolina. He died on 23 Dec 1971 in Philadelphia, Pa..

iii. EDITH IRENE NAPPER was born on 19 Jun 1931 in Philadelphia, Pa.. She married James S. Thomas on 18 Jun 1950 in Philadelphia, Pa.. He was born on 19 Jun 1931 in Philadelphia, Pa..

23. iv. WILBUR JAMES NAPPER was born on 22 Sep 1935 in Philadelphia, Pa.. He married MARION LEWIS.

v. ANNA NAPPER was born in 1932 in Philadelphia, Pa..

14. **Cora L.**[4] **Robinson** (Lorenzo[3], Dunbar[2], John[1]) was born in 1915 in Philadelphia, Pa.. She married Daniel Peterson.

   Daniel Peterson and Cora L. Robinson had the following children:

   24. i. Ellen J.[5] Peterson was born on 03 Dec 1933 in Philadelphia, Pa.. She married Jr Robert E. Lucas, son of Robert Lucas and Dorothy on 29 Jun 1957 in Philadelphia, Pa.. He was born on 14 May 1931 in Willow Grove, Pa..

   25. ii. Daniel E. Peterson was born on 08 Oct 1936 in Philadelphia, Pa.. He married Severa in Philippines. She was born on 01 Jan 1944 in Philippines.

   26. iii. Warren L. Peterson was born on 22 Mar 1938 in Philadelphia, Pa.. He married Meridel Jeffery. She was born on 05 Mar 1947 in Philadelphia, Pa..

   27. iv. Russell Peterson was born on 14 Sep 1940 in Philadelphia, Pa.. He married Francine Feggans. He married (2) Elizabeth Davis on 30 Jun 1994 in Los Angeles, California. She was born on 06 Jan 1944 in Little Rock, Arkansas.

   28. v. Edna E. Peterson was born on 05 Sep 1942 in Philadelphia, Pa.. She married (1) Jr William C. Smith on 16 Jul 1967 in Killeen, Texas. He was born on 02 Feb 1943 in Chicago, Illinois. She married (2) Jonathan A. Blaine in Aug 1972 in Philadelphia, Pa..

   29. vi. Margaret Peterson was born on 02 Feb 1945 in Philadelphia, Pa.. She married James Cross. He died in Philadelphia, Pa.. She married (2) Sr Kent E. Arline in Philadelphia, Pa..

30. vii. ROBERT T. PETERSON was born on 24 Apr 1948 in Philadelphia, Pa.. He married (1) ANNETTE STEPHENS on 26 Jan 2001. She was born on 21 Oct 1956 in San Pedro, California. He married UNKNOWN. He married UNKNOWN.

viii. GWENDOLYN D. PETERSON was born on 29 Apr 1951 in Philadelphia, Pa.. She married GEORGE GASKINS. She married (2) WALTER M. FRANKLIN, son of Willie Franklin and Pauline on 07 Mar 1987 in Philadelphia, Pa.. He was born on 29 Aug 1945 in Massilon, Ohio.

15. EARL[4] LOCKLEY (Thomas[3], Melvina[2] Robinson, John[1] Robinson) was born on 03 Dec 1911 in Middlesex County, Va.. He died on 02 Feb 1973. He married ELIZABETH GARNETT. He married (2) THELMA T. JORDAN, daughter of John Kelly Jordan and Eva S. Morris in 1955. She was born on 05 Apr 1915 in Middlesex County, Va.. She died on 20 Mar 2000 in Middlesex County, Va..

Earl Lockley and Elizabeth Garnett had the following children:

31. i. QUEEN[5] LOCKLEY was born on 04 Aug 1942.

32. ii. DELOISE LOCKLEY was born on 20 Jan 1940.

16. PHILIP MCKENLEY[4] LOCKLEY (Thomas[3], Melvina[2] Robinson, John[1] Robinson) was born on 16 Jan 1917 in Middlesex County, Va.. He died on 15 Sep 1990 in Philadelphia, Pa.. He married Mertine Virginia Foster, daughter of James Foster and Otelia Kidd on 30 Sep 1939 in Middlesex County Va.. She was born on 31 May 1921 in Middlesex County, Virginia. She died in Jul 1977.

Philip McKenley Lockley and Mertine Virginia Foster had the following children:

33. i. DIANE[5] LOCKLEY was born on 27 Jul 1947 in Philadelphia, Pa.. She married SR OLIVER LEE MATHEW. He was born on 27 Sep 1943 in Philadelphia, Pa..

> 34. ii. JACQUELINE LOCKLEY was born on 13 Oct 1948 in Philadelphia, Pa.. She married (1) WAYNE E. ROBINSON on 14 Nov 1998 in Philadelphia, Pa.. He was born on 14 Aug 1949 in Philadelphia, Pa.. She married JAMES HART. He was born on 11 Nov 1936. She married WILLIAM H. GREEN. She married ULYSSES KENT.

17. **ELMORE**[4] **LOCKLEY** (Thomas[3], Melvina[2] Robinson, John[1] Robinson) was born on 30 Apr 1918 in Middlesex County, Va.. He died on 22 May 1984. He married RUSSELL CHRISTIAN. She was born on 02 Jul 1915.

Elmore Lockley and Russell Christian had the following children:

> 35. i. ELMYRTH[5] LOCKLEY was born on 08 Mar 1948 in Yorktown, Virginia. She married SR MARTIN TALIFERRO. He was born on 18 Mar 1947.
>
> 36. ii. ZELDA LOCKLEY was born on 23 Oct 1949 in Yorktown, Virginia. She married EDWARD STEWART. He was born on 17 Jun 1951.
>
> 37. iii. ELMORE LOCKLEY JR. was born on 08 Nov 1953 in Yorktown, Virginia. He married BRENDA ATKINS. She was born on 12 Oct 1947.

18. **PEARL VIRGINIA**[4] **LOCKLEY** (Thomas[3], Melvina[2] Robinson, John[1] Robinson) was born on 10 Apr 1921 in Middlesex County, Va.. She died on 13 Oct 1999. She married THOMAS BRIGHT. He was born on 09 Sep 1914. He died on 04 Apr 1921.

Thomas Bright and Pearl Virginia Lockley had the following child:

> i. LINDA PEARL[5] BRIGHT was born on 09 Sep 1958.

19. **NANCY MARY**[4] **LOCKLEY** (Thomas[3], Melvina[2] Robinson, John[1] Robinson) was born on 26 Aug 1929 in Middlesex County, Va.. She married Robert Edward Smith, son of Ernest Augusta Smith

and Mattie Susan Fleet on 12 Aug 1957 in Middlesex County Va..
He was born on 08 Sep 1935 in Peary, Va. He died on 19 May 1979.

Robert Edward Smith and Nancy Mary Lockley had the following children:

 38. i. JAMES ROBERT[5] SMITH was born on 13 Aug 1958 in Mathews, Virginia. He married KARALEEN LIBCOMB.

 39. ii. MARY ANN SMITH was born on 05 Sep 1959 in Mathews, Virginia. She married WILLIAM DAVIS JR..

   iii. THOMAS EDWARD SMITH was born on 15 Aug 1960 in Mathews, Virginia. He died on 17 Jul 2007 in Mathews, Va..

   iv. ALICE MAY SMITH was born on 31 Aug 1961 in Mathews, Virginia.

 40. v. LUCY ELLEN SMITH was born on 10 Sep 1963 in Mathews, Virginia.

 41. vi. LINDA RUTH SMITH was born on 20 Jan 1968 in Mathews, Virginia.

20. **SR IVERSON[4] LOCKLEY** (Thomas[3], Melvina[2] Robinson, John[1] Robinson) was born on 22 Jul 1930 in Middlesex County, Va.. He married Flora Ruth Rice on 03 Dec 1957 in Boston, Mass. She was born on 17 Apr 1935 in Memphis, Tennessee.

Sr Iverson Lockley and Flora Ruth Rice had the following children:

 42. i. JR IVERSON[5] LOCKLEY was born on 03 Dec 1958 in Boston, Mass.

 43. ii. MONICE ANITA LOCKLEY was born on 30 Nov 1960 in Boston, Mass..

   iii. IASHA DEE LOCKLEY was born on 21 Nov 1981 in Boston, Mass.

Generation 5

21. **ISSAC B.[5] NAPPER II** (Ethel Irene[4] Robinson, Lorenzo[3] Robinson, Dunbar[2] Robinson, John[1] Robinson) was born on 02 Apr 1934 in Philadelphia, Pa.. He married **OLIVIA DOSSANTA**. She was born on 20 Mar 1930 in South Wales, England. She died on 07 Feb 2008 in Philadelphia, Pa..

Issac B. Napper II and Olivia Dossanta had the following children:

    44.   i.   BONITA[6] NAPPER was born on 31 Jul 1958.

    45.   ii.   ISSAC NAPPER III was born on 09 Jan 1969. He married LINDA STONE.

    46.   iii. JOHN NAPPER was born on 21 May 1966 in Philadelphia, Pa.. He married CHRISTIANA.

22. **ETHEL LUCY[5] NAPPER** (Ethel Irene[4] Robinson, Lorenzo[3] Robinson, Dunbar[2] Robinson, John[1] Robinson) was born on 24 Feb 1930 in Philadelphia, Pa.. She married John Henry Johnson on 03 Sep 1946 in De;ware. He was born on 03 Sep 1903 in Greensboro, North Carolina. He died on 23 Dec 1971 in Philadelphia, Pa..

John Henry Johnson and Ethel Lucy Napper had the following children:

    47.   i.   DEDORIAD LITHIAH[6] NAPPER was born on 24 Apr 1947 in Philadelphia, Pa.. She died in Oct 2003 in Philadelphia, Pa.. She married BILLY HIPP. He was born on 24 Apr 1947 in Philadelphia, Pa.. He died on 16 May 1990 in Philadelphia, Pa..

    48.   ii.   DELLAPHINE MARIE JOHNSON was born on 20 Apr 1948 in New jersey. She married Gerald Bingham. She married DENNIS IVY.

    49.   iii. DOREEN PATRICIA JOHNSON was born on 28 Nov 1949 in Philadelphia, Pa..

50.   iv.   Dow Lorenzo Johnson was born on 09 Mar 1951 in Philadelphia, Pa.. He died on 15 May 2011 in Texas. He married Dara Holcomb. He married Rachel Brown.

　　 v.   Derward John Johnson was born on 01 Feb 1952 in Philadelphia, Pa.. He married Gale Stevens Channel.

　　 vi.   Dartaniel Henry Johnson was born on 25 Jan 1953 in Philadelphia, Pa.. He died on 15 May 2003 in New jersey. He married Linda Brown.

51.   vii. Denise Johnson was born on 15 Jul 1955 in Philadelphia, Pa.. She married (1) William Dandridge in Apr 1972. She married Carlton Meade. He died on 30 Mar 1991 in Philadelphia, Pa..

52.   viii. Donzella Johnson was born on 13 Jul 1954 in Philadelphia, Pa.. She married Jr James King.

53.   ix.   Donzeila Olivia Johnson was born on 27 Jun 1957 in Philadelphia, Pa.. She married Richard Fisher. She married Ralph Spearman.

23. **Wilbur James**[5] **Napper** (Ethel Irene[4] Robinson, Lorenzo[3] Robinson, Dunbar[2] Robinson, John[1] Robinson) was born on 22 Sep 1935 in Philadelphia, Pa.. He married **Marion Lewis**.

Wilbur James Napper and Marion Lewis had the following children:

　　 i.   Jr Wilbur James[6] Napper was born on 23 Jun 1958 in Philadelphia, Pa.. He died on 11 Nov 2013 in Philadelphia, Pa..

54.   ii.   Claire Napper. She married Paul Roberson.

　　 iii. Carl Napper.

　　 iv.   Diane Napper. She married Shawn Holster.

24. **ELLEN J.**[5] **PETERSON** (Cora L.[4] Robinson, Lorenzo[3] Robinson, Dunbar[2] Robinson, John[1] Robinson) was born on 03 Dec 1933 in Philadelphia, Pa.. She married Jr Robert E. Lucas, son of Robert Lucas and Dorothy on 29 Jun 1957 in Philadelphia, Pa.. He was born on 14 May 1931 in Willow Grove, Pa..

Jr Robert E. Lucas and Ellen J. Peterson had the following child:

    i.   CHRYTAL A.[6] LUCAS was born on 01 Jan 1967 in Philadelphia, Pa..

25. **DANIEL E.**[5] **PETERSON** (Cora L.[4] Robinson, Lorenzo[3] Robinson, Dunbar[2] Robinson, John[1] Robinson) was born on 08 Oct 1936 in Philadelphia, Pa.. He married Severa in Philippines. She was born on 01 Jan 1944 in Philippines.

Daniel E. Peterson and Severa had the following children:

    i.   JEANETTE[6] PETERSON was born on 16 Jun 1971 in Michigan.

    ii.   DANIEL PETERSON was born on 08 Aug 1974 in Sacramento, California, USA.

    iii.   BERNADETTE PETERSON was born on 15 Feb 1978 in Sacramento, California, USA.

    iv.   WILLIAM PETERSON was born on 07 Nov 1980 in Sacramento, California, USA.

26. **WARREN L.**[5] **PETERSON** (Cora L.[4] Robinson, Lorenzo[3] Robinson, Dunbar[2] Robinson, John[1] Robinson) was born on 22 Mar 1938 in Philadelphia, Pa.. He married **MERIDEL JEFFERY**. She was born on 05 Mar 1947 in Philadelphia, Pa..

Warren L. Peterson and Meridel Jeffery had the following child:

i. Shani Danielle[6] Peterson was born on 22 Dec 1982 in Philadelphia, Pa..

27. **Russell**[5] **Peterson** (Cora L.[4] Robinson, Lorenzo[3] Robinson, Dunbar[2] Robinson, John[1] Robinson) was born on 14 Sep 1940 in Philadelphia, Pa.. He married **Francine Feggans**. He married (2) **Elizabeth Davis** on 30 Jun 1994 in Los Angeles, California. She was born on 06 Jan 1944 in Little Rock, Arkansas.

Russell Peterson and Elizabeth Davis had the following child:

i. Danielle N.[6] Davis was born on 09 Sep 1997 in Los Angeles, California.

28. **Edna E.**[5] **Peterson** (Cora L.[4] Robinson, Lorenzo[3] Robinson, Dunbar[2] Robinson, John[1] Robinson) was born on 05 Sep 1942 in Philadelphia, Pa.. She married (1) **Jr William C. Smith** on 16 Jul 1967 in Killeen, Texas. He was born on 02 Feb 1943 in Chicago, Illinois. She married (2) **Jonathan A. Blaine** in Aug 1972 in Philadelphia, Pa..

Jonathan A. Blaine and Edna E. Peterson had the following children:

i. Jonathan K.r.[6] Blaine was born on 13 Aug 1974 in Philadelphia, Pa..

ii. Rahn A. Blaine was born on 27 Dec 1975 in Philadelphia, Pa..

29. **Margaret**[5] **Peterson** (Cora L.[4] Robinson, Lorenzo[3] Robinson, Dunbar[2] Robinson, John[1] Robinson) was born on 02 Feb 1945 in Philadelphia, Pa.. She married **James Cross**. He died in Philadelphia, Pa.. She married (2) **Sr Kent E. Arline** in Philadelphia, Pa..

Sr Kent E. Arline and Margaret Peterson had the following child:

    i.   JR KENT E.⁶ ARLINE was born on 10 Sep 1967 in Philadelphia, Pa..

30. **ROBERT T.⁵ PETERSON** (Cora L.⁴ Robinson, Lorenzo³ Robinson, Dunbar² Robinson, John¹ Robinson) was born on 24 Apr 1948 in Philadelphia, Pa.. He married (1) **ANNETTE STEPHENS** on 26 Jan 2001. She was born on 21 Oct 1956 in San Pedro, California. He married **UNKNOWN**. He married **UNKNOWN**.

Robert T. Peterson and Unknown had the following child:

55. i.   SHARRON⁶ PATTERSON-MCFADDEN. He married Unknown.

Robert T. Peterson and Unknown had the following children:

56. ii.   MONIQUE D. PETERSON was born on 18 Dec 1978 in Philadelphia, Pa.. She married TIMOTHY WITCHER.

     iii. NIA M. PETERSON was born on 14 Apr 1980 in Philadelphia, Pa..

31. **QUEEN⁵ LOCKLEY** (Earl⁴, Thomas³, Melvina² Robinson, John¹ Robinson) was born on 04 Aug 1942.

Queen Lockley had the following child:

57. i.   ANGELA⁶ LOCKLEY was born on 31 Dec 1960. She married EUGENE MAYS. He was born on 24 Dec 1960.

32. **Deloise[5] Lockley** (Earl[4], Thomas[3], Melvina[2] Robinson, John[1] Robinson) was born on 20 Jan 1940.

Deloise Lockley had the following children:

    i.   Nathaniel[6] Lockley was born on 23 Dec 1962.

    ii.   Clarance Lockley was born on 11 Sep 1964.

    iii.   Royal Smith was born on 23 Mar 1966.

33. **Diane[5] Lockley** (Philip McKenley[4], Thomas[3], Melvina[2] Robinson, John[1] Robinson) was born on 27 Jul 1947 in Philadelphia, Pa.. She married **Sr Oliver Lee Mathew**. He was born on 27 Sep 1943 in Philadelphia, Pa..

Sr Oliver Lee Mathew and Diane Lockley had the following children:

58.   i.   Lorraine[6] Lockley was born on 19 Sep 1963 in Philadelphia, Pa.. She married James Malachi.

59.   ii.   Jr Oliver Lee Mathews was born on 13 May 1967 in Philadelphia, Pa.. He married Lesa Chambliss. He married Enina Hamilton.

60.   iii.   Kenneth Mathews was born on 07 Aug 1969 in Philadelphia, Pa.. He married Yolanda Martin. He married Rhonda Johnson.

61.   iv.   Sabrina Mathews was born on 19 Jul 1984 in Philadelphia, Pa.. She married Brian Reed.

34. **Jacqueline[5] Lockley** (Philip McKenley[4], Thomas[3], Melvina[2] Robinson, John[1] Robinson) was born on 13 Oct 1948 in Philadelphia, Pa.. She married (1) **Wayne E. Robinson** on 14 Nov 1998 in Philadelphia, Pa.. He was born on 14 Aug 1949 in Philadelphia, Pa.. She married **James Hart**. He was born on 11 Nov 1936. She married **William H. Green**. She married **Ulysses Kent**.

James Hart and Jacqueline Lockley had the following children:

62. i. WILLIAM JAMES[6] LOCKLEY was born on 25 Jan 1971 in Philadelphia, Pa.. He married NIGERIA.

63. ii. MARCELLA EVETTE LOCKLEY was born on 31 Dec 1971 in Philadelphia, Pa.. She married JAMES PARKER. She married MALIK SWINGLER.

64. iii. DEMITRUIS ANTHONY LOCKLEY was born on 23 Dec 1972 in Philadelphia, Pa.. He married DEBRA ANN SEALY. She was born on 23 Dec 1955.

William H. Green and Jacqueline Lockley had the following child:

65. i. CYNTHIA RENEE[6] LOCKLEY was born on 05 Mar 1970 in Philadelphia, Pa.. She married ALAN WORD. He was born on 08 Mar 1966.

Ulysses Kent and Jacqueline Lockley had the following child:

i. VANESSA[6] LOCKLEY was born on 01 Jul 1968 in Philadelphia, Pa..

35. ELMYRTH[5] LOCKLEY (Elmore[4], Thomas[3], Melvina[2] Robinson, John[1] Robinson) was born on 08 Mar 1948 in Yorktown, Virginia. She married SR MARTIN TALIFERRO. He was born on 18 Mar 1947.

Sr Martin Taliferro and Elmyrth Lockley had the following children:

i. MARTIN[6] TALIFERRO JR was born on 11 Jan 1978.

ii. ADAM TALIFERRO was born on 20 Dec 1981.

36. ZELDA[5] LOCKLEY (Elmore[4], Thomas[3], Melvina[2] Robinson, John[1] Robinson) was born on 23 Oct 1949 in Yorktown, Virginia. She married EDWARD STEWART. He was born on 17 Jun 1951.

Edward Stewart and Zelda Lockley had the following children:

  i. RACHEL CHRISTINA[6] STEWART was born on 10 Dec 1978.

  ii. ISAAC EVANS STEWART was born on 22 Mar 1982.

37. **ELMORE[5] LOCKLEY JR.** (Elmore[4], Thomas[3], Melvina[2] Robinson, John[1] Robinson) was born on 08 Nov 1953 in Yorktown, Virginia. He married **BRENDA ATKINS**. She was born on 12 Oct 1947.

Elmore Lockley Jr. and Brenda Atkins had the following child:

  i. DAVID ELMORE[6] LOCKLEY was born on 07 Jul 1985.

38. **JAMES ROBERT[5] SMITH** (Nancy Mary[4] Lockley, Thomas[3] Lockley, Melvina[2] Robinson, John[1] Robinson) was born on 13 Aug 1958 in Mathews, Virginia. He married **KARALEEN LIBCOMB**.

James Robert Smith and Karaleen Libcomb had the following children:

  i. .JR JAMES ROBERT[6] SMITH was born on 09 Apr 1982.

  ii. RICHARD EDWARD SMITH was born on 06 Jul 1983.

39. **MARY ANN[5] SMITH** (Nancy Mary[4] Lockley, Thomas[3] Lockley, Melvina[2] Robinson, John[1] Robinson) was born on 05 Sep 1959 in Mathews, Virginia. She married **WILLIAM DAVIS JR.**.

William Davis Jr. and Mary Ann Smith had the following children:

  i. JALEESA TACHELLE[6] DAVIS was born on 18 May 1988.

  ii. MARIAH JADE DAVIS was born on 03 Sep 1995.

  iii. WAYMON WILLIAM DAVIS was born on 30 Jun 1999.

  iv. JESSICA TELEESA DAVIS was born on 20 Jan 1993. She died on 12 Nov 1993.

40. **Lucy Ellen[5] Smith** (Nancy Mary[4] Lockley, Thomas[3] Lockley, Melvina[2] Robinson, John[1] Robinson) was born on 10 Sep 1963 in Mathews, Virginia.

Lucy Ellen Smith had the following child:

    i.   Deanna Nancy[6] Smith was born on 30 Aug 1984.

41. **Linda Ruth[5] Smith** (Nancy Mary[4] Lockley, Thomas[3] Lockley, Melvina[2] Robinson, John[1] Robinson) was born on 20 Jan 1968 in Mathews, Virginia.

Linda Ruth Smith had the following children:

    i.   Britney Nicole[6] King was born on 12 Aug 1990.

    ii.   Bryan Nicholas Smith was born on 19 Oct 1997.

42. **Jr Iverson[5] Lockley** (Sr Iverson[4], Thomas[3], Melvina[2] Robinson, John[1] Robinson) was born on 03 Dec 1958 in Boston, Mass.

Jr Iverson Lockley had the following child:

    i.   Iasha Dee Lockley[6] Hill was born on 21 Nov 1981 in Boston, Mass..

43. **Monice Anita[5] Lockley** (Sr Iverson[4], Thomas[3], Melvina[2] Robinson, John[1] Robinson) was born on 30 Nov 1960 in Boston, Mass..

Monice Anita Lockley had the following child:

    i.   Arron Lockley[6] Young was born on 15 Oct 1986 in Boston, Mass..

Generation 6

44. **Bonita**[6] **Napper** (Issac B.[5] II, Ethel Irene[4] Robinson, Lorenzo[3] Robinson, Dunbar[2] Robinson, John[1] Robinson) was born on 31 Jul 1958.

Bonita Napper had the following child:

    i.   Jonathan[7] Norde was born on 13 Feb 1983.

45. **Issac**[6] **Napper III** (Issac B.[5] II, Ethel Irene[4] Robinson, Lorenzo[3] Robinson, Dunbar[2] Robinson, John[1] Robinson) was born on 09 Jan 1969. He married **Linda Stone**.

Issac Napper III and Linda Stone had the following children:

    i.   Bonita[7] Stone was born in Philadelphia, Pa..

    ii.   Cheasea Napper was born in Philadelphia, Pa..

    iii.   Issac Napper IV was born in Philadelphia, Pa..

46. **John**[6] **Napper** (Issac B.[5] II, Ethel Irene[4] Robinson, Lorenzo[3] Robinson, Dunbar[2] Robinson, John[1] Robinson) was born on 21 May 1966 in Philadelphia, Pa.. He married **Christiana**.

John Napper and Christiana had the following child:

    i.   John[7] Napper was born on 13 Feb 1983 in Philadelphia, Pa..

47. **Dedoriad Lithiah**[6] **Napper** (Ethel Lucy[5], Ethel Irene[4] Robinson, Lorenzo[3] Robinson, Dunbar[2] Robinson, John[1] Robinson) was born on 24 Apr 1947 in Philadelphia, Pa.. She died in Oct 2003 in Philadelphia, Pa.. She married **Billy Hipp**. He was born on 24 Apr 1947 in Philadelphia, Pa.. He died on 16 May 1990 in Philadelphia, Pa..

Billy Hipp and Dedoriad Lithiah Napper had the following children:

66. i. EDWARD LEE[7] BARNBY was born in 1964 in Houston, Texas. He married TRACIE WOODEN.

ii. CARLTON HIPP was born on 14 Apr 1971 in Philadelphia, Pa..

iii. DEDORID L. HIPP was born on 03 Dec 1974 in Philadelphia, Pa..

48. **DELLAPHINE MARIE**[6] **JOHNSON** (Ethel Lucy[5] Napper, Ethel Irene[4] Robinson, Lorenzo[3] Robinson, Dunbar[2] Robinson, John[1] Robinson) was born on 20 Apr 1948 in New jersey. She married **GERALD BINGHAM**. She married **DENNIS IVY**.

Gerald Bingham and Dellaphine Marie Johnson had the following child:

i. JR GERALD[7] BINGHAM was born on 16 Aug in Philadelphia, Pa..

Dennis Ivy and Dellaphine Marie Johnson had the following children:

67. i. Charmine[7] Johnson was born on 04 Sep 1966 in Philadelphia, Pa.. She married LANCE MACK. She married HERBERT EDMOUNDS.

68. ii. CASS AVERY JOHNSON was born on 02 Sep 1967 in Philadelphia, Pa.. He married PATRICE HAWKINS. He married TREACIE.

iii. CARVIN JOHNSON was born on 20 Jan 1968 in Philadelphia, Pa..

69. iv. CARMA M. JOHNSON was born on 24 May 1969 in Philadelphia, Pa..

49. **Doreen Patricia**[6] **Johnson** (Ethel Lucy[5] Napper, Ethel Irene[4] Robinson, Lorenzo[3] Robinson, Dunbar[2] Robinson, John[1] Robinson) was born on 28 Nov 1949 in Philadelphia, Pa..

Doreen Patricia Johnson had the following children:

- 70. i. Christopher David[7] Johnson. He married Margarte.
- 71. ii. Candice Johnson was born in 1988 in Philadelphia, Pa.. She married John Johnson.

50. **Dow Lorenzo**[6] **Johnson** (Ethel Lucy[5] Napper, Ethel Irene[4] Robinson, Lorenzo[3] Robinson, Dunbar[2] Robinson, John[1] Robinson) was born on 09 Mar 1951 in Philadelphia, Pa.. He died on 15 May 2011 in Texas. He married **Dara Holcomb**. He married **Rachel Brown**.

Dow Lorenzo Johnson and Rachel Brown had the following child:

- i. Victor[7] Steward was born in Philadelphia, Pa..

51. **Denise**[6] **Johnson** (Ethel Lucy[5] Napper, Ethel Irene[4] Robinson, Lorenzo[3] Robinson, Dunbar[2] Robinson, John[1] Robinson) was born on 15 Jul 1955 in Philadelphia, Pa.. She married (1) **William Dandridge** in Apr 1972. She married **Carlton Meade**. He died on 30 Mar 1991 in Philadelphia, Pa..

William Dandridge and Denise Johnson had the following children:

- 72. i. Cyrus Lamont[7] Dandridge was born on 22 Aug 1972 in Philadelphia, Pa..
- 73. ii. Gary Tamara Dandridge was born on 15 Mar 1974 in Philadelphia, Pa.. He married Charnelle Harris.

52. **Donzella[6] Johnson** (Ethel Lucy[5] Napper, Ethel Irene[4] Robinson, Lorenzo[3] Robinson, Dunbar[2] Robinson, John[1] Robinson) was born on 13 Jul 1954 in Philadelphia, Pa.. She married Jr James King.

Jr James King and Donzella Johnson had the following children:

    74.   i.   Shawn James[7] King was born on 03 Mar 1973 in Philadelphia, Pa.. He married Shala Jones in Jun 1996.

    75.   ii.   Jeneene Marie King was born on 26 Jul 1979 in Philadelphia, Pa..

           iii.   Marcus Edward King was born on 24 Feb 1972 in Philadelphia, Pa..

           iv.   Holly King was born in Philadelphia, Pa..

53. **Donzeila Olivia[6] Johnson** (Ethel Lucy[5] Napper, Ethel Irene[4] Robinson, Lorenzo[3] Robinson, Dunbar[2] Robinson, John[1] Robinson) was born on 27 Jun 1957 in Philadelphia, Pa.. She married **Richard Fisher**. She married **Ralph Spearman**.

Richard Fisher and Donzeila Olivia Johnson had the following child:

    76.   i.   Nicole Noel[7] Fisher was born on 31 Dec 1979 in Philadelphia, Pa.. She married Chancey Holloway.

Ralph Spearman and Donzeila Olivia Johnson had the following children:

    77.   i.   Crystal[7] Spearman was born on 26 Mar 1981 in Philadelphia, Pa.. She married Richard Cantell on 20 May 2011.

           ii.   Michael S. Spearman was born on 10 Nov 1990 in Philadelphia, Pa..

    78.   iii.   Jonathan S. Spearman was born on 16 Nov 1991 in Philadelphia, Pa..

54. **Claire**[6] **Napper** (Wilbur James[5], Ethel Irene[4] Robinson, Lorenzo[3] Robinson, Dunbar[2] Robinson, John[1] Robinson, Wilbur James[5], Sr Issac B.). She married **Paul Roberson**.

Paul Roberson and Claire Napper had the following children:

    i.   Bethlehem[7] Roberson.

    ii.   Ruth Roberson.

    iii. Agnes Roberson.

55. **Sharron**[6] **Patterson-McFadden** (Robert T.[5] Peterson, Cora L.[4] Robinson, Lorenzo[3] Robinson, Dunbar[2] Robinson, John[1] Robinson, Robert T.[5] Peterson, Daniel Peterson). He married **Unknown**.

Sharron Patterson-Mcfadden and Unknown had the following children:

    i.   Gabrielle[7] McFadden.

    ii.   Gregory McFadden.

    iii. Shelby McFadden.

56. **Monique D.**[6] **Peterson** (Robert T.[5], Cora L.[4] Robinson, Lorenzo[3] Robinson, Dunbar[2] Robinson, John[1] Robinson) was born on 18 Dec 1978 in Philadelphia, Pa.. She married **Timothy Witcher**.

Timothy Witcher and Monique D. Peterson had the following children:

    i.   Amaini[7] Witcher was born on 24 Aug 2005 in Burlington, New Jersey, USA.

    ii.   Julius R. Witcher was born on 21 Dec 2007 in Burlington, New Jersey, USA.

57. **Angela**[6] **Lockley** (Queen[5], Earl[4], Thomas[3], Melvina[2] Robinson, John[1] Robinson) was born on 31 Dec 1960. She married **Eugene Mays**. He was born on 24 Dec 1960.

Eugene Mays and Angela Lockley had the following child:

    i.   Sheanise[7] Mays was born on 15 Feb 1993.

58. **Lorraine**[6] **Lockley** (Diane[5], Philip McKenley[4], Thomas[3], Melvina[2] Robinson, John[1] Robinson) was born on 19 Sep 1963 in Philadelphia, Pa.. She married **James Malachi**.

Lorraine Lockley had the following child:

    i.   Phillip[7] Mathews.

James Malachi and Lorraine Lockley had the following children:

    i.   Lejean[7] Malachi was born on 04 Sep 1982 in Philadelphia, Pa..

79. ii.   Jacina Malachi was born on 15 Jul 1985 in Alcas, Oklahoma. She married Gary Austin. She married Rasael Davis. She married Frank Hailey. She married James Haywood.

59. **Jr Oliver Lee**[6] **Mathews** (Diane[5] Lockley, Philip McKenley[4] Lockley, Thomas[3] Lockley, Melvina[2] Robinson, John[1] Robinson) was born on 13 May 1967 in Philadelphia, Pa.. He married **Lesa Chambliss**. He married **Enina Hamilton**.

Jr Oliver Lee Mathews and Lesa Chambliss had the following children:

    i.   Oliver[7] Mathews was born on 15 Sep 1993 in Philadelphia, Pa..

    ii.   Ashley Chambliss.

Jr Oliver Lee Mathews and Enina Hamilton had the following child:

    iii.   DORA MATHEWS was born on 04 Jul 1996 in Philadelphia, Pa..

60. **KENNETH**[6] **MATHEWS** (Diane[5] Lockley, Philip McKenley[4] Lockley, Thomas[3] Lockley, Melvina[2] Robinson, John[1] Robinson) was born on 07 Aug 1969 in Philadelphia, Pa.. He married **YOLANDA MARTIN**. He married **RHONDA JOHNSON**.

Kenneth Mathews and Yolanda Martin had the following child:

    i.   KENYA[7] MATHEWS was born on 23 Nov 1991 in Philadelphia, Pa..

Kenneth Mathews and Rhonda Johnson had the following child:

    ii.   AANISA JOHNSON.

61. **SABRINA**[6] **MATHEWS** (Diane[5] Lockley, Philip McKenley[4] Lockley, Thomas[3] Lockley, Melvina[2] Robinson, John[1] Robinson) was born on 19 Jul 1984 in Philadelphia, Pa.. She married **BRIAN REED**.

Brian Reed and Sabrina Mathews had the following child:

    i.   SABREE[7] MATHEWS was born on 20 Jul 2003.

62. **WILLIAM JAMES**[6] **LOCKLEY** (Jacqueline[5], Philip McKenley[4], Thomas[3], Melvina[2] Robinson, John[1] Robinson) was born on 25 Jan 1971 in Philadelphia, Pa.. He married **NIGERIA**.

William James Lockley and Nigeria had the following child:

    i.   TAJAY[7] LOCKLEY.

63. **Marcella Evette**[6] **Lockley** (Jacqueline[5], Philip McKenley[4], Thomas[3], Melvina[2] Robinson, John[1] Robinson) was born on 31 Dec 1971 in Philadelphia, Pa.. She married **James Parker**. She married **Malik Swingler**.

James Parker and Marcella Evette Lockley had the following children:

    i.   Marcella Mertine[7] Lockley was born on 20 Jun 1988 in Philadelphia, Pa..

    ii.   James Lockley.

Malik Swingler and Marcella Evette Lockley had the following child:

    i.   James Kenneth[7] Lockley was born on 04 Feb 1984 in Philadelphia, Pa..

64. **Demitruis Anthony**[6] **Lockley** (Jacqueline[5], Philip McKenley[4], Thomas[3], Melvina[2] Robinson, John[1] Robinson) was born on 23 Dec 1972 in Philadelphia, Pa.. He married **Debra Ann Sealy**. She was born on 23 Dec 1955.

Demitruis Anthony Lockley and Debra Ann Sealy had the following child:

    i.   Rosita Junita[7] Sealy was born on 22 Jul 2001 in Philadelphia, Pa..

65. **Cynthia Renee**[6] **Lockley** (Jacqueline[5], Philip McKenley[4], Thomas[3], Melvina[2] Robinson, John[1] Robinson) was born on 05 Mar 1970 in Philadelphia, Pa.. She married **Alan Word**. He was born on 08 Mar 1966.

Alan Word and Cynthia Renee Lockley had the following children:

80. i. VANASSA RENEE[7] LOCKLEY was born on 29 Jun 1984 in Philadelphia, Pa..

ii. JACQUELINE EVETT LOCKLEY was born on 17 Jun 1985 in Philadelphia, Pa..

iii. TIFFANY NICLOE LOCKLEY was born on 27 May 1987 in Philadelphia, Pa..

iv. ALAN DEVON LOCKLEY was born on 27 Jul 1989 in Philadelphia, Pa..

v. TERANCE PHILLIP LOCKLEY was born on 21 Jun 1990 in Philadelphia, Pa..

vi. WILLIAM ANTHONY LOCKLEY was born on 01 Jul 1991 in Philadelphia, Pa..

Generation 7

66. **EDWARD LEE**^{7} **BARNBY** (Dedoriad Lithiah^6 Napper, Ethel Lucy^5 Napper, Ethel Irene^4 Robinson, Lorenzo^3 Robinson, Dunbar^2 Robinson, John^1 Robinson) was born in 1964 in Houston, Texas. He married **TRACIE WOODEN**.

Edward Lee Barnby and Tracie Wooden had the following children:

    i.   STACIA^8 BARNBY.

    ii.   JAMES BARNBY.

67. **CHARMINE**^{7} **JOHNSON** (Dellaphine Marie^6, Ethel Lucy^5 Napper, Ethel Irene^4 Robinson, Lorenzo^3 Robinson, Dunbar^2 Robinson, John^1 Robinson) was born on 04 Sep 1966 in Philadelphia, Pa.. She married **LANCE MACK**. She married **HERBERT EDMOUNDS**.

Lance Mack and Charmine Johnson had the following children:

81.   i.   LISA^8 MACK was born on 30 Sep 1982 in Philadelphia, Pa.. She married JAMES CONWAY.

      ii.   LORI MACK was born on 10 Mar 1988 in Philadelphia, Pa..

82.   iii.   LEAH MACK was born on 21 Jan 1990 in Philadelphia, Pa..

Herbert Edmounds and Charmine Johnson had the following children:

    i.   HERBERT^8 EDMOUNDS was born on 23 Sep 1991 in Philadelphia, Pa..

    ii.   CRISONA EDMOUNDS was born on 27 Jul 1997 in Philadelphia, Pa..

68. **Cass Avery[7] Johnson** (Dellaphine Marie[6], Ethel Lucy[5] Napper, Ethel Irene[4] Robinson, Lorenzo[3] Robinson, Dunbar[2] Robinson, John[1] Robinson) was born on 02 Sep 1967 in Philadelphia, Pa.. He married **Patrice Hawkins**. He married **Treacie**.

Cass Avery Johnson and Patrice Hawkins had the following child:

    i.   Amber[8] Hawkins was born in Philadelphia, Pa..

Cass Avery Johnson and Treacie had the following children:

    ii.   Khalia Johnson was born in Georgia.

    iii.   Kalise Johnson was born in Georgia.

69. **Carma M.[7] Johnson** (Dellaphine Marie[6], Ethel Lucy[5] Napper, Ethel Irene[4] Robinson, Lorenzo[3] Robinson, Dunbar[2] Robinson, John[1] Robinson) was born on 24 May 1969 in Philadelphia, Pa..

Carma M. Johnson had the following child:

    i.   Aja[8] Johnson was born on 10 Apr 1997 in Georgia.

70. **Christopher David[7] Johnson** (Doreen Patricia[6], Ethel Lucy[5] Napper, Ethel Irene[4] Robinson, Lorenzo[3] Robinson, Dunbar[2] Robinson, John[1] Robinson). He married **Margarte**.

Christopher David Johnson and Margarte had the following child:

    i.   D.J.[8] Johnson.

71. **Candice[7] Johnson** (Doreen Patricia[6], Ethel Lucy[5] Napper, Ethel Irene[4] Robinson, Lorenzo[3] Robinson, Dunbar[2] Robinson, John[1] Robinson) was born in 1988 in Philadelphia, Pa.. She married **John Johnson**.

John Johnson and Candice Johnson had the following child:

 i. Courtney[8] Johnson.

72. Cyrus Lamont[7] Dandridge (Denise[6] Johnson, Ethel Lucy[5] Napper, Ethel Irene[4] Robinson, Lorenzo[3] Robinson, Dunbar[2] Robinson, John[1] Robinson) was born on 22 Aug 1972 in Philadelphia, Pa..

Cyrus Lamont Dandridge had the following child:

 i. Nadjea[8] Campbell was born on 05 Aug 1997 in Philadelphia, Pa..

73. Gary Tamara[7] Dandridge (Denise[6] Johnson, Ethel Lucy[5] Napper, Ethel Irene[4] Robinson, Lorenzo[3] Robinson, Dunbar[2] Robinson, John[1] Robinson) was born on 15 Mar 1974 in Philadelphia, Pa.. He married Charnelle Harris.

Gary Tamara Dandridge and Charnelle Harris had the following children:

 i. Serenity[8] Harris was born on 10 Jun 2004 in Georgia.

 ii. Malani Dandridge was born on 12 Jun 2010 in Georgia.

 iii. O'ryan Tamara Dandridge was born on 09 Mar 2013 in Georgia.

74. Shawn James[7] King (Donzella[6] Johnson, Ethel Lucy[5] Napper, Ethel Irene[4] Robinson, Lorenzo[3] Robinson, Dunbar[2] Robinson, John[1] Robinson) was born on 03 Mar 1973 in Philadelphia, Pa.. He married Shala Jones in Jun 1996.

Shawn James King and Shala Jones had the following children:

i. DEMARCUS[8] JONES was born on 27 Nov 1996 in canton, Georgia.

ii. JORDAN AMIR KING was born on 30 Aug 2000 in Canton, Georgia.

iii. SHAYLA JENAE KING was born on 24 Feb 2004 in Canton, Georgia.

iv. LEILAH JAMES KING was born on 04 Feb 2008 in Canton, Georgia.

75. **JENEENE MARIE[7] KING** (Donzella[6] Johnson, Ethel Lucy[5] Napper, Ethel Irene[4] Robinson, Lorenzo[3] Robinson, Dunbar[2] Robinson, John[1] Robinson) was born on 26 Jul 1979 in Philadelphia, Pa..

Jeneene Marie King had the following children:

i. KHADEJAH[8] NEAL was born on 14 Nov 1997 in Philadelphia, Pa..

ii. GERALD LAMONT HERBERT was born on 07 Jul 2001 in Philadelphia, Pa..

76. **NICOLE NOEL[7] FISHER** (Donzeila Olivia[6] Johnson, Ethel Lucy[5] Napper, Ethel Irene[4] Robinson, Lorenzo[3] Robinson, Dunbar[2] Robinson, John[1] Robinson) was born on 31 Dec 1979 in Philadelphia, Pa.. She married **CHANCEY HOLLOWAY**.

Chancey Holloway and Nicole Noel Fisher had the following child:

i. MADISON[8] HOLLOWAY was born on 17 Jun 2004 in Philadelphia, Pa..

77. **CRYSTAL[7] SPEARMAN** (Donzeila Olivia[6] Johnson, Ethel Lucy[5] Napper, Ethel Irene[4] Robinson, Lorenzo[3] Robinson, Dunbar[2] Robinson, John[1] Robinson) was born on 26 Mar 1981 in Philadelphia, Pa.. She married Richard Cantell on 20 May 2011.

Richard Cantell and Crystal Spearman had the following children:

    i.   ASHLEY[8] SPEARMAN was born on 19 Oct 1998 in Philadelphia, Pa..

    ii.   ANGEL RICHARDSON was born on 04 Jul 2001 in Riverdale, Georgia.

    iii.   KEENAN SPEARMAN was born on 30 Aug 2005 in Canton, Georgia.

    iv.   KEIRA HAYES was born on 15 Feb 2007 in Canton, Georgia.

78. **JONATHAN S.[7] SPEARMAN** (Donzeila Olivia[6] Johnson, Ethel Lucy[5] Napper, Ethel Irene[4] Robinson, Lorenzo[3] Robinson, Dunbar[2] Robinson, John[1] Robinson) was born on 16 Nov 1991 in Philadelphia, Pa..

Jonathan S. Spearman had the following child:

    i.   TAYLOR MARIE[8] HAMBRICK was born on 24 Jun 2011 in Riverdale, Georgia.

79. **JACINA[7] MALACHI** (Lorraine[6] Lockley, Diane[5] Lockley, Philip McKenley[4] Lockley, Thomas[3] Lockley, Melvina[2] Robinson, John[1] Robinson) was born on 15 Jul 1985 in Alcas, Oklahoma. She married **GARY AUSTIN**. She married **RASAEL DAVIS**. She married **FRANK HAILEY**. She married **JAMES HAYWOOD**.

Gary Austin and Jacina Malachi had the following child:

    i.   MANYA[8] AUSTIN was born on 26 Jul 2001 in Philadelphia, Pa..

Rasael Davis and Jacina Malachi had the following child:

i. CIANNI[8] MALACHI was born on 29 Sep 2004 in Philadelphia, Pa..

Frank Hailey and Jacina Malachi had the following child:

i. DAMADE[8] MATHEWS was born on 18 Mar 2002 in Philadelphia, Pa..

James Haywood and Jacina Malachi had the following child:

i. DAQUINE[8] MATHEWS was born on 01 Apr 2004.

80. **VANASSA RENEE**[7] **LOCKLEY** (Cynthia Renee[6], Jacqueline[5], Philip McKenley[4], Thomas[3], Melvina[2] Robinson, John[1] Robinson) was born on 29 Jun 1984 in Philadelphia, Pa..

Vanassa Renee Lockley had the following child:

i. MARISSA RENEE[8] LOCKLEY was born on 21 Mar 2008 in Philadelphia, Pa..

Generation 8

81. **Lisa**[8] **Mack** (Charmine[7] Johnson, Dellaphine Marie[6] Johnson, Ethel Lucy[5] Napper, Ethel Irene[4] Robinson, Lorenzo[3] Robinson, Dunbar[2] Robinson, John[1] Robinson) was born on 30 Sep 1982 in Philadelphia, Pa.. She married **James Conway**.

James Conway and Lisa Mack had the following children:

   i. Rugaiyyah[9] Conway was born on 24 Apr 2002 in Philadelphia, Pa..

   ii. Abdullah Conway was born on 11 Jan 2004 in Philadelphia, Pa..

   iii. Damir Conway was born on 05 Jan 2009 in Philadelphia, Pa..

82. **Leah**[8] **Mack** (Charmine[7] Johnson, Dellaphine Marie[6] Johnson, Ethel Lucy[5] Napper, Ethel Irene[4] Robinson, Lorenzo[3] Robinson, Dunbar[2] Robinson, John[1] Robinson) was born on 21 Jan 1990 in Philadelphia, Pa..

Leah Mack had the following children:

   i. Rahyyah[9] Banton was born on 05 Jun 2006 in Philadelphia, Pa..

   ii. Raaiyah Sido was born on 31 May 2011 in Philadelphia, Pa..

MELVINA ROBINSON 1850 – 1878

Melvina the daughter of John Robinson & Mary Harris, Married Robert Lockley the son of Daniel Lockley and Milly Redmon on June 29, 1869 at his home in Gloucester County, Va. Robert had purchased 5 acres of land in Gloucester in 1867, from Archer Bland for $100.00. There they raised their four children, Jack 1868, Thomas 1870, Milly 1874, Robert, 1875 & Goalder 1876.

Descendants of Melvina Robinson

Generation 1

1. **MELVINA¹ ROBINSON** was born in 1849 in Gloucester County, Va.. She died in Apr 1878 in Gloucester County, Va.. She married Robert Lockley, son of Daniel Lockley and Milly Redmon on 29 Jun 1869 in Gloucester County, Va.. He was born in 1842 in Gloucester County, Va..

Robert Lockley and Melvina Robinson had the following children:

    2.   i.   THOMAS² LOCKLEY was born in 1870 in Gloucester County, Va.. He married (1) FRANCIS SUTHERLIN, daughter of John Sutherlin and Eliza Lockley on 29 Dec 1892 in Middlesex County, Virginia. She was born on 15 Jan 1868 in Middlesex County, Virginia. He married (2) BESSIE ANN BANKS, daughter of Lewis Banks and Nancy Lomax on 14 Nov 1909 in Middlesex County Va.. She was born in 1889 in Middlesex County, Virginia.

ii. MILLY LOCKLEY was born in 1874 in Gloucester County, Va..

iii. ROBERT LOCKLEY was born in 1875 in Gloucester County, Va..

iv. JACK LOCKLEY was born in 1868 in Gloucester County, Va.. He died on 15 Jun 1873 in Gloucester County, Va..

v. GOALDER LOCKLEY was born in 1876 in Gloucester County, Va.. She died in Nov 1876 in Gloucester County, Va..

Generation 2

2. **Thomas**[2] **Lockley** (Melvina[1] Robinson) was born in 1870 in Gloucester County, Va.. He married (1) **Francis Sutherlin**, daughter of John Sutherlin and Eliza Lockley on 29 Dec 1892 in Middlesex County, Virginia. She was born on 15 Jan 1868 in Middlesex County, Virginia. He married (2) **Bessie Ann Banks**, daughter of Lewis Banks and Nancy Lomax on 14 Nov 1909 in Middlesex County Va.. She was born in 1889 in Middlesex County, Virginia.

Thomas Lockley and Francis Sutherlin had the following children:

    i.   Clarence[3] Lockley was born in 1894.

    ii.   John Lockley was born in 1895. He married Josephine.

    iii.   Eliza Lockley was born in 1898.

    iv.   Nora Lockley was born in 1899.

Thomas Lockley and Bessie Ann Banks had the following children:

    v.   Robert Lewis Lockley was born on 10 Dec 1910 in Middlesex County, Virginia. He died on 26 Sep 1961 in Middlesex County, Va.. He married Emma Lee, daughter of Andrew Lee and Mollie Holmes-Lee on 16 Feb 1942 in Middlesex County Va.. She was born in 1918 in Middlesex County, Virginia.

3.   vi.   Earl Lockley was born on 03 Dec 1911 in Middlesex County, Va.. He died on 02 Feb 1973. He married Elizabeth Garnett. He married (2) Thelma T. Jordan, daughter of John Kelly Jordan and Eva S. Morris in 1955. She was born on 05 Apr 1915 in Middlesex County, Va.. She died on 20 Mar 2000 in Middlesex County, Va..

4. vii. PHILIP MCKENLEY LOCKLEY was born on 16 Jan 1917 in Middlesex County, Va.. He died on 15 Sep 1990 in Philadelphia, Pa.. He married Mertine Virginia Foster, daughter of James Foster and Otelia Kidd on 30 Sep 1939 in Middlesex County Va.. She was born on 31 May 1921 in Middlesex County, Virginia. She died in Jul 1977.

5. viii. ELMORE LOCKLEY was born on 30 Apr 1918 in Middlesex County, Va.. He died on 22 May 1984. He married RUSSELL CHRISTIAN. She was born on 02 Jul 1915.

6. ix. PEARL VIRGINIA LOCKLEY was born on 10 Apr 1921 in Middlesex County, Va.. She died on 13 Oct 1999. She married THOMAS BRIGHT. He was born on 09 Sep 1914. He died on 04 Apr 1921.

x. RUTH LOCKLEY was born on 09 Jul 1925 in Middlesex County, Va.. She died on 07 Jun 2005 in Brooklyn, N.Y.. She married MAJOR HARRIS.

7. xi. NANCY MARY LOCKLEY was born on 26 Aug 1929 in Middlesex County, Va.. She married Robert Edward Smith, son of Ernest Augusta Smith and Mattie Susan Fleet on 12 Aug 1957 in Middlesex County Va.. He was born on 08 Sep 1935 in Peary, Va. He died on 19 May 1979.

8. xii. SR IVERSON LOCKLEY was born on 22 Jul 1930 in Middlesex County, Va.. He married Flora Ruth Rice on 03 Dec 1957 in Boston, Mass. She was born on 17 Apr 1935 in Memphis, Tennessee.

xiii. ALICE LILLIAN LOCKLEY was born on 10 Aug 1932 in Middlesex County, Va..

Generation 3

3. **Earl**[3] **Lockley** (Thomas[2], Melvina[1] Robinson) was born on 03 Dec 1911 in Middlesex County, Va.. He died on 02 Feb 1973. He married **Elizabeth Garnett**. He married (2) **Thelma T. Jordan**, daughter of John Kelly Jordan and Eva S. Morris in 1955. She was born on 05 Apr 1915 in Middlesex County, Va.. She died on 20 Mar 2000 in Middlesex County, Va..

Earl Lockley and Elizabeth Garnett had the following children:

- 9. i. Queen[4] Lockley was born on 04 Aug 1942.

- 10. ii. Deloise Lockley was born on 20 Jan 1940.

4. **Philip McKenley**[3] **Lockley** (Thomas[2], Melvina[1] Robinson) was born on 16 Jan 1917 in Middlesex County, Va.. He died on 15 Sep 1990 in Philadelphia, Pa.. He married Mertine Virginia Foster, daughter of James Foster and Otelia Kidd on 30 Sep 1939 in Middlesex County Va.. She was born on 31 May 1921 in Middlesex County, Virginia. She died in Jul 1977.

Philip McKenley Lockley and Mertine Virginia Foster had the following children:

- 11. i. Diane[4] Lockley was born on 27 Jul 1947 in Philadelphia, Pa.. She married Sr Oliver Lee Mathew. He was born on 27 Sep 1943 in Philadelphia, Pa..

- 12. ii. Jacqueline Lockley was born on 13 Oct 1948 in Philadelphia, Pa.. She married (1) Wayne E. Robinson on 14 Nov 1998 in Philadelphia, Pa.. He was born on 14 Aug 1949 in Philadelphia, Pa.. She married James Hart. He was born on 11 Nov 1936. She married William H. Green. She married Ulysses Kent.

5. **Elmore**[3] **Lockley** (Thomas[2], Melvina[1] Robinson) was born on 30 Apr 1918 in Middlesex County, Va.. He died on 22 May 1984. He married **Russell Christian**. She was born on 02 Jul 1915.

Elmore Lockley and Russell Christian had the following children:

13.   i.   Elmyrth[4] Lockley was born on 08 Mar 1948 in Yorktown, Virginia. She married Sr Martin Taliferro. He was born on 18 Mar 1947.

14.   ii. Zelda Lockley was born on 23 Oct 1949 in Yorktown, Virginia. She married Edward Stewart. He was born on 17 Jun 1951.

15.   iii. Elmore Lockley Jr. was born on 08 Nov 1953 in Yorktown, Virginia. He married Brenda Atkins. She was born on 12 Oct 1947.

6. **Pearl Virginia**[3] **Lockley** (Thomas[2], Melvina[1] Robinson) was born on 10 Apr 1921 in Middlesex County, Va.. She died on 13 Oct 1999. She married **Thomas Bright**. He was born on 09 Sep 1914. He died on 04 Apr 1921.

Thomas Bright and Pearl Virginia Lockley had the following child:

   i.   Linda Pearl[4] Bright was born on 09 Sep 1958.

7. **Nancy Mary**[3] **Lockley** (Thomas[2], Melvina[1] Robinson) was born on 26 Aug 1929 in Middlesex County, Va.. She married Robert Edward Smith, son of Ernest Augusta Smith and Mattie Susan Fleet on 12 Aug 1957 in Middlesex County Va.. He was born on 08 Sep 1935 in Peary, Va. He died on 19 May 1979.

Robert Edward Smith and Nancy Mary Lockley had the following children:

16.   i.   James Robert[4] Smith was born on 13 Aug 1958 in Mathews, Virginia. He married Karaleen Libcomb.

17.	ii.	Mary Ann Smith was born on 05 Sep 1959 in Mathews, Virginia. She married William Davis Jr..
	iii.	Thomas Edward Smith was born on 15 Aug 1960 in Mathews, Virginia. He died on 17 Jul 2007 in Mathews, Va..
	iv.	Alice May Smith was born on 31 Aug 1961 in Mathews, Virginia.
18.	v.	Lucy Ellen Smith was born on 10 Sep 1963 in Mathews, Virginia.
19.	vi.	Linda Ruth Smith was born on 20 Jan 1968 in Mathews, Virginia.

8. **Sr Iverson³ Lockley** (Thomas², Melvina¹ Robinson) was born on 22 Jul 1930 in Middlesex County, Va.. He married Flora Ruth Rice on 03 Dec 1957 in Boston, Mass. She was born on 17 Apr 1935 in Memphis, Tennessee.

Sr Iverson Lockley and Flora Ruth Rice had the following children:

20.	i.	Jr Iverson⁴ Lockley was born on 03 Dec 1958 in Boston, Mass.
21.	ii.	Monice Anita Lockley was born on 30 Nov 1960 in Boston, Mass..
	iii.	Iasha Dee Lockley was born on 21 Nov 1981 in Boston, Mass.

Generation 4

9. **Queen**[4] **Lockley** (Earl[3], Thomas[2], Melvina[1] Robinson) was born on 04 Aug 1942.

   Queen Lockley had the following child:

   i. Angela[5] Lockley was born on 31 Dec 1960. She married Eugene Mays. He was born on 24 Dec 1960

10. **Deloise**[4] **Lockley** (Earl[3], Thomas[2], Melvina[1] Robinson) was born on 20 Jan 1940.

    Deloise Lockley had the following children:

    i. Nathaniel[5] Lockley was born on 23 Dec 1962.

    ii. Clarance Lockley was born on 11 Sep 1964.

    iii. Royal Smith was born on 23 Mar 1966.

11. **Diane**[4] **Lockley** (Philip McKenley[3], Thomas[2], Melvina[1] Robinson) was born on 27 Jul 1947 in Philadelphia, Pa.. She married **Sr Oliver Lee Mathew**. He was born on 27 Sep 1943 in Philadelphia, Pa..

    Sr Oliver Lee Mathew and Diane Lockley had the following children:

    i. Lorraine[5] Lockley was born on 19 Sep 1963 in Philadelphia, Pa.. She married James Malachi.

    ii. Jr Oliver Lee Mathews was born on 13 May 1967 in Philadelphia, Pa.. He married Lesa Chambliss. He married Enina Hamilton.

    iii. Kenneth Mathews was born on 07 Aug 1969 in Philadelphia, Pa.. He married Yolanda Martin. He married Rhonda Johnson.

    iv. Sabrina Mathews was born on 19 Jul 1984 in Philadelphia, Pa.. She married Brian Reed.

12. **JACQUELINE**[4] **LOCKLEY** (Philip McKenley[3], Thomas[2], Melvina[1] Robinson) was born on 13 Oct 1948 in Philadelphia, Pa.. She married (1) **WAYNE E. ROBINSON** on 14 Nov 1998 in Philadelphia, Pa.. He was born on 14 Aug 1949 in Philadelphia, Pa.. She married **JAMES HART**. He was born on 11 Nov 1936. She married **WILLIAM H. GREEN**. She married **ULYSSES KENT**.

James Hart and Jacqueline Lockley had the following children:

    i. WILLIAM JAMES[5] LOCKLEY was born on 25 Jan 1971 in Philadelphia, Pa.. He married NIGERIA.

    ii. MARCELLA EVETTE LOCKLEY was born on 31 Dec 1971 in Philadelphia, Pa.. She married JAMES PARKER. She married MALIK SWINGLER.

    iii. DEMITRUIS ANTHONY LOCKLEY was born on 23 Dec 1972 in Philadelphia, Pa.. He married DEBRA ANN SEALY. She was born on 23 Dec 1955.

William H. Green and Jacqueline Lockley had the following child:

    i. CYNTHIA RENEE[5] LOCKLEY was born on 05 Mar 1970 in Philadelphia, Pa.. She married ALAN WORD. He was born on 08 Mar 1966.

Ulysses Kent and Jacqueline Lockley had the following child:

    i. VANESSA[5] LOCKLEY was born on 01 Jul 1968 in Philadelphia, Pa..

13. **ELMYRTH**[4] **LOCKLEY** (Elmore[3], Thomas[2], Melvina[1] Robinson) was born on 08 Mar 1948 in Yorktown, Virginia. She married SR MARTIN TALIFERRO. He was born on 18 Mar 1947.

Sr Martin Taliferro and Elmyrth Lockley had the following children:

    i. MARTIN[5] TALIFERRO JR was born on 11 Jan 1978.

    ii. ADAM TALIFERRO was born on 20 Dec 1981.

14. **Zelda**[4] **Lockley** (Elmore[3], Thomas[2], Melvina[1] Robinson) was born on 23 Oct 1949 in Yorktown, Virginia. She married **Edward Stewart**. He was born on 17 Jun 1951.

    Edward Stewart and Zelda Lockley had the following children:

    i. Rachel Christina[5] Stewart was born on 10 Dec 1978.

    ii. Isaac Evans Stewart was born on 22 Mar 1982.

15. **Elmore**[4] **Lockley Jr.** (Elmore[3], Thomas[2], Melvina[1] Robinson) was born on 08 Nov 1953 in Yorktown, Virginia. He married **Brenda Atkins**. She was born on 12 Oct 1947.

    Elmore Lockley Jr. and Brenda Atkins had the following child:

    i. David Elmore[5] Lockley was born on 07 Jul 1985.

16. **James Robert**[4] **Smith** (Nancy Mary[3] Lockley, Thomas[2] Lockley, Melvina[1] Robinson) was born on 13 Aug 1958 in Mathews, Virginia. He married **Karaleen Libcomb**.

    James Robert Smith and Karaleen Libcomb had the following children:

    i. .jr James Robert[5] Smith was born on 09 Apr 1982.

    ii. Richard Edward Smith was born on 06 Jul 1983.

17. **Mary Ann**[4] **Smith** (Nancy Mary[3] Lockley, Thomas[2] Lockley, Melvina[1] Robinson) was born on 05 Sep 1959 in Mathews, Virginia. She married **William Davis Jr.**.

    William Davis Jr. and Mary Ann Smith had the following children:

    i. Jaleesa Tachelle[5] Davis was born on 18 May 1988.

    ii. Mariah Jade Davis was born on 03 Sep 1995.

    iii.   WAYMON WILLIAM DAVIS was born on 30 Jun 1999.

    iv.   JESSICA TELEESA DAVIS was born on 20 Jan 1993. She died on 12 Nov 1993.

18. **LUCY ELLEN**[4] **SMITH** .(Nancy Mary[3] Lockley, Thomas[2] Lockley, Melvina[1] Robinson) was born on 10 Sep 1963 in Mathews, Virginia.

Lucy Ellen Smith had the following child:

    i.   DEANNA NANCY[5] SMITH was born on 30 Aug 1984.

19. **LINDA RUTH**[4] **SMITH** (Nancy Mary[3] Lockley, Thomas[2] Lockley, Melvina[1] Robinson) was born on 20 Jan 1968 in Mathews, Virginia.

Linda Ruth Smith had the following children:

    i.   BRITNEY NICOLE[5] KING was born on 12 Aug 1990.

    ii.   BRYAN NICHOLAS SMITH was born on 19 Oct 1997.

20. **JR IVERSON**[4] **LOCKLEY** (Sr Iverson[3], Thomas[2], Melvina[1] Robinson) was born on 03 Dec 1958 in Boston, Mass.

Jr Iverson Lockley had the following child:

    i.   IASHA DEE LOCKLEY[5] HILL was born on 21 Nov 1981 in Boston, Mass..

21. **MONICE ANITA**[4] **LOCKLEY** (Sr Iverson[3], Thomas[2], Melvina[1] Robinson) was born on 30 Nov 1960 in Boston, Mass..

Monice Anita Lockley had the following child:

    i.   ARRON LOCKLEY[5] YOUNG was born on 15 Oct 1986 in Boston, Mass..

Descendants of Melvina Robinson

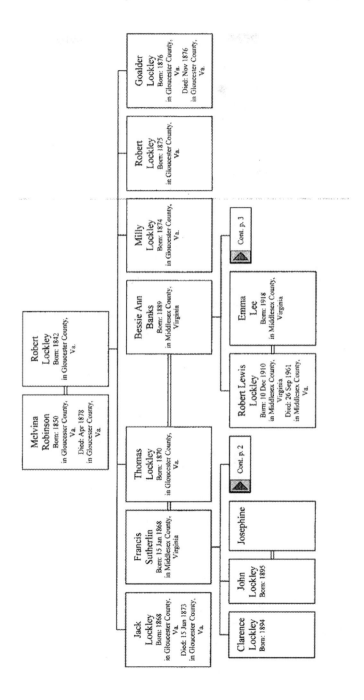

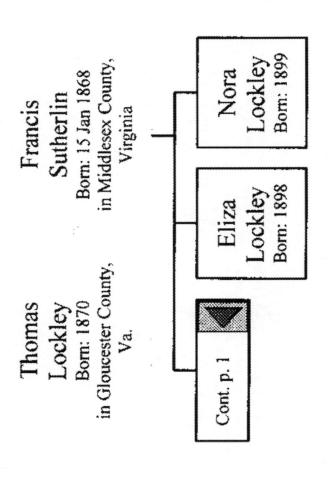

Descendants of Melvina Robinson (3 of 15)

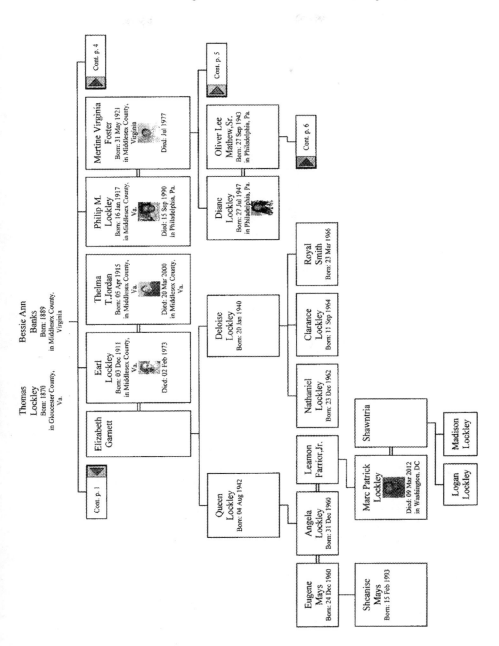

Descendants of Melvina Robinson (4 of 15)

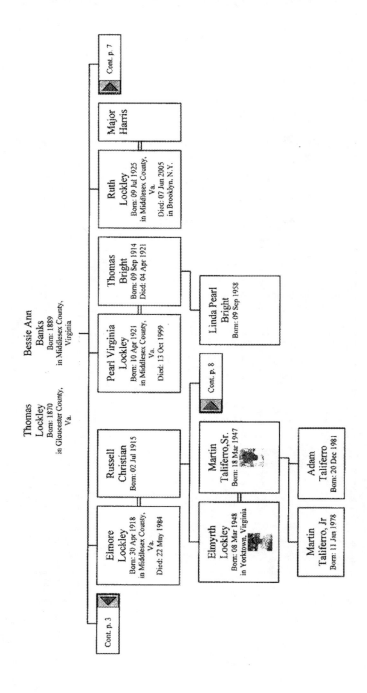

Descendants of Melvina Robinson

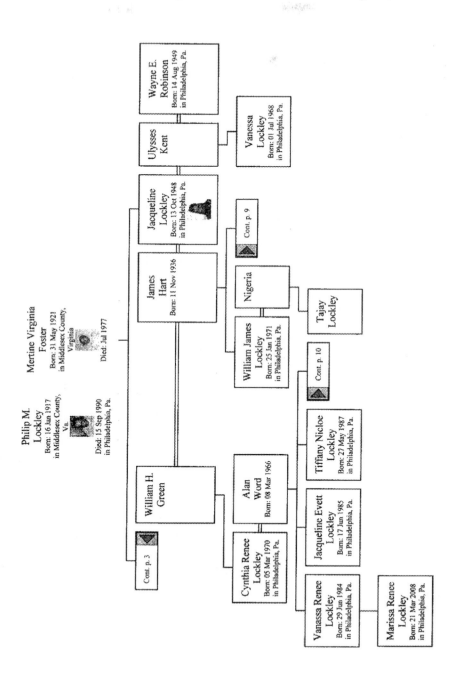

Descendants of Melvina Robinson (6 of 15)

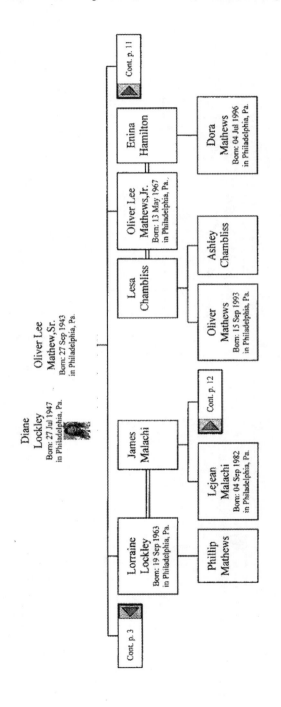

Descendants of Melvina Robinson (7 of 15)

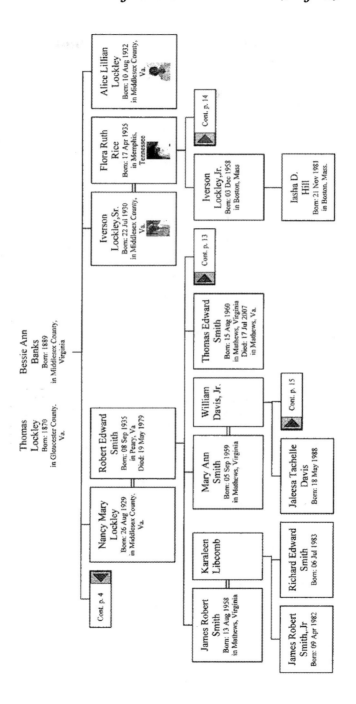

Descendants of Melvina Robinson

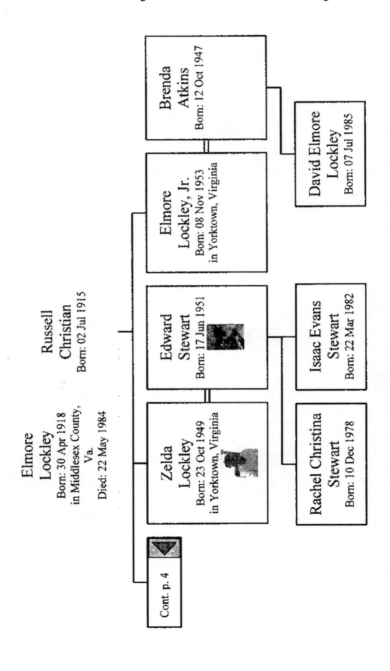

Descendants of Melvina Robinson

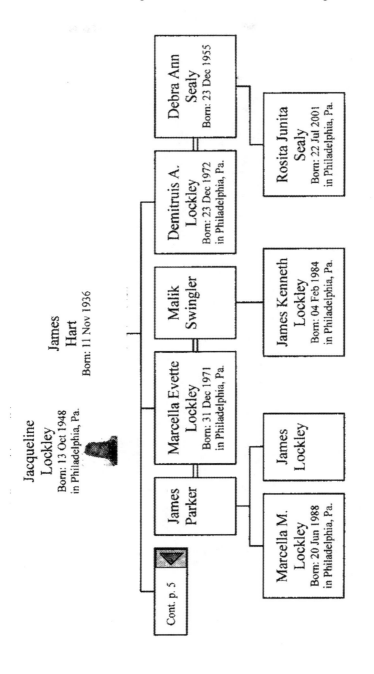

Descendants of Melvina Robinson

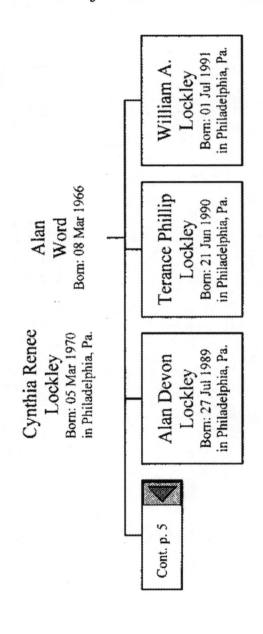

Descendants of Melvina Robinson

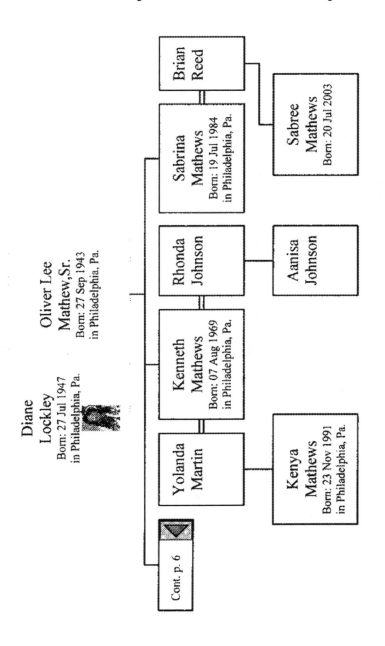

Descendants of Melvina Robinson

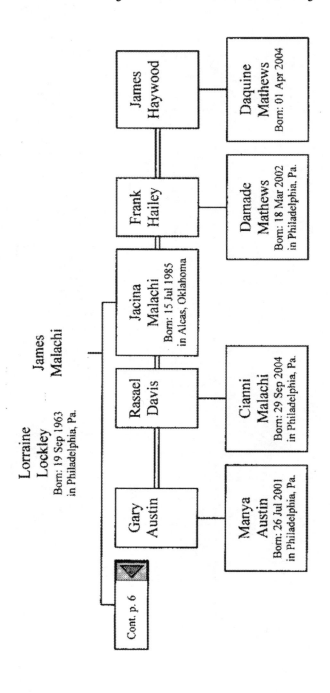

Descendants of Melvina Robinson

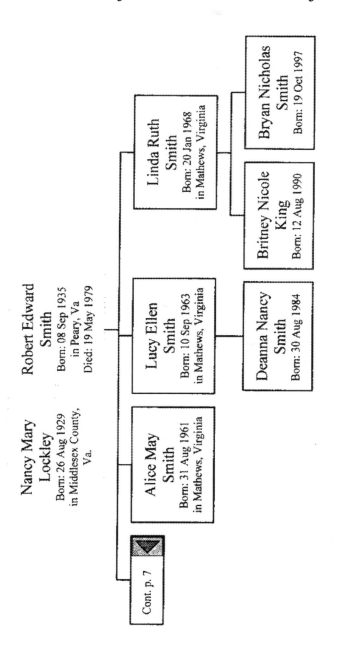

Descendants of Melvina Robinson

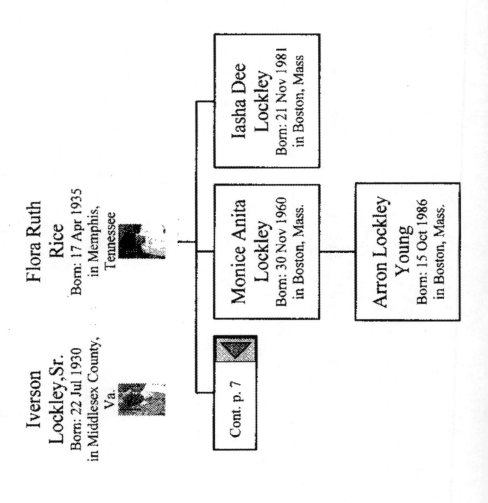

Iverson Lockley, Sr.
Born: 22 Jul 1930 in Middlesex County, Va.

Flora Ruth Rice
Born: 17 Apr 1935 in Memphis, Tennessee

Iasha Dee Lockley
Born: 21 Nov 1981 in Boston, Mass

Monice Anita Lockley
Born: 30 Nov 1960 in Boston, Mass.

Arron Lockley Young
Born: 15 Oct 1986 in Boston, Mass.

Cont. p. 7

Descendants of Melvina Robinson

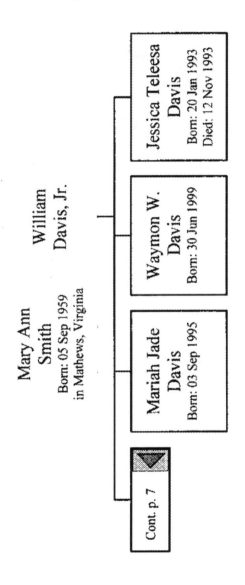

THOMAS LOCKLEY 1870

Thomas married his first wife Francis Sutherlin, January 15. 1892, they were the parents of four children, Clarence 1894, John 1895, Eliza 1898 & Nora 1899. After her death he married Bessie Ann Banks, November 14, 1909 in Middlesex County, Va., from this union nine children were born.

EARL LOCKLEY 1911 – 1973

Earl married Elizabeth Garnett in Middlesex County, Va. They were the parents of Queen 1942 and Deloise 1940. At the time of his death he was married to his second wife Thelma Jordan, they had no children together.

IVERSON LOCKLEY 1930

Ike entered the United States Air Force after graduating from High School in Middlesex County, Va. After completing his military service he married Flora Ruth Rice December 3, 1957 and settled in Boston, Massachusetts where they raised their children, Iverson, JR Monice Anita and Iasha Dee.

ELMORE LOCKLEY 1918 – 1984

Elmore moved to Yorktown, VA where he met and married Russell Christian. They were the parents of 3 children, Elmyrth 1948, Zelda 1949 and Elmore, JR 1953.

PHILIP MCKENLEY LOCKLEY
1917 – 1990

Philip the son of Thomas Lockley & Bessie Ann banks was married to Mertine Virginia Foster September 30, 1939 in Middlesex County, Va. The family moved to Philadelphia, Pa. where their daughters Diane and Jacqueline were born.

Diane, Jacqueline, Bonita

DABNEY ROBINSON 1835

In 1880 Dabney was living with his family on a 45 Acre farm in King & Queen County, Va.

Descendants of Dabney Robinson

Generation No. 1

1. DABNEY[2] ROBINSON *(JOHN[1])* was born 1835 in King & Queen County, Va.. He married (1) MARY E., daughter of JOHN HUDGINS and MARTHA. She was born 1835 in King & Queen, Virginia. He married (2) SARAH JANE JORDAN 26 Dec 1875 in King & Queen County, Va., daughter of GEORGE JORDAN and MARGARETT ROBINSON. She was born 1849 in King & Queen County, Va..

Notes for DABNEY ROBINSON:

The 1875 Marriage to Sarah Jordan was performed by his uncle Lorenzo Dow Robinson

Notes for MARY E.:

MARY E. was a Hudgins when she married James Kauffman. After his death she married Dabney Robinson,

More About MARY E.:

Nationality: Mulatto

Notes for SARAH JANE JORDAN:

Sarah Jane Jordan took the sirname of her step father. Her father was Alexander Gilmore her mothers first husband.

More About SARAH JANE JORDAN:

Caste: Mulatto

Children of DABNEY ROBINSON and MARY E. are:

    i.   VICTORIA[3] ROBINSON, b. 1866.

    ii.   FATIMA ROBINSON, b. 1867.

    iii.   KETUIA ROBINSON, b. 1868.

Children of DABNEY ROBINSON and SARAH JORDAN are:

    iv.   HARRIET[3] ROBINSON, b. 1879.

    v.   MARGARET ROBINSON, b. 1882; m. O. KADEMY.

    vi.   FANNIE E. ROBINSON, b. 1885; m. O. McDONALD.

    vii.   JULIE A. ROBINSON, b. 1886, King & Queen County, Va.; m. JOHN H. PATTERSON, 20 Jan 1907, King & Queen County, Va.; b. 1880, Albemarle County, Va..

    viii.   ALFRED G. ROBINSON, B. 1888, King & Queen County, Va.; m. REBECCA KIDD, 01 Jul 1916, King & Queen County, Va.; b. 1890, King & Queen County, Va..

DUNBAR ROBINSON 1834

After the death of his father in 1855 Dunbar became very attached to his uncle Lorenzo D. Robinson and his son Archibald Robinson. During the Civil War Archibald was taken to work on the fortifications at Gloucester Point, Virginia by the Confederate Army. He states that he stayed from 1861 to 1863. Dunbar was also taken to Gloucester Point; he stayed 6 or 7 months. They were paid 50 cents a day plus rations.

After the Civil War was over Dunbar signed as a witness to his Uncle Lorenzo Dow Robinson's claim against the government, for food taken from his farm in June 1864 by Union troops under the command of General Phillip Sheridan.

The United States Census of 1900 lists in his household only his two youngest daughters Emma & Luvanna. The older children had migrated to Philadelphia, Pa. By 1910 his wife Margarette was deceased and he had married the 15 year old Gertrude Hampton on December 15, 1909 he was 76 years old at the time. They lived on a small farm in King & Queen County. Va.

1870 Agriculture Schedule - Dunbar Robinson

1880 Agriculture Schedule County/State: King & Queen County, VA   District: 39
Page ....   NARA Mfm ....   1. Owner/Agent/Mgr: Dunbar Robinson

Description	Col	Value		Description	Col	Value		Description	Col	Value		Description	Col	Value
Owner	2	Acres		Other Cows	27			Barley – Crop	53	Bu		Maple Molasses	79	Gals
Rents for Fixed Money	3	Acres		Calves dropped	28			Buckwheat – Area	54	Acres		Pulse; Cow Peas	80	Bu
Rents for Share of Product	4	Acres		Cattle purchased	29			Buckwheat – Crop	55	Bu		Beans, Dry	81	Bu
Tilled, incl fallow & grass in rotation	5	Acres 10		Cattle sold living	30			Indian Corn – Area	56	Acres 10		Irish Potatoes – Area	82	Acres
Perm. Pastures, orchards, vineyards	6	Acres		Cattle slaughtered	31			Indian Corn – Crop	57	Bu 200		Irish Potatoes – Crop	83	Bu
Woodland & forest	7	Acres 10		Cattle died, strayed	32			Oats – Area	58	Acres		Sweet Potatoes – Area	84	Acres
Other unimproved	8	Acres		Milk sold or sent for Cheese	33	Lbs 100		Oats – Crop	59	Bu		Sweet Potatoes – Crop	85	Bu
Value, Farm, land, fences & buildings	9	$ 160		Butter produced on farm	34	Lbs		Rye – Area	60	Acres		Tobacco – Area	86	Acres
Farm implements & machinery value	10	$ 10		Cheese produced on farm	35	Gals		Rye – Crop	61	Bu		Tobacco – Crop	87	Lbs
Livestock value	11	$ 100		Sheep on hand June 1, 1880	36			Wheat – Area	62	Acres 1		Apples – Area	88	Acres
Bldg & repairs in 1879	12	$		Lambs dropped	37			Wheat – Crop	63	Bu 10		Apples – Trees	89	
Fertilizer in 1879	13	$		Lambs purchased	38			Cotton – Area	64	Acres		Apples	90	Bu
Wages for farm labor incl board	14	$		Lambs sold live	39			Cotton – Bales	65			Peach – Area	91	Acres
Weeks hired labor (White) & household	15			Sheep/lambs slaughtered	40			Flax – Area	66	Acres		Peach Trees	92	
Weeks hired labor (Colored) & household	16	120		Sheep/lambs killed by dogs	41			Flaxseed	67	Bu		Peaches	93	Bu
Value, farm product sold, used & on hand	17			Sheep/lambs died of disease	42			Flax Straw	68	Tons		Value Orchard Products	94	$
Grass lands, mown	18	Acres		Sheep/lambs d. of weather stress	43			Flax Fiber	69	Lbs		Nurseries – Area	95	Acres
Grass lands, not mown	19	Acres		No. of Fleeces	44			Hemp – Area	70	Acres		Value of Nursery Produce	96	$
Hay harvest in 1879	20	Tons		Weight of Fleece	45	Lbs 9		Hemp – Crop	71	Tons		Vineyards – Area	97	Acres
Clover seed	21	Bu		Swine on hand June 1, 1880	46	11		Cane Sugar – Area	72	Acres		Grapes sold	98	Lbs
Grass seed	22	Bu 1		Barnyard Poultry June 1, 1880	47			Cane Sugar	73	Hhds		Wine made 1879	99	Gals
Horses	23			Other Poultry on hand	48	30		Cane Molasses	74	Gals		Value Garden Product sold	100	$
Mules & Asses	24	2		Eggs	49	Doz		Sorghum – Area	75	Acres		Honey	101	Lbs
Oxen	25	2		Rice 1879 – Area	50	Acres		Sorghum Sugar	76	Lbs		Wax	102	Lbs
Milk Cows	26	2		Rice – Crop	51	Bu		Sorghum Molasses	77	Gals		Amt of wood cut 1879	103	Cords
				Barley – Area	52	Acres		Maple Sugar	78	Lbs		Value of forest product sold/used	104	$

1880 Agriculture Schedule - Dunbar Robinson

Two of his sons Joshua Dunbar Robinson and John Thomas Robinson registered for the World War 1 1917-1918 Draft from their homes in Philadelphia, Pa.

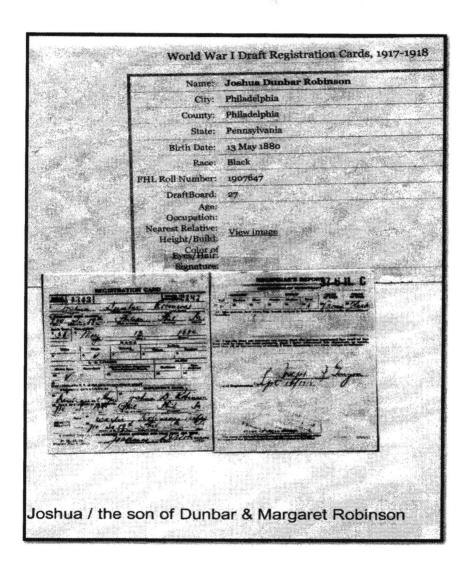

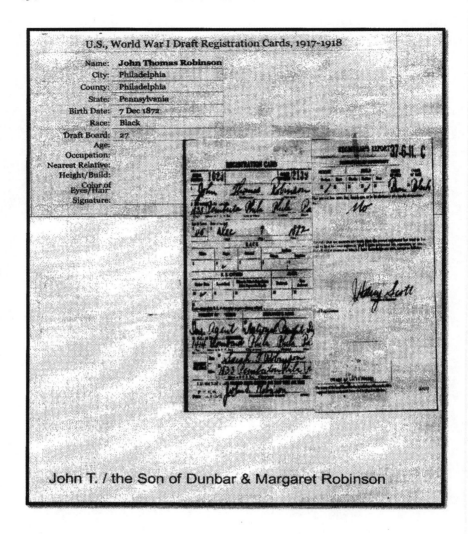

At the time of his death Dunbar Robinson is Identified in a March 12, 1918 Suite in the Commissioner of Chancery, Pending in the Circuit Court of King & Queen County. Claim for 50 Acres of land owned by his father, John Robinson at the time of his death. Suite is filed by Sarah L. Jordan granddaughter of John Robinson.

Descendants of Dunbar Robinson

Generation No. 1

1. DUNBAR² ROBINSON *(JOHN¹)* was born 1834 in King & Queen County, Va.. He married (1) MARGARETTE J. 1863 in King & Queen County, Va.. She was born 1841 in King & Queen County, Va.. He married (2) GERTRUDE HAMPTON 15 Dec 1909 in King & Queen County, Va.. She was born 1895 in King & Queen County, Va..

Children of DUNBAR ROBINSON and MARGARETTE J. are:

    i.   ISAIAH P.³ ROBINSON, b. 1865, King & Queen County, Va.; m. LUCY B. BAKER, 28 May 1895, Richmond, Virginia; b. 1871, Richmond, Va..

    ii.   ANN ELIZA ROBINSON, b. 1867, King & Queen County, Va..

2.   iii.   LORENZO ROBINSON, b. 1868, King & Queen County, Va..

    iv.   JAMES A. ROBINSON, b. 1870, King & Queen County, Va..

    v.   JOHN THOMAS ROBINSON, b. 1873, King & Queen County, Va.; m. SARAH T., 1902, Pennsylvania; b. 1880, Virginia.

    vi.   JOSHUA DUNBAR ROBINSON, b. 1879, King & Queen County, Va.; m. CARE BERNICE ROWE, 31 Oct 1907, King & Queen County, Va.; b. 1880, King & Queen County, Va..

    vii.   EMMA ROBINSON, b. 1883, King & Queen County, Va..

    viii.   LUVANNA ROBINSON, b. 1888, King & Queen County, Va..

Generation No. 2

2. LORENZO[3] ROBINSON *(DUNBAR[2], JOHN[1])* was born 1868 in King & Queen County, Va.. He married TEXANA ROBINSON 1898 in Philadelphia, Pa., daughter of ALBERT ROBINSON and SOPHIA. She was born Sep 1872 in Louisa, Virginia.

Children of LORENZO ROBINSON and TEXANA ROBINSON are:

	i.	WILBUR[4] ROBINSON, b. 1899, Philadelphia, Pa.; d. 03 Feb 1901, Philadelphia, Pa..
3.	ii.	EDITH MADELINE ROBINSON, b. 1901, Philadelphia, Pa..
	iii.	MARGARET D. ROBINSON, b. 1902, Philadelphia, Pa.; m. LUTHER MATHIS.
	iv.	CHANCELLOR D. ROBINSON, b. 1904, Philadelphia, Pa.; d. 21 Apr 1905, Philadelphia, Pa..
4.	v.	EVA LADOCIA ROBINSON, b. 06 Mar 1906, Philadelphia, Pa..
5.	vi.	ANNA BESSIE ROBINSON, b. 1908, Philadelphia, Pa..
6.	vii.	ETHEL IRENE ROBINSON, b. 15 Mar 1912, Philadelphia, Pa.; d. Apr 1957, Philadelphia, Pa..
7.	viii.	CORA L. ROBINSON, b. 1915, Philadelphia, Pa..

Generation No. 3

3. EDITH MADELINE[4] ROBINSON *(LORENZO[3], DUNBAR[2], JOHN[1])* was born 1901 in Philadelphia, Pa.. She married WILLARD MOORE.

Notes for EDITH MADELINE ROBINSON:

Unmarried

Child of EDITH ROBINSON and WILLARD MOORE is:

    i.   WILLIAM[5] MOORE, b. 1925, Philadelphia, Pa..

4. EVA LADOCIA[4] ROBINSON *(LORENZO[3], DUNBAR[2], JOHN[1])* was born 06 Mar 1906 in Philadelphia, Pa.. She married FREDERICK K. FORD.

Children of EVA ROBINSON and FREDERICK FORD are:

    i.   PHILLIP BROOKS[5] FORD, b. Philadelphia, Pa.; d. 1959, Philadelphia, Pa..

8.   ii.   FREDERICK K. FORD. JR., b. 31 Oct 1942, Philadelphia, Pa.; d. 22 May 1989, Wilmington Delaware.

    iii.   JOHN RUSSELL FORD, b. Philadelphia, Pa.; m. DARLENE.

9.   iv.   EDWARD FORD, b. 29 Aug 1947, Philadelphia, Pa..

    v.   ROBERT FORD, b. 24 Aug 1950, Philadelphia, Pa..

5. ANNA BESSIE[4] ROBINSON *(LORENZO[3], DUNBAR[2], JOHN[1])* was born 1908 in Philadelphia, Pa..

Child of ANNA BESSIE ROBINSON is:

10.   i.   GENEVIEVE A.[5] ROBINSON, b. 07 Feb 1933, Philadelphia, Pa..

6. ETHEL IRENE[4] ROBINSON *(LORENZO[3], DUNBAR[2], JOHN[1])* was born 15 Mar 1912 in Philadelphia, Pa., and died Apr 1957 in Philadelphia, Pa.. She married (1) ISAAC B. NAPPER, SR., son of BENJAMIN NAPPER and LUCY BELL. He was born 10 Mar 1911 in Philadelphia, Pa., and died 01 Mar 1943 in Philadelphia, Pa.. She married (2) EDWARD MULLEN.

Children of ETHEL ROBINSON and ISAAC NAPPER are:

11. i. ISSAC B.[5] NAPPER II, b. 02 Apr 1934, Philadelphia, Pa..
12. ii. ETHEL LUCY NAPPER, b. 24 Feb 1930, Philadelphia, Pa..
13. iii. EDITH IRENE NAPPER, b. 19 Jun 1931, Philadelphia, Pa..
14. iv. WILBER JAMES NAPPER, b. 22 Sep 1935, Philadelphia, Pa..
    v. ANNA NAPPER, b. 1932, Philadelphia, Pa..

7. CORA L.[4] ROBINSON *(LORENZO[3], DUNBAR[2], JOHN[1])* was born 1915 in Philadelphia, Pa.. She married DANIEL PETERSON 1933 in Philadelphia, Pa..

Children of CORA ROBINSON and DANIEL PETERSON are:

15. i. ELLEN J.[5] PETERSON, b. 03 Dec 1933, Philadelphia, Pa..
16. ii. DANIEL E. PETERSON, b. 08 Oct 1936, Philadelphia, Pa..
17. iii. WARREN L. PETERSON, b. 22 Mar 1938, Philadelphia, Pa..
18. iv. RUSSELL PETERSON, b. 14 Sep 1940, Philadelphia, Pa..
19. v. EDNA E. PETERSON, b. 05 Sep 1942, Philadelphia, Pa..
20. vi. MARGARET PETERSON, b. 02 Feb 1945, Philadelphia, Pa..
21. vii. ROBERT T. PETERSON, b. 24 Apr 1948, Philadelphia, Pa..

viii. GWENDOLYN D. PETERSON, b. 29 Apr 1951, Philadelphia, Pa.; m. (1) GEORGE GASKIN; m. (2) WALTER FRANKLIN, 07 Mar 1987, Philadelphia, Pa.; b. 29 Aug 1945, Massilon, Ohio.

More About GWENDOLYN D. PETERSON:

Divorced: George Gaskin

Generation No. 4

8. FREDERICK K.[5] FORD. JR. *(EVA LADOCIA[4] ROBINSON, LORENZO[3], DUNBAR[2], JOHN[1])* was born 31 Oct 1942 in Philadelphia, Pa., and died 22 May 1989 in Wilmington Delaware. He married JUANITA GREEN 31 Jul 1965, daughter of HORTON GREEN and ANLIZAR. She was born 16 Apr 1947 in Philadelphia, Pa..

Children of FREDERICK FORD. JR. and JUANITA GREEN are:

22. i.   FREDERICK RAYMOND[6] FORD, b. 15 Sep 1966, Philadelphia, Pa..

23. ii. RONALD LEE FORD, b. 23 May 1967, Waldorf, Maryland.

    iii. REGINALD HORTON FORD, b. 21 Apr 1971.

24. iv. RUSSELL LAMARR FORD, b. 03 May 1983.

9. EDWARD[5] FORD *(EVA LADOCIA[4] ROBINSON, LORENZO[3], DUNBAR[2], JOHN[1])* was born 29 Aug 1947 in Philadelphia, Pa.. He married EDITH PENDER.

Children of EDWARD FORD and EDITH PENDER are:

    i.   FRANKLIN[6] PENDER, b. 19 Dec 1975, Philadelphia, Pa..

    ii. AZIA PENDER, b. 12 Apr 1976, Philadelphia, Pa..

25. iii. EBONY PENDER, b. 08 Mar 1980, Philadelphia, Pa..

26. iv. SONYA PENDER, b. 24 May 1983, Philadelphia, Pa..

27. v.   NADINE PENDER, b. 08 Feb 1988, Philadelphia, Pa..

10. GENEVIEVE A.[5] ROBINSON *(ANNA BESSIE[4], LORENZO[3], DUNBAR[2], JOHN[1])* was born 07 Feb 1933 in Philadelphia, Pa.. She married JOHNNIE L. WELCH 10 May 1951 in Philadelphia, Pa.. He was born 17 Mar 1927 in Tarpon Springs, Florida.

Children of Genevieve Robinson and Johnnie Welch are:

28. i. Judith E.[6] Welch, b. 15 May 1951, Philadelphia, Pa..
29. ii. Jacqueline Flora Welch, b. 11 Nov 1952, Tarpon Springs, Florida.
30. iii. Quineseta A. Welch, b. 06 May 1956, Philadelphia, Pa..
31. iv. Joyce M. Welch, b. 26 Sep 1956, Philadelphia, Pa..
    v. Johnnie L. Welch, b. 05 Mar 1958, Tarpon Springs, Florida; m. Tracie.

Notes for Johnnie L. Welch:

Divorced

32. vi. Denise A. Welch, b. 13 Jul 1960, Philadelphia, Pa..
33. vii. Cynthia A. Welch, b. 24 Jun 1962, Philadelphia, Pa..

11. Issac B.[5] Napper II *(Ethel Irene[4] Robinson, Lorenzo[3], Dunbar[2], John[1])* was born 02 Apr 1934 in Philadelphia, Pa.. He married Olivia Dossanta. She was born 20 Mar 1930 in South Wales, England, and died 07 Feb 2008.

Children of Issac Napper and Olivia Dossanta are:

34. i. Bonita[6] Napper, b. 31 Jul 1958.
35. ii. Issac Napper III, b. 09 Jan 1969.
36. iii. John Napper, b. 21 May 1966, Philadelphia, Pa..

12. Ethel Lucy[5] Napper *(Ethel Irene[4] Robinson, Lorenzo[3], Dunbar[2], John[1])* was born 24 Feb 1930 in Philadelphia, Pa.. She married John Henry Johnson 03 Sep 1946 in Deleware. He was born 03 Sep 1903 in Greenboro, North Carolina, and died 23 Dec 1971 in Philadelphia, Pa..

Children of Ethel Napper and John Johnson are:

37. i.   Dedoriad Lithiah[6] Napper, b. 24 Apr 1947, Philadelphia, Pa.; d. Oct 2003, Philadelphia, Pa..

38. ii.   Dellaphine Marie Johnson, b. 20 Apr 1948, New Jersey.

39. iii. Doreen Patricia Johnson, b. 28 Nov 1949, Philadelphia, Pa..

40. iv.   Dow Lorenzo Johnson, b. 09 Mar 1951, Philadelphia, Pa.; d. 15 May 2011, Texas.

     v.   Derward John Johnson, b. 01 Feb 1952, Philadelphia, Pa.; m. Gale Stevens Channel.

     vi.   Dartaniel Henry Johnson, b. 25 Jan 1953, Philadelphia, Pa.; d. 15 May 2003, New Jersey; m. Linda Brown, 10 Apr 1999.

41. vii. Donzella Johnson, b. 13 Jul 1954, Philadelphia, Pa..

42. viii. Denise Johnson, b. 24 Jul 1955, Philadelphia, Pa..

43. ix.   Donzeila Olivia Johnson, b. 27 Jun 1957, Philadelphia, Pa..

13. Edith Irene[5] Napper *(Ethel Irene[4] Robinson, Lorenzo[3], Dunbar[2], John[1])* was born 19 Jun 1931 in Philadelphia, Pa.. She married James S. Thomas 18 Jun 1950. He was born 19 Jun 1931 in Philadelphia, Pa..

Child of Edith Napper and James Thomas is:

44. i.   Edith Elizabeth[6] Thomas, b. 04 Oct 1951, Philadelphia, Pa..

14. Wilber James[5] Napper *(Ethel Irene[4] Robinson, Lorenzo[3], Dunbar[2], John[1])* was born 22 Sep 1935 in Philadelphia, Pa.. He married Marion Lewis.

Children of WILBER NAPPER and MARION LEWIS are:

      i.   WILBER JAMES[6] NAPPER, JR., b. 23 Jun 1958, Philadelphia, Pa.; d. 11 Nov 2013, Philadelphia, Pa..

45. ii.   CLAIRE NAPPER.

     iii. CARL M. NAPPER.

     iv. DIANE NAPPER, m. SHAWN HOLSTER.

15. ELLEN J.[5] PETERSON *(CORA L.[4] ROBINSON, LORENZO[3], DUNBAR[2], JOHN[1])* was born 03 Dec 1933 in Philadelphia, Pa.. She married ROBERT E. LUCAS, JR. 29 Jun 1957 in Philadelphia, Pa., son of ROBERT LUCAS and DOROTHY. He was born 14 May 1931 in Willow Grove, Pa..

Child of ELLEN PETERSON and ROBERT LUCAS is:

      i.   CHRYSTAL A.[6] LUCAS, b. 01 Jan 1967, Philadelphia, Pa..

16. DANIEL E.[5] PETERSON *(CORA L.[4] ROBINSON, LORENZO[3], DUNBAR[2], JOHN[1])* was born 08 Oct 1936 in Philadelphia, Pa.. He married SEVERA in Philippines. She was born 01 Jan 1944 in Philippines.

Children of DANIEL PETERSON and SEVERA are:

46. i.   JEANETTE[6] PETERSON, b. 16 Jun 1971, Michigan.

47. ii. DANIEL PETERSON, b. 08 Aug 1974, Sacramento, California.

     iii. BERNADETTE PETERSON, b. 15 Feb 1978, Sacramento, California.

     iv. WILLIAM PETERSON, b. 07 Nov 1980, Sacramento, California.

17. WARREN L.[5] PETERSON *(CORA L.[4] ROBINSON, LORENZO[3], DUNBAR[2], JOHN[1])* was born 22 Mar 1938 in Philadelphia, Pa.. He married MERIDEL JEFFERY 07 Dec 1980 in Philadelphia, Pa., daughter of

JAMES JEFFERY and ROSA ROLLIAS. She was born 05 Mar 1947 in Philadelphia, Pa..

Child of WARREN PETERSON and MERIDEL JEFFERY is:

48. i.   SHANI DANIELLE[6] PETERSON, b. 22 Dec 1982, Philadelphia, Pa..

18. RUSSELL[5] PETERSON *(CORA L.[4] ROBINSON, LORENZO[3], DUNBAR[2], JOHN[1])* was born 14 Sep 1940 in Philadelphia, Pa.. He married (1) FRANCINE FEGGANS. He married (2) ELIZABETH DAVIS 30 Jun 1994 in Los Angeles, California. She was born 06 Jan 1944 in Little Rock, Arkansas.

Child of RUSSELL PETERSON and ELIZABETH DAVIS is:

i.   DANIELLE N.[6] DAVIS, b. 09 Sep 1997, Los Angeles, California.

19. EDNA E.[5] PETERSON *(CORA L.[4] ROBINSON, LORENZO[3], DUNBAR[2], JOHN[1])* was born 05 Sep 1942 in Philadelphia, Pa.. She married (1) WILLIAM C. SMITH, JR. 16 Jul 1967 in Killeen, Texas. He was born 02 Feb 1943 in Chicago, Illinois. She married (2) JONATHAN A. BLAINE Aug 1972 in Philadelphia, Pa..

Children of EDNA PETERSON and JONATHAN BLAINE are:

49. i.   JONATHAN K.R.[6] BLAINE, b. 13 Aug 1974, Philadelphia, Pa..

50. ii. RAHN A. BLAINE, b. 27 Dec 1975, Philadelphia, Pa..

20. MARGARET[5] PETERSON *(CORA L.[4] ROBINSON, LORENZO[3], DUNBAR[2], JOHN[1])* was born 02 Feb 1945 in Philadelphia, Pa.. She married (1) JAMES CROSS. He died in Philadelphia, Pa.. She married (2) KENT E. ARLINE, SR. in Philadelphia, Pa..

More About Margaret Peterson:

Divorced: Kent E. Arline, Sr.

    Child of Margaret Peterson and Kent Arline is:

    51.   i.   Kent E.[6] Arline, Jr., b. 10 Sep 1967, Philadelphia, Pa..

21. Robert T.[5] Peterson *(Cora L.[4] Robinson, Lorenzo[3], Dunbar[2], John[1])* was born 24 Apr 1948 in Philadelphia, Pa.. He married (3) Annette Stephens 26 Jan 2001 in Burlington, New Jersey. She was born 21 Oct 1956 in San Pedro, California.

Children of Robert T. Peterson are:

        i.   Monique[6] Peterson, b. 18 Dec 1978, Philadelphia, Pa.; m. Timothy Witcher.

        ii.   Nia M. Peterson, b. 14 Apr 1980, Philadelphia, Pa..

Child of Robert T. Peterson is:

    52.   iii.   Sharron[6] Patterson-McFadden, b. Aug 1965.

Generation No. 5

22. FREDERICK RAYMOND[6] FORD *(FREDERICK K.[5] FORD. JR., EVA LADOCIA[4] ROBINSON, LORENZO[3], DUNBAR[2], JOHN[1])* was born 15 Sep 1966 in Philadelphia, Pa.. He married TRACEY LEME. She was born 20 Feb 1965.

Children of FREDERICK FORD and TRACEY LEME are:

    i.   WHITNEY DENISE[7] FORD, b. 26 Jun 1988.

    ii.   ERICK RAYMOND FORD, b. 07 Apr 1997.

23. RONALD LEE[6] FORD *(FREDERICK K.[5] FORD. JR., EVA LADOCIA[4] ROBINSON, LORENZO[3], DUNBAR[2], JOHN[1])* was born 23 May 1967 in Waldorf, Maryland. He married JAQUEL JACKSON.

Notes for RONALD LEE FORD:

Not Married

Child of RONALD FORD and JAQUEL JACKSON is:

    i.   JUSTIN[7] JACKSON, b. 26 Jun 1986.

24. RUSSELL LAMARR[6] FORD *(FREDERICK K.[5] FORD. JR., EVA LADOCIA[4] ROBINSON, LORENZO[3], DUNBAR[2], JOHN[1])* was born 03 May 1983. He married VICTORIA ACRESS.

Child of RUSSELL FORD and VICTORIA ACRESS is:

    i.   RUSSELL LAMAAR[7] FORD, JR., B. 15 FEB 2009.

25. EBONY[6] PENDER *(EDWARD[5] FORD, EVA LADOCIA[4] ROBINSON, LORENZO[3], DUNBAR[2], JOHN[1])* was born 08 Mar 1980 in Philadelphia, Pa.. She married CARL STEVENSON.

Children of EBONY PENDER and CARL STEVENSON are:

  i. JAHMEER[7] PENDER, b. 18 Dec 1995, Philadelphia, Pa..

  ii. ALEXIS PENDER, b. 25 Sep 1998, Philadelphia, Pa..

  iii. MARQUES PENDER, b. 02 Mar 2001, Philadelphia, Pa..

  iv. TREY BROWN, JR., b. 12 Sep 2002, Philadelphia, Pa..

  v. JERVIER STEVENSON, b. 04 Jul 2008, Philadelphia, Pa..

  vi. CARL STEVENSON, b. 11 May 2011, Philadelphia, Pa..

26. SONYA[6] PENDER *(EDWARD[5] FORD, EVA LADOCIA[4] ROBINSON, LORENZO[3], DUNBAR[2], JOHN[1])* was born 24 May 1983 in Philadelphia, Pa..

Notes for SONYA PENDER:

Not Married

Children of SONYA PENDER are:

  i. EMANI[7] PENDER, b. 19 Jul 2003, Philadelphia, Pa..

  ii. RIMAJ PENDER, b. 05 Jan 2004, Philadelphia, Pa..

  iii. EMYIA PENDER, b. 17 Nov 2008, Philadelphia, Pa..

  iv. EDWARD FORD, b. 16 Feb 2011, Philadelphia, Pa..

27. NADINE[6] PENDER *(EDWARD[5] FORD, EVA LADOCIA[4] ROBINSON, LORENZO[3], DUNBAR[2], JOHN[1])* was born 08 Feb 1988 in Philadelphia, Pa..

Children of NADINE PENDER are:

  i. AANIR[7] PENDER, b. 04 May 2005, Philadelphia, Pa..

  ii. QUISEEM WASHINGTON, b. 02 Jul 2010, Philadelphia, Pa..

28. JUDITH E.[6] WELCH *(GENEVIEVE A.[5] ROBINSON, ANNA BESSIE[4], LORENZO[3], DUNBAR[2], JOHN[1])* was born 15 May 1951 in Philadelphia, Pa.. She married (2) HENRY BAKER STURGIS 22 Apr 2006. He was born 1945.

Children of JUDITH E. WELCH are:

53. i.   ERIK STEPHEN[7] WELCH, b. 11 Dec 1969, Philadelphia, Pa..

54. ii. SOLOMON ELLIOTT WELCH, b. 08 Aug 1973, Philadelphia, Pa..

     iii. GMERICE JOIA WELCH, b. 26 Sep 1981, Philadelphia, Pa.; m. ALPHONSO DANDRIGE.

29. JACQUELINE FLORA[6] WELCH *(GENEVIEVE A.[5] ROBINSON, ANNA BESSIE[4], LORENZO[3], DUNBAR[2], JOHN[1])* was born 11 Nov 1952 in Tarpon Springs, Florida.

Child of JACQUELINE FLORA WELCH is:

55. i.   JONELLE MARQUETTE[7] WELCH, b. 08 Nov 1972, Philadelphia, Pa..

30. QUINESETA A.[6] WELCH *(GENEVIEVE A.[5] ROBINSON, ANNA BESSIE[4], LORENZO[3], DUNBAR[2], JOHN[1])* was born 06 May 1956 in Philadelphia, Pa..

Notes for QUINESETA A. WELCH:

Unmarried

Children of QUINESETA A. WELCH are:

56. i.   ZANISHA A.[7] WELCH, b. 24 Oct 1973, Philadelphia, Pa..

     ii. QUINZELL P CHAMPANGE, b. 06 Mar 1974, Philadelphia, Pa..

31. Joyce M.[6] Welch *(Genevieve A.[5] Robinson, Anna Bessie[4], Lorenzo[3], Dunbar[2], John[1])* was born 26 Sep 1956 in Philadelphia, Pa.. She married (1) Greg Alston 1979. She married (2) Leon Grant 1990.

Notes for Joyce M. Welch:

Divorced

Children of Joyce Welch and Greg Alston are:

57. i. Calia N.[7] Alston, b. 06 Aug 1974, Tarpon Springs, Florida.

58. ii. April D. Alston, b. 27 Mar 1979, Philadelphia, Pa..

32. Denise A.[6] Welch *(Genevieve A.[5] Robinson, Anna Bessie[4], Lorenzo[3], Dunbar[2], John[1])* was born 13 Jul 1960 in Philadelphia, Pa.. She married Douglas Wallace 27 Jun 1996 in Orlando, Florida. He was born 03 Apr 1965 in Tarpon Springs, Florida.

Children of Denise Welch and Douglas Wallace are:

i. Brandon R.[7] Lowery, b. 04 Sep 1981, Philadelphia, Pa..

ii. Douglas N. Wallace, b. 22 Mar 1989, Tarpon Springs, Florida.

iii. Elijah K. Wallace, b. 26 Oct 1996, Orlando, Florida.

33. Cynthia A.[6] Welch *(Genevieve A.[5] Robinson, Anna Bessie[4], Lorenzo[3], Dunbar[2], John[1])* was born 24 Jun 1962 in Philadelphia, Pa.. She married Marshal Conley 1985 in Florida.

Children of Cynthia Welch and Marshal Conley are:

59. i. Marcia J.[7] Welch, b. 22 May 1981, Tarpon Springs, Florida.

60. ii. MARSHALL WELCH, b. 09 Jul 1982, Tarpon Springs, Florida.

61. iii. MARCO CONLEY, b. 12 Jan 1989, Clearwater, Florida.

iv. MARKEISHA G. CONLEY, b. 17 May 1991, Clearwater, Florida.

62. v. MARZINNIA CONLEY, b. 18 Oct 1992, Clearwater, Florida.

vi. MARLIASHA CONLEY, b. 28 Mar 1994, Clearwater, Florida.

34. BONITA[6] NAPPER *(ISSAC B.[5], ETHEL IRENE[4] ROBINSON, LORENZO[3], DUNBAR[2], JOHN[1])* was born 31 Jul 1958.

Child of BONITA NAPPER is:

i. JONATHAN[7] NORDE, b. 13 Feb 1983.

35. ISSAC[6] NAPPER III *(ISSAC B.[5], ETHEL IRENE[4] ROBINSON, LORENZO[3], DUNBAR[2], JOHN[1])* was born 09 Jan 1969. He married LINDA STONE.

Children of ISSAC NAPPER and LINDA STONE are:

i. BONITA[7] STONE, b. Philadelphia, Pa..

ii. CHEASEA NAPPER, b. Philadelphia, Pa..

iii. ISSAC NAPPER IV, b. Philadelphia, Pa..

36. JOHN[6] NAPPER *(ISSAC B.[5], ETHEL IRENE[4] ROBINSON, LORENZO[3], DUNBAR[2], JOHN[1])* was born 21 May 1966 in Philadelphia, Pa.. He married CHRISTIANA.

Child of JOHN NAPPER and CHRISTIANA is:

i. JOHN[7] NAPPER, b. 13 Feb 1983, Philadelphia, Pa..

37. Dedoriad Lithiah[6] Napper *(Ethel Lucy[5], Ethel Irene[4] Robinson, Lorenzo[3], Dunbar[2], John[1])* was born 24 Apr 1947 in Philadelphia, Pa., and died Oct 2003 in Philadelphia, Pa.. She married Billy Hipp. He was born 24 Apr 1947 in Philadelphia, Pa., and died 16 May 1990 in Philadelphia, Pa..

Children of Dedoriad Napper and Billy Hipp are:

63.	i.	Edward Lee[7] Barnby, b. 1964, Houston, Texas.
	ii.	Carlton Hipp, b. 14 Apr 1971, Philadelphia, Pa..
	iii.	Dedorid L. Hipp, b. 03 Dec 1974, Philadelphia, Pa..

38. Dellaphine Marie[6] Johnson *(Ethel Lucy[5] Napper, Ethel Irene[4] Robinson, Lorenzo[3], Dunbar[2], John[1])* was born 20 Apr 1948 in New Jersey. She married (1) Gerald Bingham. She married (2) Dennis Ivy.

Child of Dellaphine Johnson and Gerald Bingham is:

	i.	Gerald[7] Bingham, Jr., b. 16 Aug, Philadelphia, Pa..

Children of Dellaphine Johnson and Dennis Ivy are:

64.	ii.	Charmine[7] Johnson, b. 04 Sep 1966, Philadelphia, Pa..
65.	iii.	Cass Avery Johnson, b. 02 Sep 1967, Philadelphia, Pa..
66.	iv.	Carin Johnson, b. 20 Jan 1968, Philadelphia, Pa..
67.	v.	Carma M. Johnson, b. 24 May 1969, Philadelphia, Pa..

39. Doreen Patricia[6] Johnson *(Ethel Lucy[5] Napper, Ethel Irene[4] Robinson, Lorenzo[3], Dunbar[2], John[1])* was born 28 Nov 1949 in Philadelphia, Pa..

Notes for Doreen Patricia Johnson:

Married to Walter Dean who died 5/15/2005 - No children

Married to George Porcchea - No children

Children of Doreen Patricia Johnson are:

68.   i.   Christopher David[7] Johnson, b. Philadelphia, Pa..

69.   ii. Candice Johnson, b. 1988, Philadelphia, Pa..

40. Dow Lorenzo[6] Johnson *(Ethel Lucy[5] Napper, Ethel Irene[4] Robinson, Lorenzo[3], Dunbar[2], John[1])* was born 09 Mar 1951 in Philadelphia, Pa., and died 15 May 2011 in Texas. He married (1) Dara Holcomb. He married (2) Rachel Brown.

Child of Dow Johnson and Rachel Brown is:

   i.   Victor[7] Steward.

41. Donzella[6] Johnson *(Ethel Lucy[5] Napper, Ethel Irene[4] Robinson, Lorenzo[3], Dunbar[2], John[1])* was born 13 Jul 1954 in Philadelphia, Pa.. She married James King, Jr. 12 Jan 2007.

Children of Donzella Johnson and James King are:

70.   i.   Shawn James[7] King, b. 03 Mar 1973, Philadelphia, Pa..

71.   ii. Jeneene Marie King, b. 26 Jul 1979, Philadelphia, Pa..

      iii. Marcus Edward King, b. 24 Feb 1972, Philadelphia, Pa..

      iv. Holly King.

42. Denise[6] Johnson *(Ethel Lucy[5] Napper, Ethel Irene[4] Robinson, Lorenzo[3], Dunbar[2], John[1])* was born 24 Jul 1955 in Philadelphia, Pa.. She married (1) Carlton Meade. He died 30 Mar 1991 in Philadelphia, Pa.. She married (2) William Dandridge Apr 1972.

Children of Denise Johnson and William Dandridge are:

72. i.   CYRUS LAMONT[7] DANDRIDGE, b. 22 Aug 1972, Philadelphia, Pa..

73. ii. GARY TAMARA DANDRIDGE, b. 15 Mar 1974, Philadelphia, Pa..

43. DONZEILA OLIVIA[6] JOHNSON *(ETHEL LUCY[5] NAPPER, ETHEL IRENE[4] ROBINSON, LORENZO[3], DUNBAR[2], JOHN[1])* was born 27 Jun 1957 in Philadelphia, Pa.. She married (1) RICHARD FISHER. She married (2) RALPH SPEARMAN 15 Jul 2002.

Child of DONZEILA JOHNSON and RICHARD FISHER is:

74. i.   NICOLE NOEL[7] FISHER, b. 31 Dec 1979, Philadelphia, Pa..

Children of DONZEILA JOHNSON and RALPH SPEARMAN are:

75. ii. CRYSTAL[7] SPEARMAN, b. 26 Mar 1981, Philadelphia, Pa..

     iii. MICHAEL S. SPEARMAN, b. 10 Nov 1990, Philadelphia, Pa..

76. iv. JONATHAN S. SPEARMAN, b. 16 Nov 1991, Philadelphia, Pa..

44. EDITH ELIZABETH[6] THOMAS *(EDITH IRENE[5] NAPPER, ETHEL IRENE[4] ROBINSON, LORENZO[3], DUNBAR[2], JOHN[1])* was born 04 Oct 1951 in Philadelphia, Pa.. She married (1) JOSEPH L. HOBBS. She married (2) FRANK BESTER,. SR..

Child of EDITH THOMAS and JOSEPH HOBBS is:

77. i.   DEBORAH VICTORIA[7] HOBBS, b. 11 Jul 1976, Philadelphia, Pa..

Child of EDITH THOMAS and FRANK BESTER is:

78. ii. ANTHONY PATRICK[7] BESTER, SR., b. 01 May 1986, Philadelphia, Pa..

45. CLAIRE[6] NAPPER *(WILBER JAMES[5], ETHEL IRENE[4] ROBINSON, LORENZO[3], DUNBAR[2], JOHN[1])* She married PAUL ROBERSON.

Children of CLAIRE NAPPER and PAUL ROBERSON are:

    i. BETHLEHEM[7] ROBERSON.

    ii. RUTH ROBERSON.

    iii. AGNES ROBERSON.

46. JEANETTE[6] PETERSON *(DANIEL E.[5], CORA L.[4] ROBINSON, LORENZO[3], DUNBAR[2], JOHN[1])* was born 16 Jun 1971 in Michigan. She married (1) RODNEY JOHNSON.

Children of JEANETTE PETERSON are:

    i. CARLIA JANAJ[7] JACKSON, b. 03 Dec, Douglasville, Ga..

    ii. AUDRINA JACKSON, b. 17 Jun 2012, Douglasville, Ga..

47. DANIEL[6] PETERSON *(DANIEL E.[5], CORA L.[4] ROBINSON, LORENZO[3], DUNBAR[2], JOHN[1])* was born 08 Aug 1974 in Sacramento, California. He married WENDY.

Child of DANIEL PETERSON and WENDY is:

    i. SEAN DANIEL[7] PETERSON, b. 28 Feb 2013, La Guana Hills, California.

48. SHANI DANIELLE[6] PETERSON *(WARREN L.[5], CORA L.[4] ROBINSON, LORENZO[3], DUNBAR[2], JOHN[1])* was born 22 Dec 1982 in Philadelphia, Pa..

Child of SHANI DANIELLE PETERSON is:

i. CAMERON DANIELLE[7] PETERSON, b. 30 Mar 2005, Philadelphia, Pa..

49. JONATHAN K.R.[6] BLAINE *(EDNA E.[5] PETERSON, CORA L.[4] ROBINSON, LORENZO[3], DUNBAR[2], JOHN[1])* was born 13 Aug 1974 in Philadelphia, Pa.. He married MONICA A. FERRON 20 Jun 1993 in Philadelphia, Pa., daughter of ROBERTO FERRON and FREDRICKA MORRIS. She was born 05 Jul 1970 in Philadelphia, Pa..

Children of JONATHAN BLAINE and MONICA FERRON are:

i. DEVIN I.[7] FERRON, b. 12 Jun 1990, Philadelphia, Pa..

ii. DAJEN M. BLAINE, b. 15 Sep 1997, Philadelphia, Pa..

iii. KHALISA M. BLAINE, b. 03 Jun 2002, Willingboro, New Jersey.

iv. KHYRA A. BLAINE, b. 09 Nov 2004, Willingboro, New Jersey.

v. DENYM M. BLAINE, b. 25 Jan 2012, Voorhees, New Jersey.

50. RAHN A.[6] BLAINE *(EDNA E.[5] PETERSON, CORA L.[4] ROBINSON, LORENZO[3], DUNBAR[2], JOHN[1])* was born 27 Dec 1975 in Philadelphia, Pa.. He married ANGEL E. WRIGHT 08 Oct 2011 in Philadelphia, Pa., daughter of MELVIN WRIGHT and DOROTHY MCMANUS. She was born 27 Dec 1973 in Philadelphia, Pa..

Child of RAHN BLAINE and ANGEL WRIGHT is:

i. MYR N.[7] BLAINE, b. 22 Sep 2000, Philadelphia, Pa..

51. KENT E.[6] ARLINE, JR. *(MARGARET[5] PETERSON, CORA L.[4] ROBINSON, LORENZO[3], DUNBAR[2], JOHN[1])* was born 10 Sep 1967 in Philadelphia, Pa.. He married MELISSA MCDADE 19 Aug 2003.

Child of KENT ARLINE and MELISSA MCDADE is:

i. JACK K.[7] ARLINE, b. 2005, Winslow, New Jersey.

52. SHARRON[6] PATTERSON-MCFADDEN *(ROBERT T.[5] PETERSON, CORA L.[4] ROBINSON, LORENZO[3], DUNBAR[2], JOHN[1])* was born Aug 1965.

Children of SHARRON PATTERSON-MCFADDEN are:

i. GABRIELLE[7] MCFADDEN.

ii. GREGORY MCFADDEN.

iii. SHELBY MCFADDEN.

Generation No. 6

53. ERIK STEPHEN[7] WELCH (JUDITH E.[6], GENEVIEVE A.[5] ROBINSON, ANNA BESSIE[4], LORENZO[3], DUNBAR[2], JOHN[1]) was born 11 Dec 1969 in Philadelphia, Pa.. He married VONETTA.

Children of ERIK WELCH and VONETTA are:

  i. ZOE ALYSSA[8] WELCH, b. 18 May, Atlanta, Georgia.

  ii. MYLLES HENRII WELCH, b. 10 Aug 2009, Atlanta, Georgia.

54. SOLOMON ELLIOTT[7] WELCH (JUDITH E.[6], GENEVIEVE A.[5] ROBINSON, ANNA BESSIE[4], LORENZO[3], DUNBAR[2], JOHN[1]) was born 08 Aug 1973 in Philadelphia, Pa..

Children of SOLOMON ELLIOTT WELCH are:

  i. RA-QUANNA ALEXANDRIA[8] WELCH, b. 07 Sep 1994, Agusta, Georgia.

  ii. SAUL ELIJAH CAIN WELCH, b. 14 Jan 1997, Agusta, Georgia.

  iii. XENIA CYAUANA KALI WELCH, b. 11 Jan 2004, Springfield, Mass..

  iv. WINTER LEKETMIA RENII WELCH, b. 15 Nov 2007, Springfield, Mass..

  v. DESARI QANNADI ZAEIR WELCH, b. 16 Apr 2010, Springfield, Mass..

55. JONELLE MARQUETTE[7] WELCH (JACQUELINE FLORA[6], GENEVIEVE A.[5] ROBINSON, ANNA BESSIE[4], LORENZO[3], DUNBAR[2], JOHN[1]) was born 08 Nov 1972 in Philadelphia, Pa..

Children of JONELLE MARQUETTE WELCH are:

 i. PHILLIP MARQUES[8] WELCH, b. 22 Apr 1991, Philadelphia, Pa..

 ii. THADER JEAN WELCH, b. 14 Dec 2002, Philadelphia, Pa..

56. ZANISHA A.[7] WELCH *(QUINESETA A.[6], GENEVIEVE A.[5] ROBINSON, ANNA BESSIE[4], LORENZO[3], DUNBAR[2], JOHN[1])* was born 24 Oct 1973 in Philadelphia, Pa..

Child of ZANISHA A. WELCH is:

 i. JESUS R.[8] WELCH, B. 20 AUG 1989, PHILADELPHIA, PA..

57. CALIA N.[7] ALSTON *(JOYCE M.[6] WELCH, GENEVIEVE A.[5] ROBINSON, ANNA BESSIE[4], LORENZO[3], DUNBAR[2], JOHN[1])* was born 06 Aug 1974 in Tarpon Springs, Florida. She married JEFF YOUNG.

Child of CALIA ALSTON and JEFF YOUNG is:

 i. MYA BLAIN[8] YOUNG, b. 24 Sep 1999, Philadelphia, Pa..

58. APRIL D.[7] ALSTON *(JOYCE M.[6] WELCH, GENEVIEVE A.[5] ROBINSON, ANNA BESSIE[4], LORENZO[3], DUNBAR[2], JOHN[1])* was born 27 Mar 1979 in Philadelphia, Pa..

Child of APRIL D. ALSTON is:

 i. TAKIRA TULL[8] ALSTON, b. 31 Dec 1994, Philadelphia, Pa..

59. MARCIA J.[7] WELCH *(CYNTHIA A.[6], GENEVIEVE A.[5] ROBINSON, ANNA BESSIE[4], LORENZO[3], DUNBAR[2], JOHN[1])* was born 22 May 1981 in Tarpon Springs, Florida.

Children of MARCIA J. WELCH are:

i. Jacques[8] Welch, b. 26 Mar 2001, Florida.

ii. Ashant Welch, b. 23 Oct 2003, Florida.

iii. Demarion Boyd, b. 30 Jan 2005, Florida.

iv. Malayia Boyd, b. 25 Apr 2006, Florida.

v. Maliak Boyd, b. 25 Dec 2007, Florida.

60. Marshall[7] Welch *(Cynthia A.[6], Genevieve A.[5] Robinson, Anna Bessie[4], Lorenzo[3], Dunbar[2], John[1])* was born 09 Jul 1982 in Tarpon Springs, Florida.

Child of Marshall Welch is:

i. Iasiah[8] Welch, b. 23 Sep 2004, Florida.

61. Marco[7] Conley *(Cynthia A.[6] Welch, Genevieve A.[5] Robinson, Anna Bessie[4], Lorenzo[3], Dunbar[2], John[1])* was born 12 Jan 1989 in Clearwater, Florida.

Child of Marco Conley is:

i. Maleah[8] Conley, b. 26 Jan 2011, Florida.

62. Marzinnia[7] Conley *(Cynthia A.[6] Welch, Genevieve A.[5] Robinson, Anna Bessie[4], Lorenzo[3], Dunbar[2], John[1])* was born 18 Oct 1992 in Clearwater, Florida.

Child of Marzinnia Conley is:

i. Lardarius[8] Conley, b. 04 Aug 2011, Florida.

63. Edward Lee[7] Barnby *(Dedoriad Lithiah[6] Napper, Ethel Lucy[5], Ethel Irene[4] Robinson, Lorenzo[3], Dunbar[2], John[1])* was born 1964 in Houston, Texas. He married Tracie Wooden.

Children of EDWARD BARNBY and TRACIE WOODEN are:

    i.   STACIA[8] BARNBY.

    ii.   JAMES BARNBY.

64. CHARMINE[7] JOHNSON *(DELLAPHINE MARIE[6], ETHEL LUCY[5] NAPPER, ETHEL IRENE[4] ROBINSON, LORENZO[3], DUNBAR[2], JOHN[1])* was born 04 Sep 1966 in Philadelphia, Pa.. She married (1) LANCE MACK. She married (2) HERBERT EDMOUNDS.

Children of CHARMINE JOHNSON and HERBERT EDMOUNDS are:

    i.   HERBERT[8] EDMOUNDS, b. 23 Sep 1991, Philadelphia, Pa..

    ii.   CRISONA EDMOUNDS, b. 27 Jul 1997, Philadelphia, Pa..

65. CASS AVERY[7] JOHNSON *(DELLAPHINE MARIE[6], ETHEL LUCY[5] NAPPER, ETHEL IRENE[4] ROBINSON, LORENZO[3], DUNBAR[2], JOHN[1])* was born 02 Sep 1967 in Philadelphia, Pa.. He married (1) PATRICE HAWKINS. He married (2) TREACIE.

Child of CASS JOHNSON and PATRICE HAWKINS is:

    i.   AMBER[8] HAWKINS, b. 21 Jul 1987, Philadelphia, Pa..

Children of CASS JOHNSON and TREACIE are:

    ii.   KHALIA[8] JOHNSON, b. Georgia.

    iii.   KALISE JOHNSON, b. Georgia.

66. CARIN[7] JOHNSON *(DELLAPHINE MARIE[6], ETHEL LUCY[5] NAPPER, ETHEL IRENE[4] ROBINSON, LORENZO[3], DUNBAR[2], JOHN[1])* was born 20 Jan 1968 in Philadelphia, Pa.. She married APPLEBE.

Child of CARIN JOHNSON and APPLEBE is:

    i.   AARON[8] APPLEBE, b. 17 Nov 1991, Philadelphia, Pa..

67. CARMA M.[7] JOHNSON *(DELLAPHINE MARIE[6], ETHEL LUCY[5] NAPPER, ETHEL IRENE[4] ROBINSON, LORENZO[3], DUNBAR[2], JOHN[1])* was born 24 May 1969 in Philadelphia, Pa..

Child of CARMA M. JOHNSON is:

    i.   AJA[8] JOHNSON, b. 10 Apr 1997, Georgia.

68. CHRISTOPHER DAVID[7] JOHNSON *(DOREEN PATRICIA[6], ETHEL LUCY[5] NAPPER, ETHEL IRENE[4] ROBINSON, LORENZO[3], DUNBAR[2], JOHN[1])* was born in Philadelphia, Pa.. He married MARGARET.

Child of CHRISTOPHER JOHNSON and MARGARET is:

    i.   D.J.[8] JOHNSON.

69. CANDICE[7] JOHNSON *(DOREEN PATRICIA[6], ETHEL LUCY[5] NAPPER, ETHEL IRENE[4] ROBINSON, LORENZO[3], DUNBAR[2], JOHN[1])* was born 1988 in Philadelphia, Pa.. She married JOHN JOHNSON, son of MARY ALICE JOHNSON.

Child of CANDICE JOHNSON and JOHN JOHNSON is:

    i.   COURTNEY[8] JOHNSON.

70. SHAWN JAMES[7] KING *(DONZELLA[6] JOHNSON, ETHEL LUCY[5] NAPPER, ETHEL IRENE[4] ROBINSON, LORENZO[3], DUNBAR[2], JOHN[1])* was born 03 Mar 1973 in Philadelphia, Pa.. He married SHALA JONES Jun 1996.

Children of SHAWN KING and SHALA JONES are:

    i.   DEMARCUS[8] JONES, b. 27 Nov 1996, Canton, Georgia.

ii. JORDAN AMIN KING, b. 30 Aug 2000, Canton, Georgia.

iii. SHAYLA JENAE KING, b. 24 Feb 2004, Canton, Georgia.

iv. LEILAH JAMES KING, b. 04 Feb 2008, Canton, Georgia.

71. JENEENE MARIE[7] KING *(DONZELLA[6] JOHNSON, ETHEL LUCY[5] NAPPER, ETHEL IRENE[4] ROBINSON, LORENZO[3], DUNBAR[2], JOHN[1])* was born 26 Jul 1979 in Philadelphia, Pa..

Children of JENEENE MARIE KING are:

i. KHADEJAH[8] NEAL, b. 14 Nov 1997, Philadelphia, Pa..

ii. GERALD LAMONT HERBERT, b. 07 Jul 2001, Philadelphia, Pa..

72. CYRUS LAMONT[7] DANDRIDGE *(DENISE[6] JOHNSON, ETHEL LUCY[5] NAPPER, ETHEL IRENE[4] ROBINSON, LORENZO[3], DUNBAR[2], JOHN[1])* was born 22 Aug 1972 in Philadelphia, Pa..

Child of CYRUS LAMONT DANDRIDGE is:

i. NADJEA[8] CAMPBELL, b. 05 Aug 1997, Philadelphia, Pa..

73. GARY TAMARA[7] DANDRIDGE *(DENISE[6] JOHNSON, ETHEL LUCY[5] NAPPER, ETHEL IRENE[4] ROBINSON, LORENZO[3], DUNBAR[2], JOHN[1])* was born 15 Mar 1974 in Philadelphia, Pa.. He married CHARNELLE HARRIS.

Children of GARY DANDRIDGE and CHARNELLE HARRIS are:

i. SERENITY[8] HARRIS, b. 10 Jun 2004, Georgia.

ii. MALANI DANDRIDGE, b. 12 Jun 2010, Georgia.

iii. O'RYAN TAMARA DANDRIDGE, b. 09 Mar 2013, Georgia.

74. NICOLE NOEL[7] FISHER *(DONZEILA OLIVIA[6] JOHNSON, ETHEL LUCY[5] NAPPER, ETHEL IRENE[4] ROBINSON, LORENZO[3], DUNBAR[2], JOHN[1])* was born 31 Dec 1979 in Philadelphia, Pa.. She married CHANCEY HOLLOWAY.

Child of NICOLE FISHER and CHANCEY HOLLOWAY is:

i. MADISON[8] HOLLOWAY, b. 17 Jun 2004, Philadelphia, Pa..

75. CRYSTAL[7] SPEARMAN *(DONZEILA OLIVIA[6] JOHNSON, ETHEL LUCY[5] NAPPER, ETHEL IRENE[4] ROBINSON, LORENZO[3], DUNBAR[2], JOHN[1])* was born 26 Mar 1981 in Philadelphia, Pa.. She married RICHARD CENTRELL 20 May 2011.

Children of CRYSTAL SPEARMAN and RICHARD CENTRELL are:

i. ASHLEY[8] SPEARMAN, b. 19 Oct 1998, Philadelphia, Pa..

ii. ANGEL RICHARDSON, b. 04 Jul 2001, Riverdale, Georgia.

iii. KEENAN SPEARMAN, b. 30 Aug 2005, Canton, Georgia.

iv. KEIRA HAYES, b. 15 Feb 2007, Canton, Georgia.

76. JONATHAN S.[7] SPEARMAN *(DONZEILA OLIVIA[6] JOHNSON, ETHEL LUCY[5] NAPPER, ETHEL IRENE[4] ROBINSON,* Lorenzo[3]*,* Dunbar[2]*,* John[1]*)* was born 16 Nov 1991 in Philadelphia, Pa..

Child of JONATHAN S. SPEARMAN is:

i. TAYLOR MARIE[8] HAMBRICK, b. 24 Jun 2011, Riverdale, Georgia.

77. DEBORAH VICTORIA[7] HOBBS *(EDITH ELIZABETH[6] THOMAS, EDITH IRENE[5] NAPPER, ETHEL IRENE[4] ROBINSON,* Lorenzo[3]*,* Dunbar[2]*,* John[1]*)* was born 11 Jul 1976 in Philadelphia, Pa..

Child of DEBORAH VICTORIA HOBBS is:

    i.   JA'SID CHRISTOPHER[8] CITY, b. 25 Apr 2004, Philadelphia, Pa..

78. ANTHONY PATRICK[7] BESTER, SR. *(EDITH ELIZABETH[6] THOMAS, EDITH IRENE[5] NAPPER, ETHEL IRENE[4] Robinson, Lorenzo[3], Dunbar[2], John[1])* was born 01 May 1986 in Philadelphia, Pa..

Child of ANTHONY PATRICK BESTER, SR. is:

    i.   ANTHONY PATRICK[8] BESTER, JR., B. 20 MAY 2010, PHILADELPHIA, PA..

LORENZO ROBINSON 1868 - 1931

Lorenzo was born in King & Queen County, Va., the son of Dunbar Robinson. He and his siblings moved to Philadelphia, Pa. during the late 1800's. He married Texana Robinson in 1898 and raised a family of eight.

Name: Wilbur A Robinson
Birth Date: abt 1900
Death Date: 3 Feb 1901
Death Place: Philadelphia, Philadelphia, Pennsylvania
Age at Death: 14 months
Gender: Male
Father: Lorenzo Robinson
Mother: Anna Robinson
FHL Film Number: 1845286

Philadelphia, Pennsylvania, Death Certificates Index, 1803-1915
Name: **Chancellor D Robinson**
Birth Date: abt 1904
Birth Place: Phila
Death Date: 21 Apr 1905
Death Place: Philadelphia, Pennsylvania
Age at Death: 1 year 7 months
Burial Date: 24 Apr 1905
Gender: Male
Race: Black
Residence: Philadelphia, Pennsylvania
Father: Lorenzo Robinson
Mother: Anna Robinson

Descendants of Lorenzo Robinson

Generation No. 1

1. LORENZO[3] ROBINSON *(DUNBAR[2], JOHN[1])* was born 1868 in King & Queen County, Va.. He married TEXANA ROBINSON 1898 in Philadelphia, Pa., daughter of ALBERT ROBINSON and SOPHIA. She was born Sep 1872 in Louisa, Virginia.

Children of LORENZO ROBINSON and TEXANA ROBINSON are:

	i.	WILBUR[4] ROBINSON, b. 1899, Philadelphia, Pa.; d. 03 Feb 1901, Philadelphia, Pa..
2.	ii.	EDITH MADELINE ROBINSON, b. 1901, Philadelphia, Pa..
	iii.	MARGARET D. ROBINSON, b. 1902, Philadelphia, Pa.; m. LUTHER MATHIS.
	iv.	CHANCELLOR D. ROBINSON, b. 1904, Philadelphia, Pa.; d. 21 Apr 1905, Philadelphia, Pa..
3.	v.	EVA LADOCIA ROBINSON, b. 06 Mar 1906, Philadelphia, Pa..
4.	vi.	ANNA BESSIE ROBINSON, b. 1908, Philadelphia, Pa..
5.	vii.	ETHEL IRENE ROBINSON, b. 15 Mar 1912, Philadelphia, Pa.; d. Apr 1957, Philadelphia, Pa..
6.	viii.	CORA L. ROBINSON, b. 1915, Philadelphia, Pa..

Generation No. 2

2. EDITH MADELINE[4] ROBINSON *(LORENZO[3], DUNBAR[2], JOHN[1])* was born 1901 in Philadelphia, Pa.. She married WILLARD MOORE.

Notes for EDITH MADELINE ROBINSON:

Unmarried

Child of EDITH ROBINSON and WILLARD MOORE is:

    i.   WILLIAM[5] MOORE, b. 1925, Philadelphia, Pa..

3. EVA LADOCIA[4] ROBINSON *(LORENZO[3], DUNBAR[2], JOHN[1])* was born 06 Mar 1906 in Philadelphia, Pa.. She married FREDERICK K. FORD.

Children of EVA ROBINSON and FREDERICK FORD are:

    i.   PHILLIP BROOKS[5] FORD, b. Philadelphia, Pa.; d. 1959, Philadelphia, Pa..

    ii.   FREDERICK K. FORD. JR., b. 31 Oct 1942, Philadelphia, Pa.; d. 22 May 1989, Wilmington Delaware; m. JUANITA GREEN, 31 Jul 1965; b. 16 Apr 1947, Philadelphia, Pa..

    iii.   JOHN RUSSELL FORD, b. Philadelphia, Pa.; m. DARLENE.

    iv.   EDWARD FORD, b. 29 Aug 1947, Philadelphia, Pa.; m. EDITH PENDER.

    v.   ROBERT FORD, b. 24 Aug 1950, Philadelphia, Pa..

4. ANNA BESSIE[4] ROBINSON *(LORENZO[3], DUNBAR[2], JOHN[1])* was born 1908 in Philadelphia, Pa..

Child of ANNA BESSIE ROBINSON is:

    i.   GENEVIEVE A.[5] ROBINSON, b. 07 Feb 1933, Philadelphia, Pa.; m. JOHNNIE L. WELCH, 10 May 1951, Philadelphia, Pa.; b. 17 Mar 1927, Tarpon Springs, Florida.

5. ETHEL IRENE[4] ROBINSON *(LORENZO[3], DUNBAR[2], JOHN[1])* was born 15 Mar 1912 in Philadelphia, Pa., and died Apr 1957 in Philadelphia, Pa.. She married (1) ISAAC B. NAPPER, SR., son of BENJAMIN NAPPER and LUCY BELL. He was born 10 Mar 1911 in Philadelphia, Pa., and died 01 Mar 1943 in Philadelphia, Pa.. She married (2) EDWARD MULLEN.

Children of ETHEL ROBINSON and ISAAC NAPPER are:

- i. ISSAC B.[5] NAPPER II, b. 02 Apr 1934, Philadelphia, Pa.; m. OLIVIA DOSSANTA; b. 20 Mar 1930, South Wales, England; d. 07 Feb 2008.
- ii. ETHEL LUCY NAPPER, b. 24 Feb 1930, Philadelphia, Pa.; m. JOHN HENRY JOHNSON, 03 Sep 1946, Deleware; b. 03 Sep 1903, Greenboro, North Carolina; d. 23 Dec 1971, Philadelphia, Pa..
- iii. EDITH IRENE NAPPER, b. 19 Jun 1931, Philadelphia, Pa.; m. JAMES S. THOMAS, 18 Jun 1950; b. 19 Jun 1931, Philadelphia, Pa..
- iv. WILBER JAMES NAPPER, b. 22 Sep 1935, Philadelphia, Pa.; m. MARION LEWIS.
- v. ANNA NAPPER, b. 1932, Philadelphia, Pa..

6. CORA L.[4] ROBINSON *(LORENZO[3], DUNBAR[2], JOHN[1])* was born 1915 in Philadelphia, Pa.. She married DANIEL PETERSON 1933 in Philadelphia, Pa..

Children of CORA ROBINSON and DANIEL PETERSON are:

- i. ELLEN J.[5] PETERSON, b. 03 Dec 1933, Philadelphia, Pa.; m. ROBERT E. LUCAS, JR., 29 Jun 1957, Philadelphia, Pa.; b. 14 May 1931, Willow Grove Pa..
- ii. DANIEL E. PETERSON, b. 08 Oct 1936, Philadelphia, Pa.; m. SEVERA, Philippines; b. 01 Jan 1944, Philippines.

iii. WARREN L. PETERSON, b. 22 Mar 1938, Philadelphia, Pa.; m. MERIDEL JEFFERY, 07 Dec 1980, Philadelphia, Pa.; b. 05 Mar 1947, Philadelphia, Pa..

iv. RUSSELL PETERSON, b. 14 Sep 1940, Philadelphia, Pa.; m. (1) FRANCINE FEGGANS; m. (2) ELIZABETH DAVIS, 30 Jun 1994, Los Angeles, California; b. 06 Jan 1944, Little Rock, Arkansas.

v. EDNA E. PETERSON, b. 05 Sep 1942, Philadelphia, Pa.; m. (1) WILLIAM C. SMITH, JR., 16 Jul 1967, Killeen, Texas; b. 02 Feb 1943, Chicago, Illinois; m. (2) JONATHAN A. BLAINE, Aug 1972, Philadelphia, Pa..

vi. MARGARET PETERSON, b. 02 Feb 1945, Philadelphia, Pa.; m. (1) JAMES CROSS; d. Philadelphia, Pa.; m. (2) KENT E. ARLINE, SR., Philadelphia, Pa..

More About Margaret Peterson:

Divorced: Kent E. Arline, Sr.

vii. ROBERT T. PETERSON, b. 24 Apr 1948, Philadelphia, Pa.; m. (3) ANNETTE STEPHENS, 26 Jan 2001, Burlington, New Jersey; b. 21 Oct 1956, San Pedro, California.

viii. GWENDOLYN D. PETERSON, b. 29 Apr 1951, Philadelphia, Pa.; m. (1) GEORGE GASKIN; m. (2) WALTER FRANKLIN, 07 Mar 1987, Philadelphia, Pa.; b. 29 Aug 1945, Massilon, Ohio.

More About GWENDOLYN D. PETERSON:

Divorced: George Gaskin

ETHEL LUCY NAPPER 2/24/1930

Ethel the great granddaughter of Lorenzo Robinson was born and raised in Philadelphia, Pa. She married John Henry Johnson September 3, 1946.

Eight of their nine children were born and raised in Philadelphia, Pa. All members of her family and those of her siblings were active members of Calvary Baptist Church of West Philadelphia located at 6122 Haverford Avenue, Philadelphia, Pa. In her early years Ethel was one of its Ministers. In recent years she only works with the Sunday School Program.

Descendants of Ethel Lucy Napper (1 of 12)

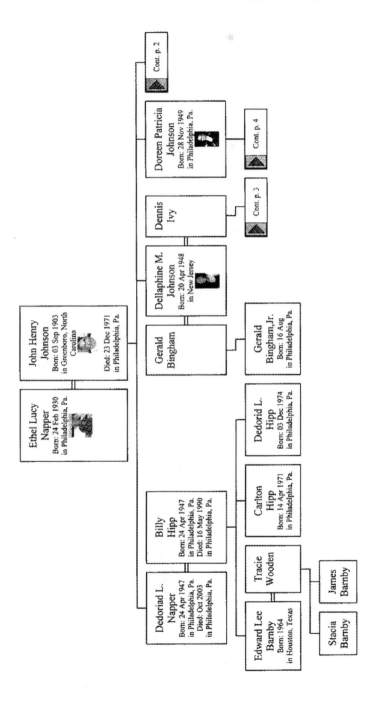

Descendants of Ethel Lucy Napper (2 of 12)

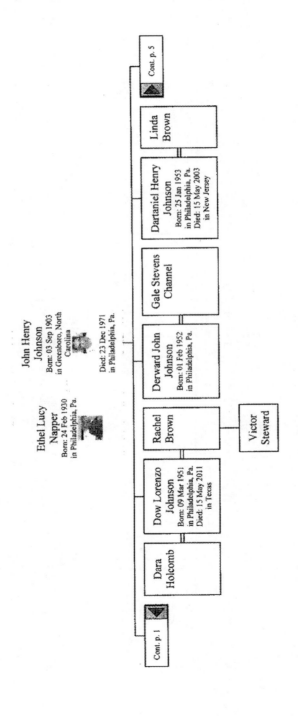

Descendants of Ethel Lucy Napper (3 of 12)

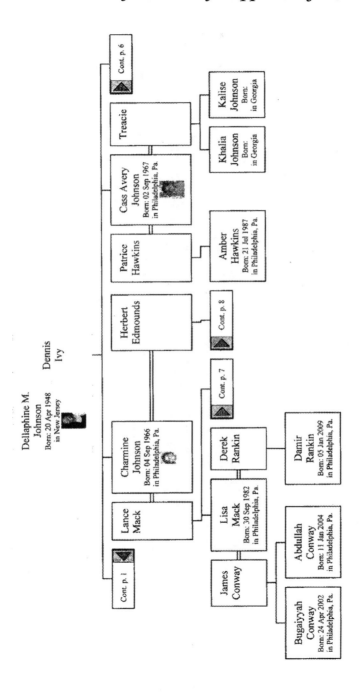

Descendants of Ethel Lucy Napper

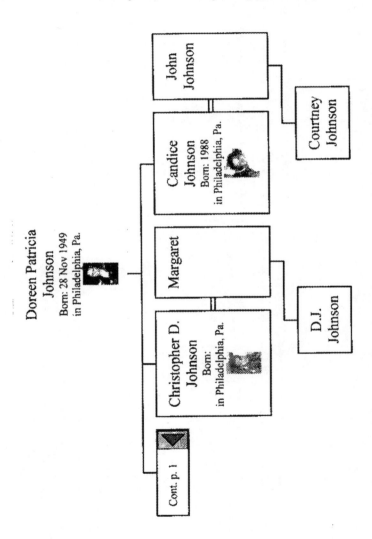

Descendants of Ethel Lucy Napper (5 of 12)

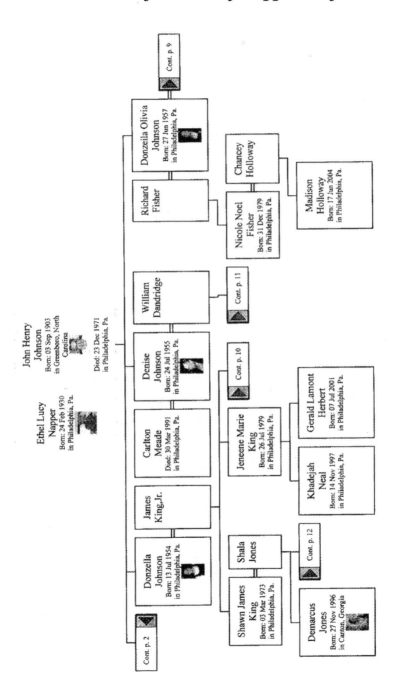

Descendants of Ethel Lucy Napper

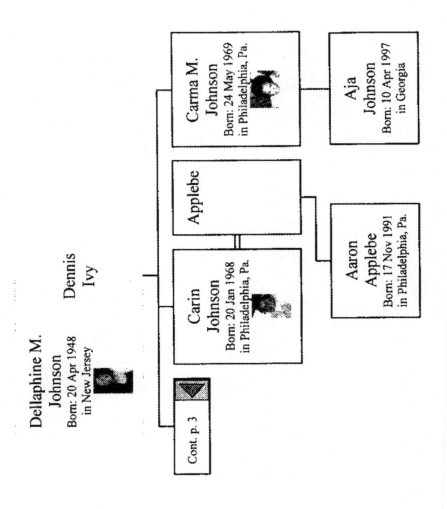

Descendants of Ethel Lucy Napper

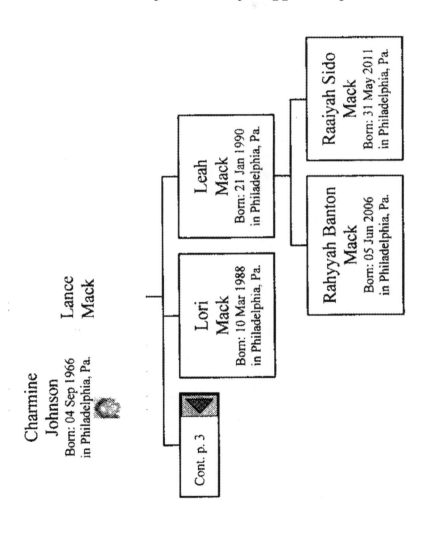

Descendants of Ethel Lucy Napper

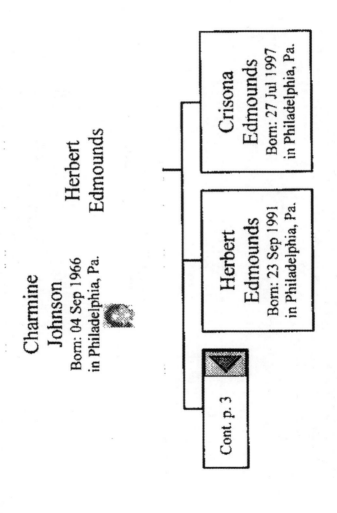

Descendants of Ethel Lucy Napper

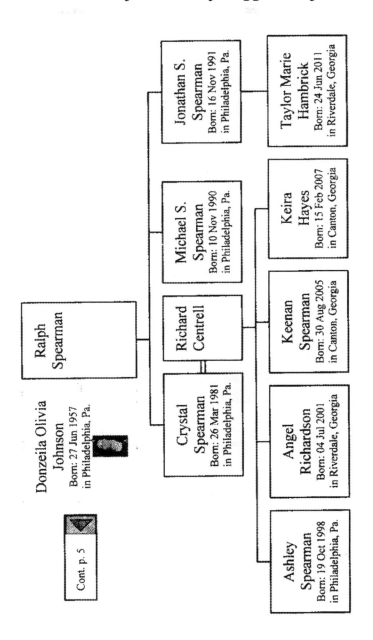

Descendants of Ethel Lucy Napper

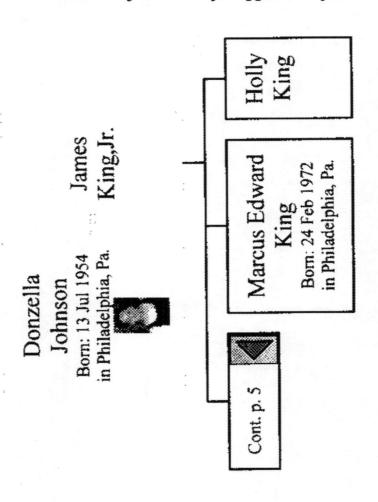

Descendants of Ethel Lucy Napper

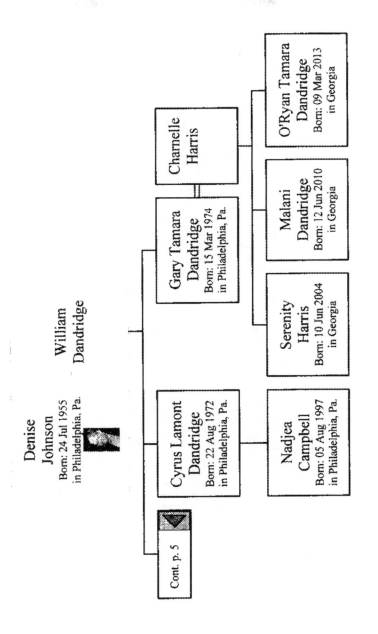

Descendants of Ethel Lucy Napper

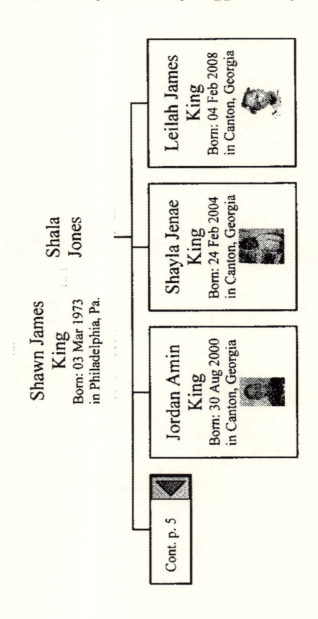

CHAPTER 4

POLLY ROBINSON 1803 - 1881

Polly and her husband George Kauffman lived on a 120 Acre farm in King & Queen County, Va. The 1950 Agriculture Schedule for King & Queen County indicates that the family would have been living well for families during this period. By 1851 their family had grown to five with the birth of their youngest son Richard in 1851.

1850 Agriculture Schedule		
County/State	KING + QUEEN, VA	
District	STRATTON MAJOR PARISH	
Page		
NARA M#		
Owner/Agent/Mgr		
Row #		

Description	Col	Value	
Name of Owner, Agent or Manager of the Farm	1	GEORGE KAUFFMAN	
Total Acres Improved	2	120	Acres
Total Acres Unimproved	3	60	Acres
Cash Value of Farm	4	$ 400	
Farm implements & machinery value	5	$ 35	
Horses (no. of)	6		
Asses and Mules	7		
Milch Cows	8	4	
Working Oxen	9	6	
Other Cattle	10	4	
Sheep	11	7	
Swine	12	20	
Value of Livestock	13	$ 208	
Wheat	14	12	Bu
Rye	15		Bu
Indian Corn	16	400	Bu
Oats	17		Bu
Rice	18		Lbs
Tobacco	19		Lbs
Ginned cotton (400# bales)	20		Bales
Wool	21	10	Lbs

Description	Col	Value	
Peas & Beans	22	1	Bu
Irish Potatoes	23	3	Bu
Sweet Potatoes	24	10	Bu
Barley	25		Bu
Buckwheat	26		Bu
Value of Orchard Products	27	$	
Wine	28		Gals
Market Gardens Produce Value	29	$	
Butter	30	25	Lbs
Cheese	31		Lbs
Hay	32		Tons
Clover seed	33		Bu
Other Grass seeds	34		Bu
Hops	35		Lbs
Dew rotted Hemp	36		Tons
Water rotted Hemp	37		Tons
Flax	38		Lbs
Flaxseed	39		Bu
Silk Cocoons	40		Lbs
Maple Sugar	41		Lbs
Cane Sugar (1000 # hhds)	42		Hhds
Molasses	43		Gals
Beeswax and Honey	44		Lbs
Value of Homemade Manufactures	45	$ 20	
Value of Animals slaughtered	46	$ 50	

All rights reserved ©2007 J. Mark Lowe

George Kauffman is the husband of Polly Robinson sister of Lorenzo D. Robinson.

207

George Kauffman died in July 1859. Polly continued to live on the farm with the help of her sons John, Richard and Jeremiah. The 1865 County Land records show that Polly Kauffman was paying taxes on 248 Acres of land.

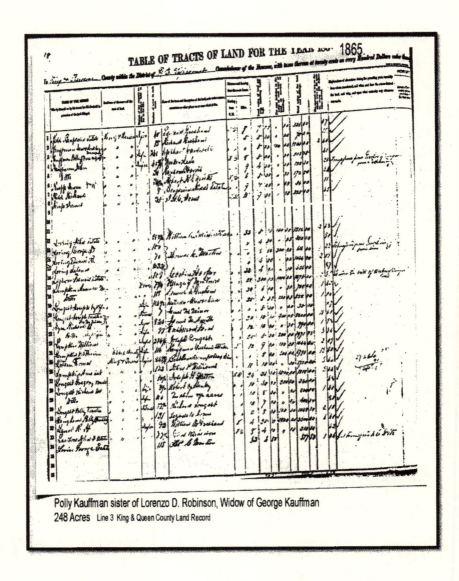

Polly Kauffman sister of Lorenzo D. Robinson, Widow of George Kauffman
248 Acres   Line 3 King & Queen County Land Record

Descendants of Polly Robinson

Generation 1

1. **Polly**[1] **Robinson** was born in 1803 in King & Queen County, Va.. She married **George Kaufman**. He was born about 1784 in King & Queen County, Va.. He died in Jul 1859 in King & Queen County, Va..

George Kaufman and Polly Robinson had the following children:

    2.   i.   John[2] Kaufman was born in 1823 in King & Queen County, Va.. He married Lucy Jones.

        ii.   James Kaufman was born in 1829 in King & Queen County, Va.. He died on 13 Aug 1862 in King & Queen County, Va..

        iii.   Mary Francis Kaufman was born in 1832.

    3.   iv.   Jeremia Kaufman was born in 1834 in King & Queen County, Va.. He died on 01 Sep 1870 in King & Queen County, Va.. He married Pinky Robinson, daughter of Lorenzo D. Robinson and Betsy on 06 Mar 1856 in King & Queen County, Va.. She was born in 1840 in King & Queen County, Va..

        v.   Henrietta Kaufman was born in 1836.

        vi.   Martha Ellen Kaufman was born in 1839.

        vii.   Catherine Kaufman was born in 1842.

    4.   viii.   Grace Kaufman was born in 1845 in King & Queen County, Va.. She died on 27 Nov 1876 in King & Queen County, Va.. She married Robert Logan Williams on 20 Jan 1869 in King & Queen County, Va.. He was born in 1847 in King & Queen County, Va..

5. ix. PHILLIS ANN KAUFMAN was born in 1849 in King & Queen County, Virginia. She married Wiley Lockley, son of John Gilmore and Fanny Lockley on 19 Dec 1872 in King & Queen County, Virginia. He was born in 1847 in King & Queen County, Virginia.

x. RICHARD KAUFMAN was born in 1851 in King & Queen County, Va.. He married Atlanta Dungy, daughter of Richard Dungy and Kiturah Key on 26 Jan 1876 in King & Queen County, Va.. She was born in 1855 in King & Queen County, Va..

Generation 2

2. **John² Kaufman** (Polly¹ Robinson) was born in 1823 in King & Queen County, Va.. He married **Lucy Jones**.

   John Kaufman and Lucy Jones had the following children:

   i. Mirian³ Kaufman was born in 1853 in King & Queen County, Virginia. She died on 30 Jan 1887 in King & Queen County, Va.. She married Benjamin Lockley, son of Betty Lockley on 25 Jan 1874 in Mount Olivet Baptist Church, K&Q County, Va.. He was born in 1852 in King & Queen County, Virginia.

   ii. Mary F. Kaufman was born in 1847 in King & Queen County, Va..

   iii. Sarah J. Kaufman was born in 1850 in King & Queen County, Va.. She died on 15 Jul 1886 in King & Queen County, Va..

   iv. Esperilla Kaufman was born in 1856 in King & Queen County, Va..

   v. Elizabeth J. Kaufman was born in 1959 in King & Queen County, Va.. She died on 18 Mar 1870 in King & Queen County, Va..

   vi. Pinkie E. Kaufman was born in 1862 in King & Queen County, Va..

3. **Jeremia² Kaufman** (Polly¹ Robinson) was born in 1834 in King & Queen County, Va.. He died on 01 Sep 1870 in King & Queen County, Va.. He married Pinky Robinson, daughter of Lorenzo D. Robinson and Betsy on 06 Mar 1856 in King & Queen County, Va.. She was born in 1840 in King & Queen County, Va..

   Jeremia Kaufman and Pinky Robinson had the following children:

   i. Robert³ Kaufman was born in 1860.

ii. JEREMIA KAUFMAN JR. was born in 1866.

iii. MATILDA ELLEN KAUFMAN was born in 1868.

iv. PINKY KAUFMAN was born in 1869. She married SIMPSON.

v. ELVIRA KAUFMAN was born in 1865 in King & Queen, Virginia. She died on 05 Aug 1870 in King & Queen, Virginia.

4. GRACE[2] KAUFMAN (Polly[1] Robinson) was born in 1845 in King & Queen County, Va.. She died on 27 Nov 1876 in King & Queen County, Va.. She married Robert Logan Williams on 20 Jan 1869 in King & Queen County, Va.. He was born in 1847 in King & Queen County, Va..

Robert Logan Williams and Grace Kaufman had the following children:

i. CATHERINE A.[3] WILLIAMS was born in 1870 in King & Queen County, Va..

ii. POLLY WILLIAMS was born in 1872 in King & Queen County, Va.. She married Armstead Miller, son of John Miller and Susan Bagby on 12 Apr 1896 in King & Queen County, Va.. He was born on 15 Nov 1873 in Middlesex County Va..

iii. JAMES A. WILLIAMS was born in 1873 in King & Queen County, Va..

5. **PHILLIS ANN**[2] **KAUFMAN** (Polly[1] Robinson) was born in 1849 in King & Queen County, Virginia. She married Wiley Lockley, son of John Gilmore and Fanny Lockley on 19 Dec 1872 in King & Queen County, Virginia. He was born in 1847 in King & Queen County, Virginia.

Wiley Lockley and Phillis Ann Kaufman had the following children:

6. i. JAMES BEVERLY[3] LOCKLEY was born on 12 May 1875 in King & Queen County, Virginia. He married Emma Key, daughter of James Key and Phoebe Julia Conway on 16 Oct 1902 in Middlesex County, Virginia. She was born in 1887 in Middlesex County, Virginia.

7. ii. COLUMBUS LOCKLEY was born on 07 Sep 1878 in King & Queen County, Virginia. He married Pinkey Jane Kauffman, daughter of Richard Kauffman and Lanty on 12 Jun 1907 in King & Queen County, Virginia. She was born in 1885 in King & Queen County, Virginia.

iii. KNOX LOCKLEY was born in 1883 in King & Queen County, Va..

iv. CHRISTOPHER C. LOCKLEY was born in 1877 in King & Queen County, Va.

Generation 3

6. **James Beverly[3] Lockley** (Phillis Ann[2] Kaufman, Polly[1] Robinson) was born on 12 May 1875 in King & Queen County, Virginia. He married Emma Key, daughter of James Key and Phoebe Julia Conway on 16 Oct 1902 in Middlesex County, Virginia. She was born in 1887 in Middlesex County, Virginia.

Notes for James Beverly Lockley:

Info for dob from K&Q birth records

James Beverly Lockley and Emma Key had the following children:

- i. Anna B.[4] Lockley was born in 1905 in King & Queen County, Va..
- ii. Martha Lockley was born in 1907 in King & Queen County, Va..
- iii. Landonia Lockley was born in 1908 in King & Queen County, Va..
- 8. iv. Catherine Lockley was born in 1911 in King & Queen County, Va.. She married Walter Palmes. He was born in 1890.
- v. Ethel Lockley was born in 1914 in King & Queen County, Va..
- vi. James B. Lockley Jr. was born in 1919 in King & Queen County, Va..
- vii. Eva Lockley was born in 1909 in King & Queen County, Va..
- viii. Ollin Lockley was born in 1925 in Atlantic City, New Jersey.
- ix. Emmalyn Lockley was born in 1928 in Atlantic City, New Jersey.

7. **Columbus³ Lockley** (Phillis Ann², Polly¹ Robinson) was born on 07 Sep 1878 in King & Queen County, Virginia. He married Pinkey Jane Kauffman, daughter of Richard Kauffman and Lanty on 12 Jun 1907 in King & Queen County, Virginia. She was born in 1885 in King & Queen County, Virginia.

Notes for Columbus Lockley:

Mulatto 1920 Census

Notes for Pinkey Jane Kauffman:

Mulatto - 1920 Census

Columbus Lockley and Pinkey Jane Kauffman had the following children:

    i.   Aburtia⁴ Lockley was born in 1909 in King & Queen County, Va..

Notes for Aburtia Lockley:

Mulatto - 1920 Census

    ii.   Celia Lockley was born in 1911 in King & Queen County, Va..

Notes for Celia Lockley:

Mulatto - 1920 Census

    iii.   Ellen Lockley was born in 1912 in King & Queen County, Va..

Notes for Ellen Lockley:

Mulatto - 1920 Census

iv. OLIMA LOCKLEY was born in 1917 in King & Queen County, Va..

Notes for Olima Lockley:

Mulatto - 1920 Census

v. THERSA LOCKLEY was born in 1918 in King & Queen County, Va..

Notes for Thersa Lockley:

Mulatto - 1920 Census

vi. PHILLIS LOCKLEY was born in 1919 in King & Queen County, Va..

Notes for Phillis Lockley:

Mulatto - 1920 Census

vii. WARNER LOCKLEY was born in 1923 in King & Queen County, Va.. He married Catherine Hunter, daughter of Philip Hunter and Mary Howard on 01 Jan 1946 in King & Queen County, Va.. She was born in 1923 in King & Queen County, Va..

viii. WALNUT LOCKLEY was born in 1920 in King & Queen County, Va..

Generation 4

8. **Catherine**[4] **Lockley** (James Beverly[3], Phillis Ann[2] Kaufman, Polly[1] Robinson) was born in 1911 in King & Queen County, Va.. She married **Walter Palmes**. He was born in 1890.

   Walter Palmes and Catherine Lockley had the following child:

   i. Walter[5] Palmes was born in 1928 in Atlantic City, New Jersey.

Descendants of Polly Robinson

Generation 1

1. **POLLY**[1] **ROBINSON** was born in 1803 in King & Queen County, Va.. She married **GEORGE KAUFFMAN**. He was born about 1784 in King & Queen County, Va.. He died in Jul 1859 in King & Queen County, Va..

George Kauffman and Polly Robinson had the following children:

    2.   i.   JOHN[2] KAUFFMAN (son of George Kauffman and Polly Robinson) was born in 1823 in King & Queen County, Va.. He married LUCY A. JONES. She was born in 1822 in King & Queen County, Va.. He married LUCY JONES.

    3.   ii.   JAMES KAUFFMAN (son of George Kauffman and Polly Robinson) was born in 1829 in King & Queen County, Va.. He died on 13 Aug 1862 in King & Queen County, Va.. He married MARY E. HUDGINS. She was born in 1835 in King & Queen, Virginia.

        iii.   MARY FRANCIS KAUFFMAN (daughter of George Kauffman and Polly Robinson) was born in 1832.

    4.   iv.   JEREMIA KAUFFMAN (son of George Kauffman and Polly Robinson) was born in 1834 in King & Queen County, Va.. He died on 01 Sep 1870 in King & Queen County, Va.. He married Pinky Robinson (daughter of Lorenzo D. Robinson and Betsy) on 06 Mar 1856 in King & Queen County, Va.. She was born in 1840 in King & Queen County, Va..

        v.   HENRIETTA KAUFFMAN (daughter of George Kauffman and Polly Robinson) was born in 1836.

        vi.   MARTHA ELLEN KAUFFMAN (daughter of George Kauffman and Polly Robinson) was born in 1839.

vii. CATHERINE KAUFFMAN (daughter of George Kauffman and Polly Robinson) was born in 1842.

5. viii. GRACE KAUFFMAN (daughter of George Kauffman and Polly Robinson) was born in 1845 in King & Queen County, Va.. She died on 27 Nov 1876 in King & Queen County, Va.. She married Robert Logan Williams on 20 Jan 1869 in King & Queen County, Va.. He was born in 1847 in King & Queen County, Va..

6. ix. PHILLIS ANN KAUFFMAN (daughter of George Kauffman and Polly Robinson) was born in 1849 in King & Queen County, Virginia. She married Wiley Lockley (son of John Gilmore and Fanny Lockley) on 19 Dec 1872 in King & Queen County, Virginia. He was born in 1847 in King & Queen County, Virginia.

x. RICHARD KAUFFMAN (son of George Kauffman and Polly Robinson) was born in 1851 in King & Queen County, Va.. He married Atlanta Dungy (daughter of Richard Dungy and Kiturah Key) on 26 Jan 1876 in King & Queen County, Va.. She was born in 1855 in King & Queen County, Va..

Generation 2

2. **John² Kauffman** (Polly¹ Robinson) was born in 1823 in King & Queen County, Va.. He married **Lucy A. Jones**. She was born in 1822 in King & Queen County, Va.. He married **Lucy Jones**.

John Kauffman and Lucy A. Jones had the following children:

7. i.   Mary F.³ Kauffman (daughter of John Kauffman and Lucy A. Jones) was born in 1848 in King & Queen County, Va.. She died on 21 Mar 1870 in King & Queen County, Va.. She married Jackson Davenport (son of Thomas Davenport and Nancy Jones) on 26 Mar 1868 in King & Queen County, Va.. He was born in 1846 in King & Queen County, Va..

    ii. Miriam A. Kauffman (daughter of John Kauffman and Lucy A. Jones) was born in 1853 in King & Queen County, Va.. She died on 30 Jan 1887 in King & Queen County, Va.. She married Benjamin Lockley. He was born in 1852 in King & Queen County, Virginia. He died on 30 Jan 1888 in King & Queen County, Va..

    iii. Esterrilla Kauffman (daughter of John Kauffman and Lucy A. Jones) was born in 1856 in King & Queen County, Va.. She married James Campbell.

    iv. Elizabeth J. Kauffman (daughter of John Kauffman and Lucy A. Jones) was born in 1859 in King & Queen County, Va.. She died on 18 Mar 1870 in King & Queen County, Va..

    v.   Pinky Kauffman (daughter of John Kauffman and Lucy A. Jones) was born in 1862 in King & Queen County, Va..

    vi. Sarah J. Kauffman (daughter of John Kauffman and Lucy Jones) was born in 1850 in King & Queen County, Va.. She died on 15 Jul 1886 in King & Queen County, Va..

John Kauffman and Lucy Jones had the following children:

- vii. MIRIAN KAUFFMAN (daughter of John Kauffman and Lucy Jones) was born in 1853 in King & Queen County, Virginia. She died on 30 Jan 1887 in King & Queen County, Va.. She married Benjamin Lockley on 25 Jan 1874 in Mount Olivet Baptist Church, K&Q County, Va.. He was born in 1852 in King & Queen County, Virginia. He died on 30 Jan 1888 in King & Queen County, Va..

- viii. MARY F. KAUFFMAN (daughter of John Kauffman and Lucy Jones) was born in 1847 in King & Queen County, Va..

- vi. SARAH J. KAUFFMAN (daughter of John Kauffman and Lucy Jones) was born in 1850 in King & Queen County, Va.. She died on 15 Jul 1886 in King & Queen County, Va..

- x. ESPERILLA KAUFFMAN (daughter of John Kauffman and Lucy Jones) was born in 1856 in King & Queen County, Va..

- xi. ELIZABETH J. KAUFFMAN (daughter of John Kauffman and Lucy Jones) was born in 1959 in King & Queen County, Va.. She died on 18 Mar 1870 in King & Queen County, Va..

- xii. PINKIE E. KAUFFMAN (daughter of John Kauffman and Lucy Jones) was born in 1862 in King & Queen County, Va..

3. JAMES[2] KAUFFMAN (Polly[1] Robinson) was born in 1829 in King & Queen County, Va.. He died on 13 Aug 1862 in King & Queen County, Va.. He married **MARY E. HUDGINS**. She was born in 1835 in King & Queen, Virginia.

Notes for Mary E. Hudgins:

After the death of James Kauffman, Mary Married Dabney Robinson

James Kauffman and Mary E. Hudgins had the following children:

  i. WILLIAM T.³ KAUFFMAN (son of James Kauffman and Mary E. Hudgins) was born in 1853 in King & Queen, Virginia.

  ii. JOHN E. KAUFFMAN (son of James Kauffman and Mary E. Hudgins) was born in 1855 in King & Queen, Virginia.

  iii. JAMES H. KAUFFMAN (son of James Kauffman and Mary E. Hudgins) was born in 1859 in King & Queen, Virginia.

  iv. ELIAS KAUFFMAN (son of James Kauffman and Mary E. Hudgins) was born in 1862 in King & Queen County, Va..

4. JEREMIA² KAUFFMAN (Polly¹ Robinson) was born in 1834 in King & Queen County, Va.. He died on 01 Sep 1870 in King & Queen County, Va.. He married Pinky Robinson (daughter of Lorenzo D. Robinson and Betsy) on 06 Mar 1856 in King & Queen County, Va.. She was born in 1840 in King & Queen County, Va..

Jeremia Kauffman and Pinky Robinson had the following children:

  i. ROBERT³ KAUFFMAN (son of Jeremia Kauffman and Pinky Robinson) was born in 1860.

  ii. JEREMIA KAUFFMAN JR. (son of Jeremia Kauffman and Pinky Robinson) was born in 1866.

  iii. MATILDA ELLEN KAUFFMAN (daughter of Jeremia Kauffman and Pinky Robinson) was born in 1868.

  iv. PINKY KAUFFMAN (daughter of Jeremia Kauffman and Pinky Robinson) was born in 1869. She married SIMPSON.

v. ELVIRA KAUFFMAN (daughter of Jeremia Kauffman and Pinky Robinson) was born in 1865 in King & Queen, Virginia. She died on 05 Aug 1870 in King & Queen, Virginia.

5. **GRACE[2] KAUFFMAN** (Polly[1] Robinson) was born in 1845 in King & Queen County, Va.. She died on 27 Nov 1876 in King & Queen County, Va.. She married Robert Logan Williams on 20 Jan 1869 in King & Queen County, Va.. He was born in 1847 in King & Queen County, Va..

Robert Logan Williams and Grace Kauffman had the following children:

    i. CATHERINE A.[3] WILLIAMS (daughter of Robert Logan Williams and Grace Kauffman) was born in 1870 in King & Queen County, Va..

    ii. POLLY WILLIAMS (daughter of Robert Logan Williams and Grace Kauffman) was born in 1872 in King & Queen County, Va.. She married Armstead Miller (son of John Miller and Susan Bagby) on 12 Apr 1896 in King & Queen County, Va.. He was born on 15 Nov 1873 in Middlesex County Va..

    iii. JAMES A. WILLIAMS (son of Robert Logan Williams and Grace Kauffman) was born in 1873 in King & Queen County, Va..

6. **Phillis Ann² Kauffman** (Polly¹ Robinson) was born in 1849 in King & Queen County, Virginia. She married Wiley Lockley (son of John Gilmore and Fanny Lockley) on 19 Dec 1872 in King & Queen County, Virginia. He was born in 1847 in King & Queen County, Virginia.

Wiley Lockley and Phillis Ann Kauffman had the following children:

8.   i.   James Beverly³ Lockley (son of Wiley Lockley and biological son of Phillis Ann Kauffman) was born on 12 May 1875 in King & Queen County, Virginia. He married Emma Key (daughter of James Key and Phoebe Julia Conway) on 16 Oct 1902 in Middlesex County, Virginia. She was born in 1887 in Middlesex County, Virginia.

9.   ii.   Columbus Lockley (son of Wiley Lockley and biological son of Phillis Ann Kauffman) was born on 07 Sep 1878 in King & Queen County, Virginia. He married Pinkey Jane Kauffman (daughter of Richard Kauffman and Lanty) on 12 Jun 1907 in King & Queen County, Virginia. She was born in 1885 in King & Queen County, Virginia.

    iii.   Knox Lockley (son of Wiley Lockley and Phillis Ann Kauffman) was born in 1883 in King & Queen County, Va..

    iv.   Christopher C. Lockley (son of Wiley Lockley and Phillis Ann Kauffman) was born in 1877 in King & Queen County, Va..

Generation 3

7. **MARY F.³ KAUFFMAN** (John², Polly¹ Robinson) was born in 1848 in King & Queen County, Va.. She died on 21 Mar 1870 in King & Queen County, Va.. She married Jackson Davenport (son of Thomas Davenport and Nancy Jones) on 26 Mar 1868 in King & Queen County, Va.. He was born in 1846 in King & Queen County, Va..

Jackson Davenport and Mary F. Kauffman had the following child:

    10.   i.   JOHN THOMAS⁴ DAVENPORT (son of Jackson Davenport and Mary F. Kauffman) was born in 1870 in King & Queen County, Va.. He died on 07 Nov 1933 in Little Plymouth, Va.. He married (1) ROSIE JANE JORDAN (daughter of John Robert Jordan and Polly Ann Bluefoot) on 15 Nov 1900 in King & Queen County, Va.. She was born on 10 Jan 1878 in King & Queen County, Va.. She died on 19 Jun 1936 in Little Plymouth, Va.. He married (2) LIZZIE CAMPBELL (daughter of James Campbell and Kauffman) in 1896 in King & Queen, Virginia. She was born in 1875 in King & Queen County, Va..

8. **JAMES BEVERLY³ LOCKLEY** (Phillis Ann² Kauffman, Polly¹ Robinson) was born on 12 May 1875 in King & Queen County, Virginia. He married Emma Key (daughter of James Key and Phoebe Julia Conway) on 16 Oct 1902 in Middlesex County, Virginia. She was born in 1887 in Middlesex County, Virginia.

Notes for James Beverly Lockley:

Info for dob from K&Q birth records

James Beverly Lockley and Emma Key had the following children:

	i.	ANNA B.^{4} LOCKLEY (daughter of James Beverly Lockley and Emma Key) was born in 1905 in King & Queen County, Va..
	ii.	MARTHA LOCKLEY (daughter of James Beverly Lockley and Emma Key) was born in 1907 in King & Queen County, Va..
	iii.	LANDONIA LOCKLEY (daughter of James Beverly Lockley and Emma Key) was born in 1908 in King & Queen County, Va..
11.	iv.	CATHERINE LOCKLEY (daughter of James Beverly Lockley and Emma Key) was born in 1911 in King & Queen County, Va.. She married WALTER PALMES. He was born in 1890.
	v.	ETHEL LOCKLEY (daughter of James Beverly Lockley and Emma Key) was born in 1914 in King & Queen County, Va..
	vi.	JAMES B. LOCKLEY JR. (son of James Beverly Lockley and Emma Key) was born in 1919 in King & Queen County, Va..
	vii.	EVA LOCKLEY (daughter of James Beverly Lockley and Emma Key) was born in 1909 in King & Queen County, Va..
	viii.	OLLIN LOCKLEY (daughter of James Beverly Lockley and Emma Key) was born in 1925 in Atlantic City, New Jersey.
	ix.	EMMALYN LOCKLEY (daughter of James Beverly Lockley and Emma Key) was born in 1928 in Atlantic City, New Jersey.

9. **COLUMBUS^3 LOCKLEY** (Phillis Ann^2 Kauffman, Polly^1 Robinson) was born on 07 Sep 1878 in King & Queen County, Virginia. He married Pinkey Jane Kauffman (daughter of Richard Kauffman and Lanty) on 12 Jun 1907 in King & Queen County, Virginia. She was born in 1885 in King & Queen County, Virginia.

Notes for Columbus Lockley:

Mulatto 1920 Census

Notes for Pinkey Jane Kauffman:

Mulatto - 1920 Census

 Columbus Lockley and Pinkey Jane Kauffman had the following children:

    i. ABURTIA[4] LOCKLEY (daughter of Columbus Lockley and Pinkey Jane Kauffman) was born in 1909 in King & Queen County, Va..

Notes for Aburtia Lockley:

Mulatto - 1920 Census

    ii. CELIA LOCKLEY (daughter of Columbus Lockley and Pinkey Jane Kauffman) was born in 1911 in King & Queen County, Va..

Notes for Celia Lockley:

Mulatto - 1920 Census

    iii. ELLEN LOCKLEY (daughter of Columbus Lockley and Pinkey Jane Kauffman) was born in 1912 in King & Queen County, Va..

Notes for Ellen Lockley:

Mulatto - 1920 Census

    iv. OLIMA LOCKLEY (daughter of Columbus Lockley and Pinkey Jane Kauffman) was born in 1917 in King & Queen County, Va..

Notes for Olima Lockley:

Mulatto - 1920 Census

    v.   THERSA LOCKLEY (daughter of Columbus Lockley and Pinkey Jane Kauffman) was born in 1918 in King & Queen County, Va..

Notes for Thersa Lockley:

Mulatto - 1920 Census

    vi.   PHILLIS LOCKLEY (daughter of Columbus Lockley and Pinkey Jane Kauffman) was born in 1919 in King & Queen County, Va..

Notes for Phillis Lockley:

Mulatto - 1920 Census

    vii.   WARNER LOCKLEY (son of Columbus Lockley and Pinkey Jane Kauffman) was born in 1923 in King & Queen County, Va.. He married Catherine Hunter (daughter of Philip Hunter and Mary Howard) on 01 Jan 1946 in King & Queen County, Va.. She was born in 1923 in King & Queen County, Va..

    viii.   WALNUT LOCKLEY (son of Columbus Lockley and Pinkey Jane Kauffman) was born in 1920 in King & Queen County, Va..

Generation 4

10. **John Thomas**[4] **Davenport** (Mary F.[3] Kauffman, John[2] Kauffman, Polly[1] Robinson) was born in 1870 in King & Queen County, Va.. He died on 07 Nov 1933 in Little Plymouth, Va.. He married (1) **Rosie Jane Jordan** (daughter of John Robert Jordan and Polly Ann Bluefoot) on 15 Nov 1900 in King & Queen County, Va.. She was born on 10 Jan 1878 in King & Queen County, Va.. She died on 19 Jun 1936 in Little Plymouth, Va.. He married (2) **Lizzie Campbell** (daughter of James Campbell and Kauffman) in 1896 in King & Queen, Virginia. She was born in 1875 in King & Queen County, Va..

Notes for Rosie Jane Jordan:

Four of her children died as infants: Helen M, Hattie B., Hyburnies N., and John J.,

John Thomas Davenport and Rosie Jane Jordan had the following children:

    i.   Luvenia Ann[5] Davenport (daughter of John Thomas Davenport and Rosie Jane Jordan) was born on 16 Jun 1902 in King & Queen County, Va.. She died on 01 Jan 1984 in Baltimore, Md.. She married Frank Wilson. He died on 19 Aug 1975 in Baltimore, Md..

    ii.   Ella Bertha Davenport (daughter of John Thomas Davenport and Rosie Jane Jordan) was born on 21 Jun 1903 in King & Queen County, Va.. She married Oliver Campbell (son of Joseph Campbell and Susan) on 28 Dec 1924 in King & Queen County, Va.. He was born in 1903 in Middlesex County, Va.. He died in Feb 1983.

12. iii. PEARL JANE DAVENPORT (daughter of John Thomas Davenport and Rosie Jane Jordan) was born on 26 Jan 1908 in King & Queen County, Va.. She died on 20 Jul 1984. She married Perry W. Reed (son of Abe Reed and Lili) on 31 Jul 1930 in King & Queen County, Va.. He was born in Oct 1895 in Middlesex County, Va.. He died in Mar 1940.

iv. ROBERT L.T. DAVENPORT (son of John Thomas Davenport and Rosie Jane Jordan) was born on 31 Mar 1910 in King & Queen County, Va.. He died on 02 Mar 1989.

v. ETHA IRENE DAVENPORT (daughter of John Thomas Davenport and Rosie Jane Jordan) was born on 07 Jan 1912 in King & Queen County, Va.. She died in Sep 2001. She married Walter Richardson (son of Richard Richardson and Grace) on 07 Jan 1933 in King & Queen County, Va.. He was born in 1903 in Gloucester County, Va..

13. vi. MARY FRANCES DAVENPORT (daughter of John Thomas Davenport and Rosie Jane Jordan) was born on 18 Aug 1916 in King & Queen County, Va.. She married ROGER WORMLEY. He was born on 05 Dec 1910.

14. vii. ELIJAH DAVENPORT (son of John Thomas Davenport and Rosie Jane Jordan) was born on 25 Jun 1917 in King & Queen County, Va.. He married DOSHIE STEWART. She was born on 08 Aug 1919. She died on 16 Aug 1995.

15. viii. LILLIAN E. DAVENPORT (daughter of John Thomas Davenport and Rosie Jane Jordan) was born on 20 May 1919 in King & Queen County, Va.. She married BENJAMIN GUEST. He was born on 27 Nov 1916. He died on 02 Mar 1991 in Baltimore, Md..

16. ix. MISSOURI OLIVIA DAVENPORT (daughter of John Thomas Davenport and Rosie Jane Jordan) was born on 08 Aug 1921 in King & Queen County, Va.. She married BOYCE BARTON SR.. He was born on 15 Dec 1899. He died on 01 May 1994.

17. x. GEORGE MOSES DAVENPORT (son of John Thomas Davenport and biological son of Rosie Jane Jordan) was born on 10 Sep 1913 in King & Queen County, Va.. He died on 18 Jan 1990 in Rockville, Maryland. He married (1) VIRGINIA FITCHETT (daughter of Oscar Leroy Fitchett and Susie West) on 12 Jun 1935 in Middlesex County, Va.. She was born on 07 Sep 1919 in Middlesex County, Va.. She died on 30 Oct 2004 in Middlesex County, Va.. He married LUDIE HILDA WILLIAMS. She was born on 31 Dec 1921. She died on 28 Jan 1969.

xi. HELEN M. DAVENPORT (daughter of John Thomas Davenport and Rosie Jane Jordan) was born in Apr 1901. She died in In Infancy.

xii. HATTIE B. DAVENPORT (daughter of John Thomas Davenport and Rosie Jane Jordan) was born on 21 Aug 1904.

xiii. HYBURNIES N. DAVENPORT (daughter of John Thomas Davenport and Rosie Jane Jordan) was born on 05 Nov 1906.

11. CATHERINE[4] LOCKLEY (James Beverly[3], Phillis Ann[2] Kauffman, Polly[1] Robinson) was born in 1911 in King & Queen County, Va.. She married **WALTER PALMES**. He was born in 1890.

Walter Palmes and Catherine Lockley had the following child:

i. WALTER[5] PALMES (son of Walter Palmes and Catherine Lockley) was born in 1928 in Atlantic City, New Jersey.

Generation 5

12. **Pearl Jane[5] Davenport** (John Thomas[4], Mary F.[3] Kauffman, John[2] Kauffman, Polly[1] Robinson) was born on 26 Jan 1908 in King & Queen County, Va.. She died on 20 Jul 1984. She married Perry W. Reed (son of Abe Reed and Lili) on 31 Jul 1930 in King & Queen County, Va.. He was born in Oct 1895 in Middlesex County, Va.. He died in Mar 1940.

Perry W. Reed and Pearl Jane Davenport had the following children:

   i. Rosetta[6] Reed (daughter of Perry W. Reed and Pearl Jane Davenport) was born on 30 Mar 1931.

   ii. Walter Perry Reed (son of Perry W. Reed and Pearl Jane Davenport) was born on 02 Mar 1939.

   iii. Mary Reed (daughter of Perry W. Reed and Pearl Jane Davenport) was born on 29 Nov 1936.

13. **Mary Frances[5] Davenport** (John Thomas[4], Mary F.[3] Kauffman, John[2] Kauffman, Polly[1] Robinson) was born on 18 Aug 1916 in King & Queen County, Va.. She married **Roger Wormley**. He was born on 05 Dec 1910.

Roger Wormley and Mary Frances Davenport had the following children:

   i. Allen[6] Wormley (son of Roger Wormley and Mary Frances Davenport) was born on 28 Jul 1939.

   ii. Joan Wormley (daughter of Roger Wormley and Mary Frances Davenport) was born on 27 Feb 1941.

14. **Elijah[5] Davenport** (John Thomas[4], Mary F.[3] Kauffman, John[2] Kauffman, Polly[1] Robinson) was born on 25 Jun 1917 in King & Queen County, Va.. He married **Doshie Stewart**. She was born on 08 Aug 1919. She died on 16 Aug 1995.

Elijah Davenport and Doshie Stewart had the following child:

    i.   SHIRLEY[6] DAVENPORT (daughter of Elijah Davenport and Doshie Stewart) was born on 06 Dec 1940.

15. LILLIAN E.[5] DAVENPORT (John Thomas[4], Mary F.[3] Kauffman, John[2] Kauffman, Polly[1] Robinson) was born on 20 May 1919 in King & Queen County, Va.. She married **BENJAMIN GUEST**. He was born on 27 Nov 1916. He died on 02 Mar 1991 in Baltimore, Md..

Benjamin Guest and Lillian E. Davenport had the following children:

    i.   GEORGE[6] GUEST (son of Benjamin Guest and Lillian E. Davenport) was born on 19 Sep 1941. He died on 17 Apr 1996.

    ii.   JEROME GUEST (son of Benjamin Guest and Lillian E. Davenport) was born on 11 Sep 1942.

    iii.   CECIL GUEST (son of Benjamin Guest and Lillian E. Davenport) was born on 27 Sep 1946. He died in Jul 1981.

    iv.   DEBORAH GUEST (daughter of Benjamin Guest and Lillian E. Davenport) was born on 28 May 1948.

    v.   DIANE G'JEST (daughter of Benjamin Guest and Lillian E. Davenport) was born on 03 May 1950.

16. MISSOURI OLIVIA[5] DAVENPORT (John Thomas[4], Mary F.[3] Kauffman, John[2] Kauffman, Polly[1] Robinson) was born on 08 Aug 1921 in King & Queen County, Va.. She married **BOYCE BARTON SR.**. He was born on 15 Dec 1899. He died on 01 May 1994.

Boyce Barton Sr. and Missouri Olivia Davenport had the following child:

    i.   JAMES[6] DAVENPORT (son of Boyce Barton Sr. and Missouri Olivia Davenport) was born on 05 Mar 1943.

17. **George Moses[5] Davenport** (John Thomas[4], Mary F.[3] Kauffman, John[2] Kauffman, Polly[1] Robinson) was born on 10 Sep 1913 in King & Queen County, Va.. He died on 18 Jan 1990 in Rockville, Maryland. He married (1) **Virginia Fitchett** (daughter of Oscar Leroy Fitchett and Susie West) on 12 Jun 1935 in Middlesex County, Va.. She was born on 07 Sep 1919 in Middlesex County, Va.. She died on 30 Oct 2004 in Middlesex County, Va.. He married **Ludie Hilda Williams**. She was born on 31 Dec 1921. She died on 28 Jan 1969.

George Moses Davenport and Virginia Fitchett had the following child:

18. i. John[6] Davenport (son of George Moses Davenport and Virginia Fitchett) was born on 02 May 1937 in Pennsylvania. He married Priscilla Price (daughter of John Price and Bertha A. Mars) on 08 Dec 1956 in New York City, N.Y.. She was born on 10 Jun 1941 in New York, New York.

George Moses Davenport and Ludie Hilda Williams had the following children:

ii. Cheryl Davenport (daughter of George Moses Davenport and Ludie Hilda Williams) was born on 10 Dec 1953.

iii. Cynthia Davenport (daughter of George Moses Davenport and Ludie Hilda Williams) was born on 25 Jul 1957.

iv. Philbert Davenport (son of George Moses Davenport and Ludie Hilda Williams) was born on 26 Aug 1952.

Generation 6

18. **John[6] Davenport** (George Moses[5], John Thomas[4], Mary F.[3] Kauffman, John[2] Kauffman, Polly[1] Robinson) was born on 02 May 1937 in Pennsylvania. He married Priscilla Price (daughter of John Price and Bertha A. Mars) on 08 Dec 1956 in New York City, N.Y.. She was born on 10 Jun 1941 in New York, New York.

John Davenport and Priscilla Price had the following children:

19.   i.   John Patrick[7] Davenport (son of John Davenport and Priscilla Price) was born on 10 Dec 1956 in New York, New York. He married Arletha Bias.

20.   ii.   Wayne Davenport (son of John Davenport and Priscilla Price) was born on 16 Sep 1958 in New York, New York. He died on 03 Jan 2012 in Virginia. He married Wanda Petty. She was born on 01 Jan 1955.

Generation 7

19. **John Patrick[7] Davenport** (John[6], George Moses[5], John Thomas[4], Mary F.[3] Kauffman, John[2] Kauffman, Polly[1] Robinson) was born on 10 Dec 1956 in New York, New York. He married **Arletha Bias**.

John Patrick Davenport and Arletha Bias had the following child:

- i. Laura[8] Davenport (daughter of John Patrick Davenport and Arletha Bias) was born in 1986 in New York, NY..

20. **Wayne[7] Davenport** (John[6], George Moses[5], John Thomas[4], Mary F.[3] Kauffman, John[2] Kauffman, Polly[1] Robinson) was born on 16 Sep 1958 in New York, New York. He died on 03 Jan 2012 in Virginia. He married **Wanda Petty**. She was born on 01 Jan 1955.

Wayne Davenport and Wanda Petty had the following children:

- i. Caleb[8] Davenport (son of Wayne Davenport and Wanda Petty) was born in 1984.
- ii. Joshua Davenport (son of Wayne Davenport and Wanda Petty) was born in 1986.
- iii. Daniel Davenport (son of Wayne Davenport and Wanda Petty) was born in 1988.
- iv. Micah Davenport (daughter of Wayne Davenport and Wanda Petty) was born in 1990.

CHAPTER 5

LORENZO DOW ROBINSON 1810 – 1884

He first appeared in an 1833 document listing all Free Negroes and Mulattoes in King & Queen County, Va. He was born about 1810 and by the time the 1840 Federal Census was taken, he was listed as a Free Person of Color, Head of a household, that included 3 Free Males and 2 Free Female. At the time of the 1850 Federal Census he was a 40 year old widower Head of a Household of 2 Males and 4 females. By 1870 he has re-married and heading a new family including 3 female children.

1840 United States Federal Census	
Name:	Lorenzo Robinson
Home in 1840 (City, County, State):	King and Queen, Virginia
Free Colored Persons - Males - Under 10:	2
Free Colored Persons - Males - 24 thru 35:	1
Free Colored Persons - Females - Under 10:	1
Free Colored Persons - Females - 24 thru 35:	1
Persons Employed in Agriculture:	2
Total Free Colored Persons:	5
Total All Persons - Free White, Free Colored, Slaves:	5

During the twenty years, between 1850 and 1870 Lorenzo D. Robinson became a leader in St. Stephen Parrish, King and Queen, Va. Operating a 279 Acre farm on which he produced (1860 Agriculture Census) 450 bushels of corn, 90 bushels of wheat, 15 pounds of wool, 10 swt of potatoes and 20 pounds of butter. His live stock consisted of 2 horse, 3 cows, 2 oxen, 3 other cattle, 5 sheep and 11 swine. The Agriculture Census for 1860 and 1870 shows that he was still a prosperous farmer. While conducting my research at the King & Queen County Court, I was informed by one of the clerks about a book written by Mrs. Louise Eubanks Gray, who lived in Saluda, Va. Mrs. Gray had written a book on the History of Lower King and Queen Baptist Church, King & Queen County, Va. In this history I would find some information that relates to my research. Some weeks later I arranged to meet with Mrs. Gray to purchase a copy of her book. At our meeting she stated that she wished she had met me during her research. This would have allowed her to add much to the information she had about my Great Grandfather Lorenzo D. Robinson. He was listed Under Church Officers as Lorenzo Robinson (Free) Deacon in 1856. History of Lower King and Queen, Baptist Church, 1772-1980

From a picture taken early in the twentieth century and from the recollections of persons living at the time a fair idea of it appearance can be gained. A rectangular building, it had a sharply peaked roof with two windows set close to the roof. Inside the front door the pulpit platform was low with doors on either side. The upper galleries were for the colored members. No provision for heat was made in the original building.

Lower King and Queen Baptist Church circa 1915

Sample of a membership roster (1843). White male and female members are listed separately, followed by the name of colored members (slaves) listed under the owner's name in each case and the name of free colored members conclude the list.

Total for the year 1843 WERE:

White male member	42
White female members	76
Colored members, male and female	115
Free colored members	31
Total	264

In January 1856 the church voted unanimously to call Elder Isaac Diggs as pastor. At this time the membership of Lower King and Queen Baptist Church (Wares) was approximately two hundred, more than half of which were colored. In 1856 Thomas Dungy, Lorenzo D Robinson, two free colored members, and Sarah Kerr's Ellick were chosen and ordained as deacons. Their responsibilities were to minister especially to the colored members who came under church discipline. Following the Emancipation Proclamation, effective January 1, 1863, many of the former slaves, exercising their new-found freedom, had run off. Church meeting became very irregular. There were only two meetings recorded in 1861, 1862, 1863 and one in 1864, but by June 1865 the regular monthly church meeting resumed.

It was at this meeting that this entry appeared: Resolved that every colored member of the church be excommunicated that have left their Homes and

CHURCH OFFICERS
DEACONS

WHITE	COLORED
PRIOR TO 1844	1844
Benjamin Faulkner	
Thomas Spencer	Robert Spencer's Jesse
Thomas Jeffries	Minter Spencer's George
John Y. Burton	Richard Walden's Henry
Carter Trice	Samuel Tauntleroy's Moses
William Burch	
Richard Walden, Sr.	1856
	Sarah Kerr's Ellick
1844	Thomas Dungy (Free)
Robert Garrett	Lorenzo Robinson (Free)
William Hillyard	
Richard Walden, Jr.	
1847	
John W. Cullis	
Edward Walden	WHITE DEACONS
1859	1905
William J. Eubank	Andrew Revere
Garrett Carlton	E. R. Smith
	Howard Eubank
1869	
James C. Trice	1912
Robert P. Eubank	John A. Eubank
1870	Ryland Garrett
George C. Nunn	1922
1893	R. K. Walden
Logan Oliver	Bland Garrett
John C. Gibson	Joe Carlton
G. G. Glenn	J. M. Ashley
	R. M. Eubank

gone off as they are no longer under our control. The withdrawal of the majority of the colored members in 1868 to establish their own church was vividly displayed in the membership roll for that year which showed name after name with a line drawn through it and the notation "dismissed" written by it. Some of the members continued to keep their name on the roll but did not attend; as a result the church passed a resolution in 1870 that "all colored members whose names are on our Church Book shall be notified that unless they attend church or apply for letters of demission they will be excommunicated" This action reflected no racial discrimination as might be construed today, in as much as white members also were regularly excommunicated for negligence in church attendance.

After the war, in 1869 Nelson West and his wife Catherine deeded a piece of land which he had bought in 1860 to Issey Hoskins, Otteway Harris, Ransome Harris, Thomas Dungy, John Kauffman and Carter Braxton, trustees of "Mount Olley Church, one certain parcel of land on which the church now stands containing two acre." Some of these trustees were in all probability free Negros, but the majority of the membership was made up of former slaves dismissed by letter for the purpose of organizing their own church. Today the church is known as 2nd Mt. Olive Baptist Church. From the time he was ordained as a deacon in 1856 Lorenzo D Robinson used his authority to perform marriages in the 1860's, 70's & 80'. (Appendix 1)

On June 18, 1864, 75 to 100 soldiers under the command of General Philip Sheridan who were stationed near The King & Queen Court House raided the farm of Lorenzo D. Robinson. Under normal circumstances each Military unit would have an Officer who was responsible for purchasing the supplies necessary for his unit. Lorenzo stated that no officer was present, so these soldiers took whatever they wanted. They even stayed long enough to require that his wife bake some bread for them. After the Civil War ended, Congress passed an act on March 8, 1871, establishing a Commission of Claims which gave anyone who was loyal to the union, the right to file a claim for any property taken during the war. On October 7, 1872 Lorenzo appeared before the Commissioners of Claims in King & Queen County, Va. along with witnesses Martha Robinson (wife), Matilda Robinson (daughter), and Dunbar Robinson (Nephew) to file his claim. The witnesses were each questioned about the June 1864 incident. In his opening statement Lorenzo D. Robinson stated that he lived on a 270 Acre farm about 2 1/2 miles from the King and Queen Court House.

The Claim is for: disallowed	Amount of Claim	Amount Allowed	Amount
1. Two Horses	$ 300.00	$ 200.00	$ 100.00
2. One new saddle	10.00	$ 10.00	
3. 100 Bushels of Indian Corn	100.00	$ 25.00	75.00
4. 300 lbs of bacon	45.00	$ 45.00	
5. One Barrel salt Fish	10.00	$ 10.00	
6. 25 Sacks (bags)	10.00	$ 10.00	
7. ½ Barrel Flour	7.50	$ 5.00	2.50
Totals:	$ 482.50	$ 305.00	$ 177.50

In June 1864 troops under his command stationed near the King & Queen County Court raided the farms of Lorenzo D. Robinson & his son Archie Robinson. Under the Act of Congress March 8, 1871 both filed claims with the commissioners of Claims to recover payment for items taken during the raid. Lorenzo's claim was dated June 26, 1872 & Archie's November 18, 1872. Copies in Appendix #2

General Philip Sheridan
1831 - 1888

Named Robertson in 1850 by 1860 Robinson

1850 Agriculture Schedule - Lorenzo D. Robinson

1860 Agriculture Schedule - Lorenzo D. Robinson

1870 Agriculture Schedule

County/State: King & Queen County, VA
District: Stevensville
Page:
NARA M#:
Owner/Agent/Mgr: Lorenzo Robinson
Row #:

Description	Col	Value
Improved Land	2	50 Acres
Woodland	3	20 Acres
Other unimproved land	4	10 Acres
Present value	5	$ 480
Farm implements/machinery value	6	$ 15
Amt wages pd incl board	7	$ 10
Horses	8	1
Mules and Asses	9	
Milk cows	10	3
Working oxen	11	2
Other cattle	12	3
Sheep	13	1
Swine	14	7
Value all livestock	15	$ 175
Spring wheat	16	Bu
Winter wheat	17	50 Bu
Rye	18	Bu
Indian corn	19	250 Bu
Oats	20	Bu
Barley	21	Bu
Buckwheat	22	Bu
Rice	23	Lbs
Tobacco	24	Lbs
Cotton (450# bales)	25	Bales
Wool	26	Lbs
Peas and beans	27	Bu
Irish potatoes	28	Bu
Sweet potatoes	29	Bu
Orchard products value	30	$
Wine	31	Gals
Market Garden Produce	32	$
Butter	33	Lbs
Cheese	34	Lbs
Milk sold	35	Gals
Hay	36	Tons
Clover seed	37	Bu
Grass seed	38	Bu
Hops	39	Lbs
Hemp	40	Tons
Flax	41	Lbs
Flax seed	42	Bu
Silk cocoons	43	Lbs
Maple sugar	44	Lbs
Cane sugar (1000 Lb Hhds)	45	Hhds
Molasses	46	Gals
Bees wax	47	Lbs
Honey	48	Lbs
Forest products	49	$
Home manufactures	50	$
Animals slaughtered/sold	51	$
Value all farm production	52	$

1870 Agriculture Schedule - Lorenzo D. Robinson

1880 Agriculture Schedule

County/State: King & Queen County, VA
District: 39
Page:
NARA M#: NARA M9
Owner/Agent/Mgr: Lorenzo Robinson

Description	Col	Value
Owner	2	Acres
Rents for Fixed Money	3	Acres
Rents for Share of Product	4	Acres
Tilled, incl fallow & grass in rotation	5	100 Acres
Perm. Pastures, orchards, vineyards	6	Acres
Woodland & forest	7	170 Acres
Other unimproved	8	Acres
Value, Farm, land, fences & buildings	9	$ 700
Farm Implements & machinery	10	$
Livestock value	11	$ 110
Bldg & repairs in 1879	12	$
Fertilizer in 1879	13	$
Wages for farm labor incl board	14	$
Weeks hired labor (White) & housework	15	
Weeks hired labor (Colored) & housework	16	150
Value, farm product sold, used & onhand	17	
Grass lands, mown	18	Acres
Grass lands, not mown	19	Acres
Hay harvest in 1879	20	Tons
Clover seed	21	Bu
Grass seed	22	Bu 1
Horses	23	
Mules & Asses	24	3
Oxen	25	1
Milk Cows	26	2
Other Cows	27	1
Calves dropped	28	1
Cattle purchased	29	
Cattle sold living	30	
Cattle slaughtered	31	1
Cattle died, strayed	32	
Milk sold or sent for Cheese	33	50 Lbs
Butter produced on farm	34	Lbs
Cheese produced on farm	35	Gals 6
Sheep on hand June 1, 1880	36	6
Lambs dropped	37	
Lambs purchased	38	
Lambs sold live	39	
Sheep/lambs slaughtered	40	
Sheep/lambs killed by dogs	41	2
Sheep/lambs died of diseases	42	
Sheep/lambs of weather stress	43	6
No. of Fleeces	44	10
Weight of Fleece	45	7 Lbs
Swine on hand June 1, 1880	46	10
Barnyard Poultry June 1 1880	47	
Other Poultry on hand	48	30
Eggs	49	Doz
Rice 1879 - Area	50	Acres
Rice - Crop	51	Bu
Barley - Area	52	Acres
Barley - Crop	53	Bu
Buckwheat - Area	54	Acres
Buckwheat - Crop	55	Bu
Indian Corn - Area	56	Acres 15
Indian Corn - Crop	57	Bu 200
Oats - Area	58	Acres
Oats - Crop	59	Bu
Rye - Area	60	Bu 1
Rye - Crop	61	Bu
Wheat - Area	62	Acres 2
Wheat - Crop	63	Bu 10
Cotton - Area	64	Acres
Cotton - Bales	65	
Flax - Area	66	Acres
Flaxseed	67	Bu
Flax Straw	68	Tons
Flax Fiber	69	Lbs
Hemp - Area	70	Acres
Hemp - Crop	71	Tons
Cane Sugar - Area	72	Acres
Cane Sugar	73	Hhds
Cane Molasses	74	Gals
Sorghum - Area	75	Acres
Sorghum Sugar	76	Lbs
Sorghum Molasses	77	Gals
Maple Sugar	78	Lbs
Maple Molasses	79	Gals
Pulse, Cow Peas	80	Bu
Beans, Dry	81	Bu
Irish Potatoes - Area	82	Acres
Irish Potatoes - Crop	83	Bu
Sweet Potatoes - Area	84	Acres
Sweet Potatoes - Crop	85	Bu
Tobacco - Area	86	Acres
Tobacco - Crop	87	Lbs
Apples - Area	88	Acres
Apples - Trees	89	
Apples	90	Bu
Peach - Area	91	Acres
Peach Trees	92	
Peaches	93	Bu
Value Orchard Products	94	$
Nurseries - Area	95	Acres
Value of Nursery Produce	96	$
Vineyards - Area	97	Acres
Grapes sold	98	Lbs
Wine made 1879	99	Gals
Value Garden Product sold	100	$
Honey	101	Lbs
Wax	102	Lbs
Amt of wood cut 1879	103	Cords
Value of forest product sold/used	104	$

1880 Agriculture Schedule - Lorenzo D. Robinson

Lorenzo then stated that his son, Archie Robinson was carried by the Confederates to Gloucester Point, Va., to work on the fortifications. He, Lorenzo provided him with no assistance whatever. He was in favor of the union and remained so throughout the war because the Union was the colored mans salvation.

Gloucester Point Fortifications where Archie Robinson was carried by confederate forces to work from 1861 - 1863. Dunbar Robinson the nephew of Lorenzo also worked here for 6 to 7 months. They were paid .50 cents a day plus rations. Union troops were at Yorktown on the other side of the York River. The flag in the background is Yorktown.

According to the attached deed, the children and heirs of Lorenzo D. Robinson agreed to the final disposition of land owned by Lorenzo at his death, Including a share to Dunbar Robinson, his nephew.

Whereas the late Lorenzo Robinson died seized and possessed of a certain tract of land situated in the County of King & Queen in the State of Virginia, containing one hundred and seventy three and three fourth acres, lying about three miles below King & Queen Court House, adjoining the lands of Adolphus Marshall, J. M. Davis, A. C. Robinson and the lands of the late W. P. Bird and Robert F. Bailey. And whereas the said Lorenzo Robinson left as his heirs at law his widow and the following children, to wit: A. C. Robinson, Catherine Byrd, Dunbar Robinson, Matilda West, M. E. Robinson, M. N. Robinson, Lily Robinson, L. J. Robinson, Pinky Beaufort, Rebecca Robinson, Virgie Robinson, Sara D. Robinson, Eleanor Robinson and Martha A. Robinson, his widow. And whereas prior to April 20th 1890 and subsequent to the death of the said Lorenzo Robinson, the said Sara D. and Eleanor Robinson died intestate and without children, but prior to their death had agreed upon a partition of the above mentioned tract of land as set out in a certain survey made by J. T. Purcell June, 1890, whereby said last mentioned parties were entitled to lots Nos 6 & 7 as designated in said plot. And whereas since April 20th, 1890, Pinky Beaufort and A. C. Robinson, two of the aforesaid parties, have died intestate, leaving the following children, to wit: the said Pinky Beaufort leaving as her children and only heirs at law Robert Kaufman, Jeremia Kaufman, Pinky Simpson and Ellen Kaufman, the said A. C. Robinson leaving as his only children and heirs at law John D. Robinson and Nathan B. Robinson:

And whereas it is the desire of all the aforesaid parties now living to divide and partition said tract of land in accordance with a certain deed executed, but not acknowledged, by them April 20th 1903, giving to the said widow a child's part and providing for the sale and division of the proceeds thereof of lots 6 & 7.

Now Therefore, This Deed made this ninth day of September 1903, between Catherine Byrd and Thomas Byrd, her husband, parties of the first part, Dunbar Robinson and Margaret Robinson his wife of the second part, Matilda West and Andrew West, her husband, of the third part, M. E. Robinson, of the fourth part, Martha N. Warner and Frederick G. Warner, her husband, of the fifth part, Lily C. Gordon and Daniel P. Gordon, her husband, of the sixth part, L. J. Robinson of the seventh part, Rebecca Robinson of the eighth part, Virgie Robinson, of the ninth part, Martha A. Robinson, widow of Lorenzo Robinson of the tenth part, Robert Kaufman, Jeremia Kaufman, Pinky Simpson and Ellen Kaufman, of the 11th part, John D. Robinson and Nathan B. Robinson, of the twelfth part, and I. S. Lewis, Trustee of the thirteenth part, Witnesseth: That to the end and intent that a perfect partition may be had and made between the aforesaid heirs of the said Lorenzo Robinson and the descendants of his children now dead and heirs where they left as children in said tract of land except as is hereinafter provided, and to the end that the said Martha A. Robinson shall receive the portion hereinafter allotted to her in consideration of her relinquishment of her dower interest in all of said tract of land including lots 5 & 6 and that each of said parties may from henceforth severally have and enjoy in fee simple his and their portion of the said lot, piece or parcel of ground inherited by them as aforesaid, they the said parties to this deed

exclusive of the said H. D. Lewis Trustee, by their mutual consent and agreement have made partition and allotment and by these presents do for themselves and their heirs make partition and allotment of said tracts of land in manner and form as hereinafter is mentioned, not fully set out and described in the aforesaid Plat hereto attached, and made a part of this deed (That is to say)
First, the said John B Robinson and Nathaniel B Robinson, the only children and heirs at law of A. B. Robinson shall have lot No 1, containing twelve and seven eighths acres as designated on said Plat, made by J. H. Burnell and hereto annexed and made a part of this deed. Second, Catherine Bird shall have lot No 2 as designated in said Plat. Third, Margaret J. Robinson shall have lot No 3, as designated in said Plat. Fourth, Matilda Neal shall have lot No 4 as designated in said Plat. Fifth, M B Robinson shall have lot No 5 as designated in said Plat. Sixth Martha H Warner shall have lot No 8 as designated in said Plat. Seventh Lilly P Gordon shall have lot No 9 as designated in said Plat. Eighth, F. S. Robinson shall have lot No 10 as designated in said Plat. Ninth, Robert Kaufman, Jerome Kaufman, Pinky Ampson and Ellen Kaufman, only children and heirs of Pinky Newbort deceased, shall have lot No 11, as designated in said Plat. Tenth, Abram Robinson shall have lot No 12 as designated in said Plat. Eleventh, Kerpe Robinson shall have lot No 13 as designated in said Plat. Twelfth, that Martha D Robinson widow of Lorenzo Robinson, deceased, shall have lot No 14 as designated in said Plat.

Each of the aforesaid parties to have and to hold the fee simple interest in and to their respective lots of land above described and allotted to him, her or them, their heirs or assigns forever and divided from the parts and portions of the said other parties severally.

To the end that Lots Nos. 6 & 7 may be disposed of and the proceeds divided among those entitled to the same (it being understood that Martha D Robinson widow has no interest in or claim to said last mentioned tracts of land) the aforesaid parties to this deed exclusive of the said H. D. Lewis, Trustee, in consideration of the sum of one dollar and for the purposes aforesaid, do grant with special warranty unto the said H. D. Lewis the aforesaid lots of land mentioned and described on said Plat hereto attached as Lot No 6 containing twelve and one quarter acres and Lot No 7 containing twelve and three quarter acres, but each adjoining the tract conveyed heretofore to the said Martha D Robinson. In Trust, however and for the following purposes, to wit. That the said H. D. Lewis as soon as this Deed shall have been executed and duly recorded shall proceed, after advertising the time, place and terms of sale by printed hand-bills posted at three or more public places in the County of King and Queen for two successive weeks, proceed to sell at public auction on some County Court day at King and Queen Court House to each the aforesaid Lots No 6 & 7 by this deed to the said Trustee conveyed. That the said H. D. Lewis out of the proceeds of each shall pay first the costs of sale including a commission to him of ___ per centum and the balance of the purchase money he shall pay and distribute to those parties entitled to the same as follows

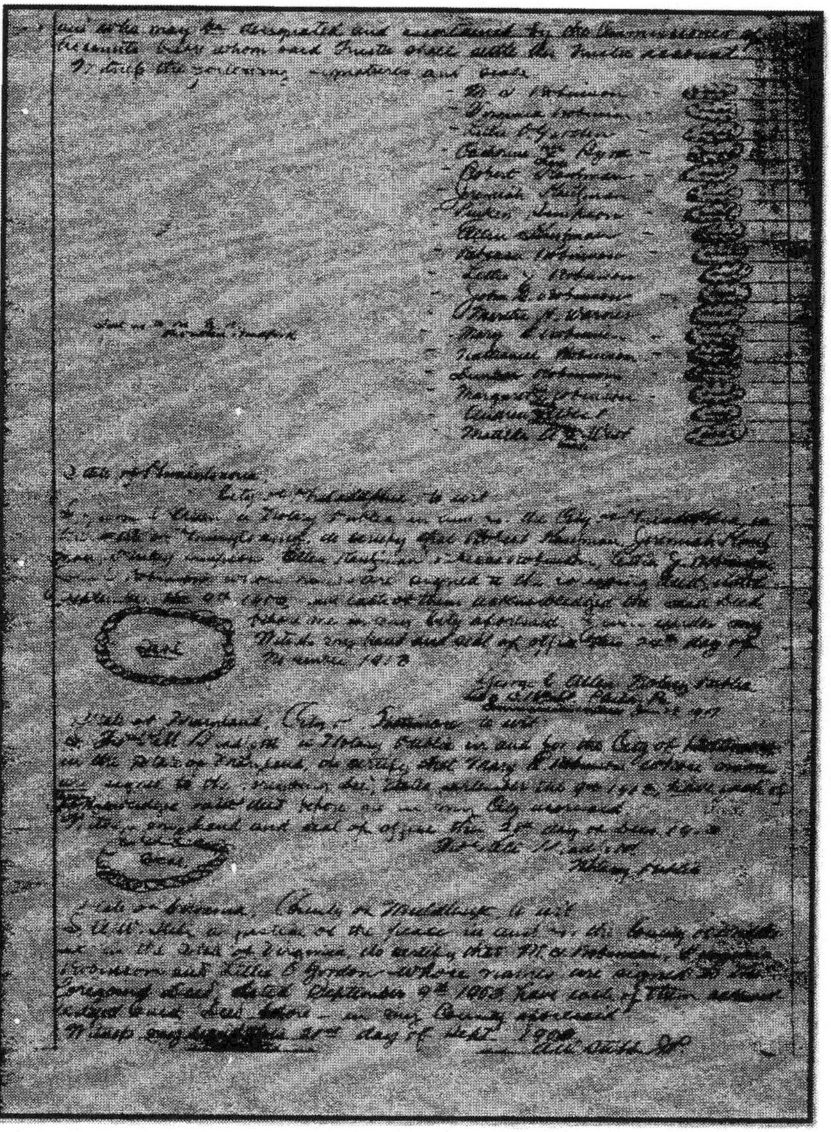

State of New York, County of Kings, on this the 19th day of December 1903, before me, personally came Nathaniel Watson to me known, and known to me to be the individual described in and who executed the foregoing instrument and .... who thereupon acknowledged to me that he executed the same

[SEAL]

John N. Gebhardt Jr.
Notary Public, Kings Co.

State of Virginia, County of King & Queen, to wit:
I, Wm. F. Bagby, a notary public in the County aforesaid, in the State of Virginia, do certify that Nathaniel Robinson, whose name is signed to the writing hereto attached, bearing date on the 9th day of September, 1903, has acknowledged the same before me in my County aforesaid.
Given under my hand this 29th day of January, 1904.

Wm. F. Bagby, N.P.
My commission expires Jan. 20, 1905.

State of Virginia, County of King & Queen, to wit:
I, Wm. F. Bagby, a notary public for the County aforesaid, in the State of Virginia, do certify that Dunbar Robinson and Margaret Robinson, his wife, whose names are signed to the writing hereto annexed, bearing date on the 9th day of September 1903, have acknowledged the same before me in my County aforesaid.
Given under my hand this 5th day of April 1904.

Wm. F. Bagby, N.P.
My commission expires Jan. 20, 1905.

State of Virginia, County of King & Queen, to wit:
I, Wm. F. Bagby, a notary public for the County aforesaid, in the State of Virginia, do certify that Matilda West and Andrew West, her husband, whose names are signed to the writing hereto annexed, bearing date on the 9th day of September, 1903, have acknowledged the same before me in said County aforesaid.
Given under my hand this 11th day of April 1904.

Wm. F. Bagby, N.P.
My commission expires Jan. 20, 1905.

State of Virginia, County of King & Queen, to wit:
I, Wm. F. Bagby, a notary public for the County aforesaid, in the State of Virginia, do certify that Catherine Boyd, whose name is signed to the writing hereto attached, bearing date on the 9th day of September 1903, has acknowledged the same before me in my County aforesaid.
Given under my hand this 18th day of November 1904.

Wm. F. Bagby, N.P.
My commission expires Jan. 20, 1905.

The figure in view represents the land owned by Edward Robinson and sub divided amongst the Legates as shown with lot numbers without exception of timber area.

J. B. Purcell
June 1890

Zion Baptist Church Seeks Families of Founders

Zion Baptist Church was formed in 1866 by colored members of Mattaponi Baptist Church. Zion is now preparing for the celebration of its sesquicentennial (150th anniversary) in 2016. We are fortunate to have the names of the founders of Zion from the minutes of Mattaponi. The goal is to identify the present day families of the founders. Please let us know whether any of the founders are your ancestors, whether you recognize the names of any of the founders, or whether you know persons with these surnames to whom we should talk. If you can provide this information or any information whatsoever about the founders of Zion Baptist Church, please contact Abigail Collins at 804-769-3252.

The following persons are founders of Zion Baptist Church:

Letters of dismission given on July 7, 1866

Joseph Braxton	Harriet Banks
Jim Brokenbrough	Judy Braxton
Jacob Brook	Joanna Carter
Washington Carter	Maria Carter
William Carter	Alice Dabney
Humphrey Garlick	Susan Fauntleroy
Abraham Homes	Agness Garlick
Ben Homes	Ellen Hampton
Henry Homes	Priscilla Hampton
John Homes	Ellen Henry
Thomas Homes	Mary Homes
John Hudgins	Martha Hudgins
Seyrus Robertson	Charlotte Lewis
Jim Robinson	Juliet Parron
Taliaferro Ross	Agness Robinson (1870)
Beverly Sparks	Sarah Robinson
John Tabb	Rachel Ross
Curtis Taylor	Nancy Sparks
Jim Taylor	Betsy Taylor
Thornton Taylor	Sarah Taylor
Robert Waller	Isabella White
Andrew White	Caroline Williams

Couples identified are highlighted above:

Beverly Sparks and Nancy Sparks
Andrew White and Isabella White
Taliaferro Ross and Rachel Ross
Humphrey Garlick and Agnes Garlick
John Hudgins and Martha Hudgins
Thornton Taylor and Sarah Taylor
Joseph Braxton and Judy Braxton
Thomas Holmes and Mary Holmes
Seyrus Robertson (Robinson) and Sarah Robinson

John & Martha Hudgins are the parents of Martha Susan Hudgins the 2nd wife of Lorenzo Dow Robinson. The 2nd grandparents of the author Robert Lorenzo Lockley

Lorenzo Dow Robinson was one of the founders of Second Mt. Olive Baptist Church constituted in 1868. Also in King & Queen County, Va.

Letters of dismission given on October 9, 1869

Mandy Bagby	Washington Carter
Harriet Banks	Tinsley Fields
Netty Berly	Joe Harris
Sally Billups	Abram Hoomes
Aggy Brit	George Lee
Roberta Brooks	Lorenzo Lockley
Rosa Brown	Thom Mitchell
Joanna Carter	Jos. Robinson
Lavinia Carter	Minter Tunstall
Lavinia Chamberlane	Andrew White
Lucy Dill	
Martha Fields	
Mary Harwood	
Judy Harris	
Ellen Hamilton	
Elvira Harris	
Anna Hoomes	
Martha Johnson	
Caroline Minor (1870, 1880) h.Samuel	
Nancy Montague	
Georganna Moody	
Hannah Muse	
Fanny Pollard	
Polly Pollard	
Ellen Robinson	
Maria Robinson	
Martha Robinson	
Judy Scott	
Hannah Smith	
Charity Tabb	
Wenny Taylor	
Barbara Walton	
Isabella White	
Mary Wiley	
Margaret Wright	

1850 United States Federal Census

Name:	**Martha Susan Hudgins**
Age:	10
Birth Year:	abt 1840
Birthplace:	Virginia
Home in 1850:	St Stephens Parish, King and Queen, Virginia
Race:	Mulatto
Gender:	Female
Family Number:	31

Family of Lorenzo Robinson's 2nd Wife - Martha Susan Hudgins

Household Members:

Name	Age	
John Hudgins	35	Black
Martha Hudgins	33	Mulatto
Mary Ellen Hudgins	14	Mulatto
Maria Elizabeth Hudgins	12	Mulatto
Martha Susan Hudgins	10	Mulatto
Anna Byrd	21	Mulatto
James Hudgins	4	Mulatto
Anna Hudgins	4	Mulatto

Descendants of Lorenzo D. Robinson

Generation 1

1. **Lorenzo D.**[1] **Robinson** was born in 1810 in King & Queen County, Va.. He died on 04 Dec 1884 in King & Queen County, Virginia. He married **Martha Hudgins**. She was born in 1840 in King & Queen County, Va.. He married **Betsy**. She was born in 1822 in Middlesex County, Va..

Notes for Lorenzo D. Robinson:

The 1st wife of Lorenzo Robinson was Betsy. Information obtained from the Marriage License of his daughter Pinky when she married Philip Bluefoot at Lorenzo's home on August 29, 1878. Betsy died between the 1846 & 1850 Census of King & Queen County.

Lorenzo D. Robinson and Martha Hudgins had the following children:

    i.   Mary E.[2] Robinson was born in 1864 in King & Queen County, Va..

    ii.   Fannie E. Robinson was born in 1866 in King & Queen County, Virginia. She died on 07 Oct 1879 in King & Queen County, Virginia.

    iii. Sarah T. Robinson was born in 1868 in King & Queen County, Va..

    iv. Lilly O. Robinson was born in 1871 in King & Queen County, Va.. She married Daniel Gordon.

    v.   Maria S. Robinson was born on 11 Nov 1872 in King & Queen County, Va..

    vi. Lecter Robinson was born in 1873 in King & Queen County, Va.. She died on 29 Apr 1890 in Philadelphia, Pa..

2.   vii. MARTHA H. ROBINSON was born on 14 Mar 1874 in King & Queen County, Va.. She married (1) FREDERICK WARNER in 1909 in New York, New York. He was born in 1873. She married (2) MARDIN in 1900 in New Jersey. She married UNKNOWN.

     viii. REBECCA ROBINSON was born in 1877 in King & Queen County, Va..

     ix.   LETHA J ROBINSON was born in 1878 in King & Queen County, Va..

3.   x.   VIRGINIA ROBINSON was born in 1880 in King & Queen, Virginia. She died in 1951 in New York City, N.Y.. She married (1) ROBERT HENRY LOCKLEY, son of Daniel Lockley I and Christy Morris on 05 Sep 1904 in Harmony Village, Virginia. He was born on 15 Dec 1877 in Christ Church, Middlesex County, Virginia. She married (2) JOSEPH HUCK HARRIS, son of Robert Harris and Fannie Lockley on 08 Apr 1916 in Middlesex County, Va.. He was born in 1855 in Middlesex County, Virginia. He died on 12 Mar 1936 in Middlesex County, Va..

Lorenzo D. Robinson and Betsy had the following children:

4.   xi.   ARCHIBALD ROBINSON was born in 1837 in King & Queen County, Va.. He married MARIA E. HUDGINS. She was born in 1836 in King & Queen County, Va.. He married (2) MARION HODGESS, daughter of John Hodgess and Mary on 24 Dec 1857 in King & Queen County, Va.. She was born in 1836 in King & Queen County, Va..

5. xii. PINKY ROBINSON was born in 1840 in King & Queen County, Va.. She married (1) JEREMIA KAUFMAN, son of George Kaufman and Polly Robinson on 06 Mar 1856 in King & Queen County, Va.. He was born in 1834 in King & Queen County, Va.. He died on 01 Sep 1870 in King & Queen County, Va.. She married (2) PHILIP BLUEFOOT, son of Phil Gatewood and Polly Bluefoot on 29 Aug 1878 in King & Queen County, Va.. He was born in 1826 in King & Queen County, Va.. She married PHILIP GATEWOOD.

xiii. MARGARETT ROBINSON was born in 1841 in King & Queen County, Va..

xiv. CATHERINE ROBINSON was born in 1843 in King & Queen County, Virginia. She married Thomas Bird on 25 Dec 1867 in Lorenzo Robinson's House. He was born in 1840 in King & Queen County, Virginia.

6. xv. MATILDA A. ROBINSON was born in 1854 in King & Queen County, Va.. She married Andrew West in 1880 in King & Queen County, Va.. He was born in Aug 1849 in King & Queen County, Va..

Generation 2

2. **MARTHA H.² ROBINSON** (Lorenzo D.¹) was born on 14 Mar 1874 in King & Queen County, Va.. She married (1) **FREDERICK WARNER** in 1909 in New York, New York. He was born in 1873. She married (2) **MARDIN** in 1900 in New Jersey. She married **UNKNOWN**.

Frederick Warner and Martha H. Robinson had the following children:

    i.   GRANVILLE³ WARNER was born on 29 Oct 1909 in New York, New York. He died in Mar 1986 in Brooklyn, N.Y..

    ii.   CLIFFORD WARNER was born on 01 Jan 1911 in New York, New York. He died in Jan 1984 in Brooklyn, N.Y..

    iii.   HELEN WARNER was born on 09 Dec 1910 in New York, New York. She died in Mar 1978 in Brooklyn, N.Y..

    iv.   LORENZO WARNER was born on 13 Nov 1913 in New York, New York. He died on 22 Dec 2004 in Brooklyn, N.Y..

    v.   CHARLES WARNER was born in 1918 in New York, New York.

Mardin and Martha H. Robinson had the following children:

    i.   MARY C.³ MARDIN was born in 1903 in Newark, NJ.

    ii.   EVERETT MARDIN was born in 1906 in New Jersey.

    iii.   RUSSELL MARDIN was born in 1908 in New Jersey.

Unknown and Martha H. Robinson had the following child:

    i.   RICHARD³ ROBINSON was born in 1900 in Essex County, Va..

3. **Virginia[2] Robinson** (Lorenzo D.[1]) was born in 1880 in King & Queen, Virginia. She died in 1951 in New York City, N.Y.. She married (1) **Robert Henry Lockley**, son of Daniel Lockley I and Christy Morris on 05 Sep 1904 in Harmony Village, Virginia. He was born on 15 Dec 1877 in Christ Church, Middlesex County, Virginia. She married (2) **Joseph Huck Harris**, son of Robert Harris and Fannie Lockley on 08 Apr 1916 in Middlesex County, Va.. He was born in 1855 in Middlesex County, Virginia. He died on 12 Mar 1936 in Middlesex County, Va..

Robert Henry Lockley and Virginia Robinson had the following children:

7. i. Robert Oceola[3] Lockley was born on 12 Aug 1905 in Christ Church, Middlesex County, Virginia. He died on 12 Aug 1979 in Tappahannock, Virginia. He married Marion Clarice Williams, daughter of Armstead Williams and Lucy Griffin on 21 Sep 1930 in Christ Church, Middlesex County, Virginia. She was born on 11 Aug 1913 in Topping Post Office, Middlesex County, Virginia. She died on 14 Jul 1978 in Tappahannock, Virginia.

   ii. Edith Alyce Lockley-White-Bell was born in 1907 in Christ Church Middlesex County, Virginia. She died in 1976 in Philadelphia, Pa.. She married William White. She married (2) Edward Bell on 07 Mar 1974 in Elkton, Maryland.

   iii. Lorenzo C. Lockley was born in 1909 in Middlesex County, Va.. He died on 14 Sep 1966 in Philadelphia, Pa..

Joseph Huck Harris and Virginia Robinson had the following child:

i. BERNARD U.³ HARRIS was born on 14 Mar 1917 in Middlesex County, Virginia. He died on 29 Oct 1984 in Middlesex County, Virginia. He married Bessie Beckwith in 1962 in New York, New York. She was born on 07 May 1918 in Hyde County, North Carolina. She died on 24 May 2000 in Middlesex County, Va..

4. ARCHIBALD² ROBINSON (Lorenzo D.¹) was born in 1837 in King & Queen County, Va.. He married **MARIA E. HUDGINS**. She was born in 1836 in King & Queen County, Va.. He married (2) **MARION HODGESS**, daughter of John Hodgess and Mary on 24 Dec 1857 in King & Queen County, Va.. She was born in 1836 in King & Queen County, Va..

Archibald Robinson and Maria E. Hudgins had the following children:

8. i. JOHN CALEB³, ROBINSON was born on 02 Dec 1873 in King & Queen County, Va.. He married NANNIE. She was born in 1875 in King & Queen County, Va..

ii. NATHAN P. ROBINSON was born in 1876 in King & Queen County, Va.. He married Mary E.W Fields, daughter of Robert Fields and Malinda on 25 Jun 1902 in Middlesex County, Virginia. She was born in 1875 in Middlesex County, Virginia.

5. PINKY² ROBINSON (LORENZO D.¹) was born in 1840 in King & Queen County, Va.. She married (1) **JEREMIA KAUFMAN**, son of George Kaufman and Polly Robinson on 06 Mar 1856 in King & Queen County, Va.. He was born in 1834 in King & Queen County, Va.. He died on 01 Sep 1870 in King & Queen County, Va.. She married (2) **PHILIP BLUEFOOT**, son of Phil Gatewood and Polly Bluefoot on 29 Aug 1878 in King & Queen County, Va.. He was born in 1826 in King & Queen County, Va.. She married **PHILIP GATEWOOD**.

Jeremia Kaufman and Pinky Robinson had the following children:

    i.   ROBERT³ KAUFMAN was born in 1860.

    ii.   JEREMIA KAUFMAN JR. was born in 1866.

    iii.   MATILDA ELLEN KAUFMAN was born in 1868.

    iv.   PINKY KAUFMAN was born in 1869. She married SIMPSON.

    v.   ELVIRA KAUFMAN was born in 1865 in King & Queen, Virginia. She died on 05 Aug 1870 in King & Queen, Virginia.

Philip Gatewood and Pinky Robinson had the following child:

    i.   MARY E.³ GATEWOOD was born in 1874.

6. **MATILDA A.² ROBINSON** (LORENZO D.¹) was born in 1854 in King & Queen County, Va.. She married Andrew West in 1880 in King & Queen County, Va.. He was born in Aug 1849 in King & Queen County, Va..

Andrew West and Matilda A. Robinson had the following children:

    i.   MATCADE³ WEST was born in 1870 in King & Queen County, Va..

    ii.   JOSEPHINE WEST was born in Nov 1878 in King & Queen County, Va..

    iii.   LAURA WEST was born in Aug 1879 in King & Queen County, Va..

    iv.   HARVEY HOLDER WEST was born in Jan 1882 in King & Queen County, Va.. He died on 17 Jan 1950 in Philadelphia, Pa..

v. GERTRUDE WEST was born in Mar 1895 in King & Queen County, Va..

vi. HOWARD T. WEST was born in Mar 1896 in King & Queen County, Va..

vii. EDWARD W. WEST was born in Jul 1898 in King & Queen County, Va..

Generation 3

7. **ROBERT OCEOLA**[3] **LOCKLEY** (Virginia[2] Robinson, Lorenzo D.[1] Robinson) was born on 12 Aug 1905 in Christ Church, Middlesex County, Virginia. He died on 12 Aug 1979 in Tappahannock, Virginia. He married Marion Clarice Williams, daughter of Armstead Williams and Lucy Griffin on 21 Sep 1930 in Christ Church, Middlesex County, Virginia. She was born on 11 Aug 1913 in Topping Post Office, Middlesex County, Virginia. She died on 14 Jul 1978 in Tappahannock, Virginia.

Robert Oceola Lockley and Marion Clarice Williams had the following children:

9. i. ROBERT LORENZO[4] LOCKLEY was born on 19 Nov 1931 in Topping Post Office, Middlesex County, Virginia. He married (2) RUIZ COELLO RAQUEL CANCEL, daughter of Manuel Cancel and Herrerra Alejandria Ruiz on 10 Oct 1983 in Laural, Maryland. She was born on 03 Dec 1944 in Quebradillas, Puerto Rico. He married (1) PATRICIA ELLIS, daughter of Edmund Otha Ellis and Mamie Parker in Aug 1955 in Philadelphia, Pa.. She was born on 12 Jan 1937 in Philadelphia, Pa..

10. ii. REGINALD ELWOOD LOCKLEY was born on 29 Aug 1933 in Topping Post Office, Middlesex County, Virginia. He died on 20 Oct 1989 in West Jersey Hospital, Berlin, New Jersey. He met ANNABELLE GLOVER. She was born on 16 Jan 1941 in Philadelphia, Pa.. He met JULIA ELIZABETH POINDEXTER. He met ELIZABETH CHERRY MORROW. She died in Nov 1989 in Philadelphia, Pa..

11. iii. HAROLD PRESTON LOCKLEY was born on 18 Aug 1937 in Topping Post Office, Middlesex County, Virginia. He died on 06 Oct 1970 in Philadelphia, Pa.. He married Maxine Norton, daughter of Ernest Bernard Norton and Guthea Green on 28 Jun 1958 in Philadelphia, Pa.. She was born on 08 Nov 1937 in Philadelphia, Pa.. She died on 11 Mar 1999 in Philadelphia, Pa.. He met JOAN DICKENS. He met CAROLYN SAUGLING.

8. JOHN CALEB[3] ROBINSON (Archibald[2], Lorenzo D.[1]) was born on 02 Dec 1873 in King & Queen County, Va.. He married **NANNIE**. She was born in 1875 in King & Queen County, Va..

John Caleb Robinson and Nannie had the following children:

i. MAUD[4] ROBINSON was born in 1903.

ii. CLARENCE ROBINSON was born in 1905 in King & Queen County, Va..

iii. WILLIE ROBINSON was born in 1909 in King & Queen County, Va..

iv. JR JOHN C. ROBINSON was born in 1913 in King & Queen County, Va..

Generation 4

9. **Robert Lorenzo**[4] **Lockley** (Robert Oceola[3], Virginia[2] Robinson, Lorenzo D.[1] Robinson) was born on 19 Nov 1931 in Topping Post Office, Middlesex County, Virginia. He married (1) **Ruiz Coello Raquel Cancel**, daughter of Manuel Cancel and Herrerra Alejandria Ruiz on 10 Oct 1983 in Laural, Maryland. She was born on 03 Dec 1944 in Quebradillas, Puerto Rico. He married (2) **Patricia Ellis**, daughter of Edmund Otha Ellis and Mamie Parker in Aug 1955 in Philadelphia, Pa.. She was born on 12 Jan 1937 in Philadelphia, Pa..

Robert Lorenzo Lockley and Ruiz Coello Raquel Cancel had the following child:

12. i. **Ashley Clarice**[5] **Lockley** was born on 24 Dec 1986 in Washington, D.C.. She married **Kevin Hall**.

Robert Lorenzo Lockley and Patricia Ellis had the following children:

13. ii. **Robin Laverne Lockley** was born on 24 May 1956 in Philadelphia, Pa.. She married **Earl Lee Andrew Miller Jr**. He was born on 25 Feb 1953 in Coatesville, Pa..

14. iii. **Robert Lorenzo Lockley Jr**. was born on 22 Jan 1960 in Philadelphia, Pa.. He married Sheryl Robin Whyte, daughter of James Melvin White and Miriam Hamburger on 04 Mar 1984 in Willingboro, New Jersey. She was born on 16 Nov 1963 in Philadelphia, Pa..

10. **Reginald Elwood**[4] **Lockley** (Robert Oceola[3], Virginia[2] Robinson, Lorenzo D.[1] Robinson) was born on 29 Aug 1933 in Topping Post Office, Middlesex County, Virginia. He died on 20 Oct 1989 in West Jersey Hospital, Berlin, New Jersey. He met **Annabelle Glover**. She was born on 16 Jan 1941 in Philadelphia, Pa.. He met **Julia Elizabeth Poindexter**. He met **Elizabeth Cherry Morrow**. She died in Nov 1989 in Philadelphia, Pa..

Reginald Elwood Lockley and Annabelle Glover had the following children:

- 15. i. Regenia Elizabeth[5] Glover was born on 29 Aug 1961 in Philadelphia, Pa.. She married (2) Rickey A. Bailey on 24 Aug 2004 in Las Vegas, NV.
- 16. ii. Rhonda Elaine Glover was born on 13 Aug 1964 in Philadelphia, Pa.. She married Walter R. Walker in Philadelphia, Pa..

Reginald Elwood Lockley and Julia Elizabeth Poindexter had the following child:

- iii. Kyle Richardson was born on 02 Apr 1966 in Philadelphia, Pa.. He married Michelle.

Reginald Elwood Lockley and Elizabeth Cherry Morrow had the following child:

- iv. Charosangina L. Morrow was born on 24 Nov 1963 in Philadelphia, Pa..

11. **HAROLD PRESTON[4] LOCKLEY** (Robert Oceola[3], Virginia[2] Robinson, Lorenzo D.[1] Robinson) was born on 18 Aug 1937 in Topping Post Office, Middlesex County, Virginia. He died on 06 Oct 1970 in Philadelphia, Pa.. He married Maxine Norton, daughter of Ernest Bernard Norton and Guthea Green on 28 Jun 1958 in Philadelphia, Pa.. She was born on 08 Nov 1937 in Philadelphia, Pa.. She died on 11 Mar 1999 in Philadelphia, Pa.. He met **JOAN DICKENS**. He met **CAROLYN SAUGLING**.

Harold Preston Lockley and Maxine Norton had the following child:

17. i. HAROLD PRESTON[5] LOCKLEY JR. was born on 18 Jan 1962 in Philadelphia, Pa.. He married (1) SHERRIE REDDICK on 02 May 1992 in East Lansdown, Pa.. She was born on 02 Sep 1959 in Camden, New Jersey. He met JANINE GIDDINGS. She died in 1996 in Philadelphia, Pa..

Harold Preston Lockley and Joan Dickens had the following child:

18. ii. DERRICK A. DICKENS was born on 19 Aug 1964 in Philadelphia, Pa.. He married Rosalind Bruce on 02 Sep 1995 in Philadelphia, Pa.. She was born on 22 May 1962 in Philadelphia, Pa..

Harold Preston Lockley and Carolyn Saugling had the following child:

iii. SANDRA SAUGLING was born in 1969.

Generation 5

12. **Ashley Clarice[5] Lockley** (Robert Lorenzo[4], Robert Oceola[3], Virginia[2] Robinson, Lorenzo D.[1] Robinson) was born on 24 Dec 1986 in Washington, D.C.. She married **Kevin Hall**.

Kevin Hall and Ashley Clarice Lockley had the following children:

    i.   Cheyanne[6] Hall was born on 20 Nov 2010.

    ii.   Manolo M. Hall was born on 28 Dec 2011.

13. **Robin Laverne[5] Lockley** (Robert Lorenzo[4], Robert Oceola[3], Virginia[2] Robinson, Lorenzo D.[1] Robinson) was born on 24 May 1956 in Philadelphia, Pa.. She married **Earl Lee Andrew Miller Jr**. He was born on 25 Feb 1953 in Coatesville, Pa..

Earl Lee Andrew Miller Jr and Robin Laverne Lockley had the following children:

19.   i.   Ryan Andrew[6] Miller was born on 19 May 1979 in New Jersey. He married (1) Andrean Sierra on 12 Mar 2001 in Cinnaminson, New Jersey. He married (2) Minerva on 08 Apr 2011 in Mount Holly, NJ.

20.   ii.   Tiffany Annette Miller was born on 27 Jun 1980 in New Jersey. She married Charles Hawkins on 11 Nov 2003 in AME Harris Temple, Camden, N.J.. He was born on 13 Jun 1980.

21.   iii. Earl Lee-andrew Miller III was born on 17 Aug 1981 in New Jersey. He married Paula Plaza, daughter of Luis Ricardo Plaza and Maria Marlen in Mar 2010 in New Jersey. She was born in Apr 1986.

22.   iv. Parrish Daneon Miller was born on 09 Jan 1983 in New Jersey. He married Lindsey Watson.

23.   v.   Tarrah A'lauri Miller was born on 15 May 1987 in New Jersey. She married Jayson Taylor.

14. **Robert Lorenzo[5] Lockley Jr.** (Robert Lorenzo[4], Robert Oceola[3], Virginia[2] Robinson, Lorenzo D.[1] Robinson) was born on 22 Jan 1960 in Philadelphia, Pa.. He married Sheryl Robin Whyte, daughter of James Melvin White and Miriam Hamburger on 04 Mar 1984 in Willingboro, New Jersey. She was born on 16 Nov 1963 in Philadelphia, Pa..

Robert Lorenzo Lockley Jr. and Sheryl Robin Whyte had the following children:

    i.   Ava Ashley[6] Lockley was born on 17 Oct 1984 in New Jersey.

    ii.   Robert Lorenzo Lockley III was born on 12 Oct 1988 in New Jersey.

15. **Regenia Elizabeth[5] Glover** (Reginald Elwood[4] Lockley, Robert Oceola[3] Lockley, Virginia[2] Robinson, Lorenzo D.[1] Robinson) was born on 29 Aug 1961 in Philadelphia, Pa.. She married (2) **Rickey A. Bailey** on 24 Aug 2004 in Las Vegas, NV.

Regenia Elizabeth Glover had the following child:

    i.   Genine Lauren[6] Stephens was born on 23 Jan 1984.

16. **Rhonda Elaine[5] Glover** (Reginald Elwood[4] Lockley, Robert Oceola[3] Lockley, Virginia[2] Robinson, Lorenzo D.[1] Robinson) was born on 13 Aug 1964 in Philadelphia, Pa.. She married Walter R. Walker in Philadelphia, Pa..

Walter R. Walker and Rhonda Elaine Glover had the following children:

    i.   Sharonda Antonette[6] Glover was born on 11 Feb 1984.

    ii.   Andre Matthew Glover was born on 08 Mar 1988.

17. **HAROLD PRESTON**[5] **LOCKLEY JR.** (Harold Preston[4], Robert Oceola[3], Virginia[2] Robinson, Lorenzo D.[1] Robinson) was born on 18 Jan 1962 in Philadelphia, Pa.. He married (1) **SHERRIE REDDICK** on 02 May 1992 in East Lansdown, Pa.. She was born on 02 Sep 1959 in Camden, New Jersey. He met **JANINE GIDDINGS**. She died in 1996 in Philadelphia, Pa..

Harold Preston Lockley Jr. and Janine Giddings had the following child:

    i.   HAROLD NYREE[6] LOCKLEY was born on 16 Sep 1985 in Philadelphia, Pa..

18. **DERRICK A.**[5] **DICKENS** (Harold Preston[4] Lockley, Robert Oceola[3] Lockley, Virginia[2] Robinson, Lorenzo D.[1] Robinson) was born on 19 Aug 1964 in Philadelphia, Pa.. He married Rosalind Bruce on 02 Sep 1995 in Philadelphia, Pa.. She was born on 22 May 1962 in Philadelphia, Pa..

Derrick A. Dickens and Rosalind Bruce had the following children:

    i.   MAXWELL ANTHONY[6] DICKENS was born on 25 Jun 1998.

    ii.   LAUREN MICHELL DICKENS was born on 13 Feb 2001.

Generation 6

19. **Ryan Andrew[6] Miller** (Robin Laverne[5] Lockley, Robert Lorenzo[4] Lockley, Robert Oceola[3] Lockley, Virginia[2] Robinson, Lorenzo D.[1] Robinson) was born on 19 May 1979 in New Jersey. He married (1) **Adrean Sierra** on 12 Mar 2001 in Cinnaminson, New Jersey. He married (2) **Minerva** on 08 Apr 2011 in Mount Holly, NJ.

Ryan Andrew Miller and Adrean Sierra had the following children:

    i.   Ryan Andrew[7] Miller Jr. was born on 28 Aug 2001 in New Jersey.

    ii.   Ariana Adrean Miller was born on 14 Dec 2002 in West Jersey Hospital, Voorhees, N.J..

    iii. Celia Margaret Patricia Miller was born on 11 Jan 2007 in West Jersey Hospital, Voorhee, N.J..

20. **Tiffany Annette[6] Miller** (Robin Laverne[5] Lockley, Robert Lorenzo[4] Lockley, Robert Oceola[3] Lockley, Virginia[2] Robinson, Lorenzo D.[1] Robinson) was born on 27 Jun 1980 in New Jersey. She married Charles Hawkins on 11 Nov 2003 in AME Harris Temple, Camden, N.J.. He was born on 13 Jun 1980.

Charles Hawkins and Tiffany Annette Miller had the following children:

    i.   Serenity Kaitlin[7] Hawkins was born on 01 Sep 2004 in New Jersey.

    ii.   Serena Karalee Hawkins was born on 08 Sep 2008 in Voorhees, New Jersey.

    iii. Seralina Kamara Hawkins was born on 01 Dec 2012 in New Jersey.

    iv. Travis Hawkins was born on 16 Apr 2008 in New Jersey.

21. **Earl Lee-Andrew**[6] **Miller** III (Robin Laverne[5] Lockley, Robert Lorenzo[4] Lockley, Robert Oceola[3] Lockley, Virginia[2] Robinson, Lorenzo D.[1] Robinson) was born on 17 Aug 1981 in New Jersey. He married Paula Plaza, daughter of Luis Ricardo Plaza and Maria Marlen in Mar 2010 in New Jersey. She was born in Apr 1986.

Earl Lee-Andrew Miller III and Paula Plaza had the following children:

    i.   Elijah[7] Miller was born on 23 Sep 2009 in New Jersey.

    ii.   Isla Miller was born on 03 Aug 2013 in New Jersey.

22. **Parrish Daneon**[6] **Miller** (Robin Laverne[5] Lockley, Robert Lorenzo[4] Lockley, Robert Oceola[3] Lockley, Virginia[2] Robinson, Lorenzo D.[1] Robinson) was born on 09 Jan 1983 in New Jersey. He married **Lindsey Watson**.

Parrish Daneon Miller and Lindsey Watson had the following child:

    i.   Leanna Cynthia[7] Miller was born on 12 Jun 2013 in New Jersey.

23. **Tarrah A'Lauri**[6] **Miller** (Robin Laverne[5] Lockley, Robert Lorenzo[4] Lockley, Robert Oceola[3] Lockley, Virginia[2] Robinson, Lorenzo D.[1] Robinson) was born on 15 May 1987 in New Jersey. She married **Jayson Taylor**.

Jayson Taylor and Tarrah A'Lauri Miller had the following child:

    i.   Jaceelyn Juliet[7] Taylor was born on 10 Oct 2010.

Descendants of Lorenzo D. Robinson (1 of 13)

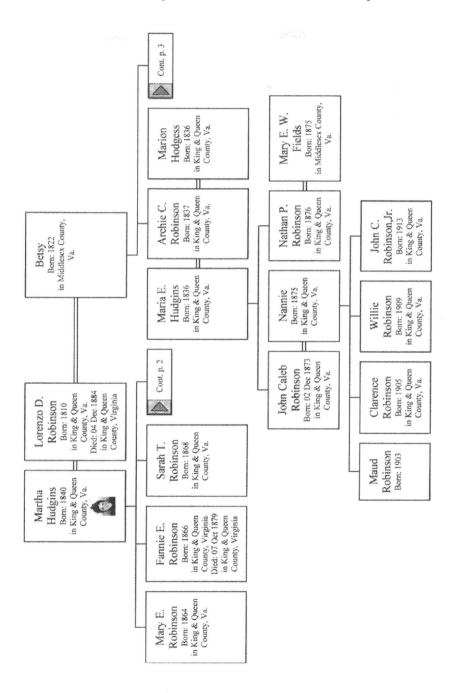

Descendants of Lorenzo D. Robinson (2 of 13)

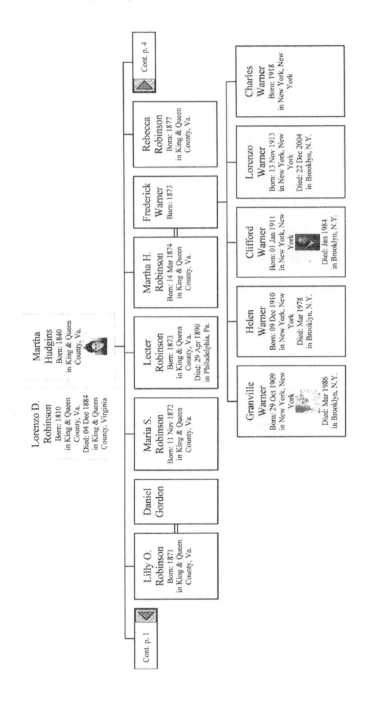

Descendants of Lorenzo D. Robinson (3 of 13)

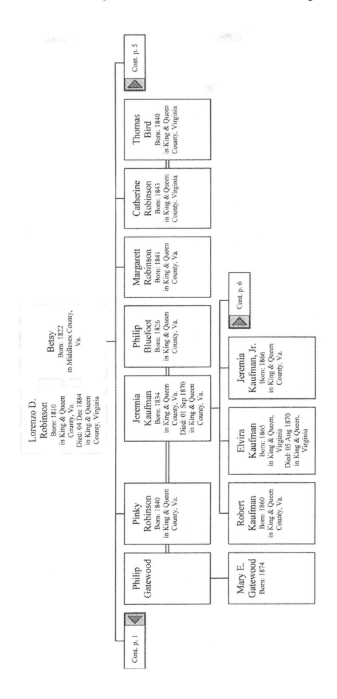

Descendants of Lorenzo D. Robinson (4 of 13)

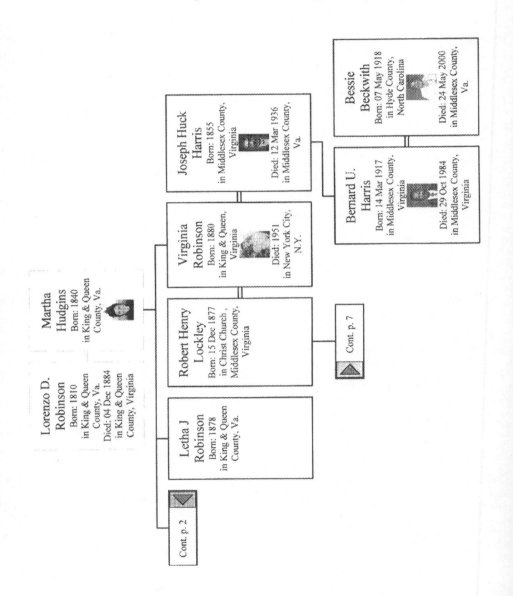

Descendants of Lorenzo D. Robinson

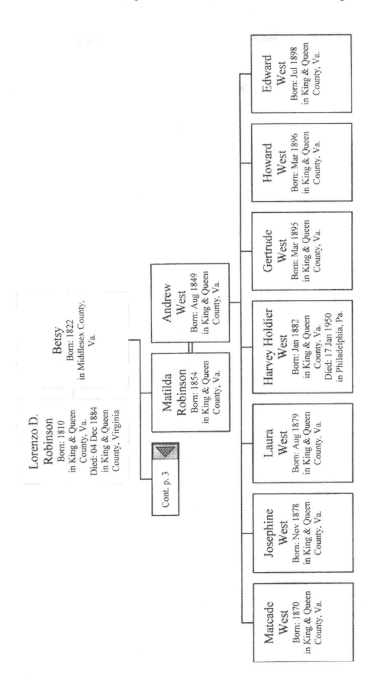

Descendants of Lorenzo D. Robinson

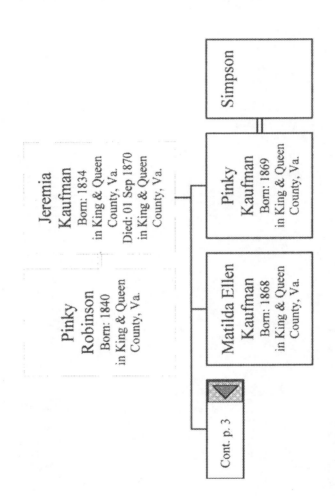

Descendants of Lorenzo D. Robinson (7 of 13)

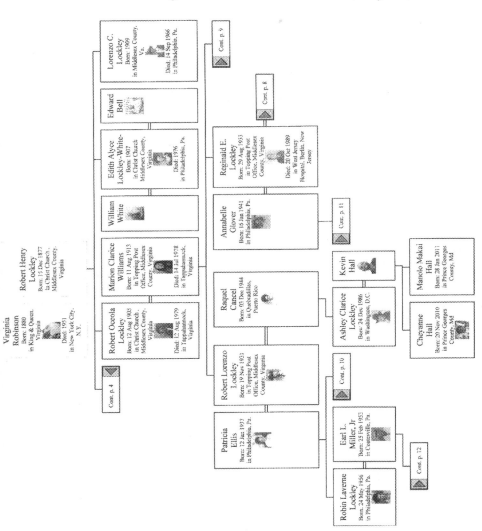

Descendants of Lorenzo D. Robinson

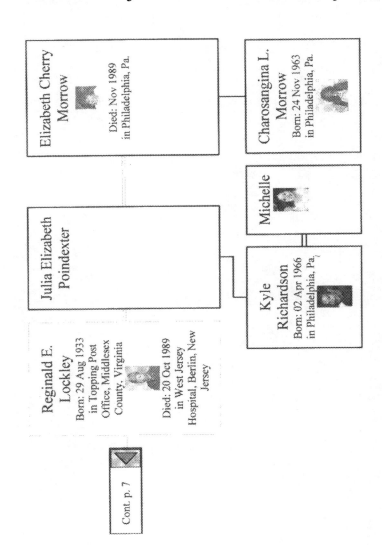

Descendants of Lorenzo D. Robinson (9 of 13)

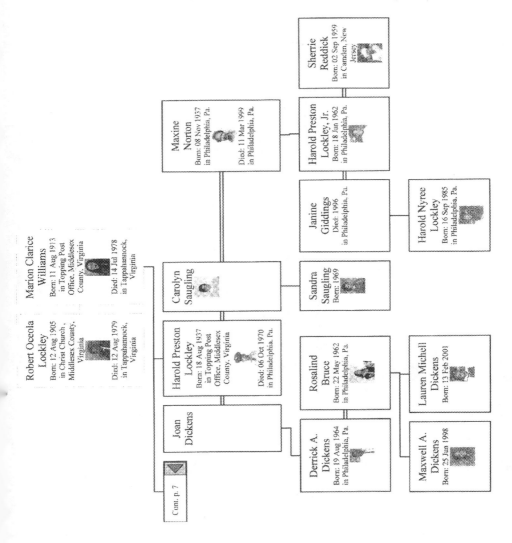

Descendants of Lorenzo D. Robinson

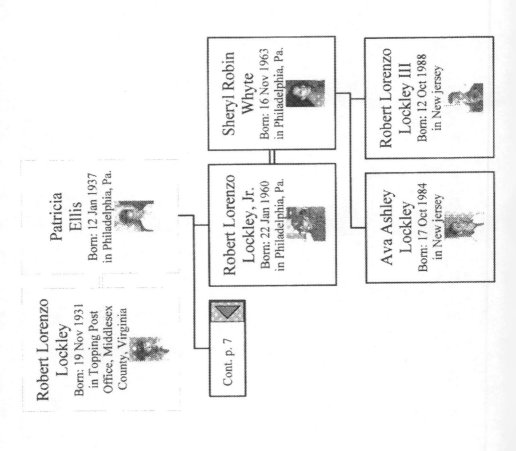

Descendants of Lorenzo D. Robinson

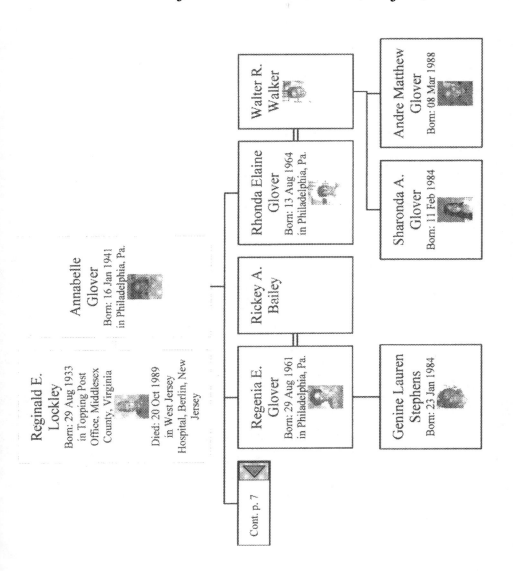

Descendants of Lorenzo D. Robinson (12 of 13)

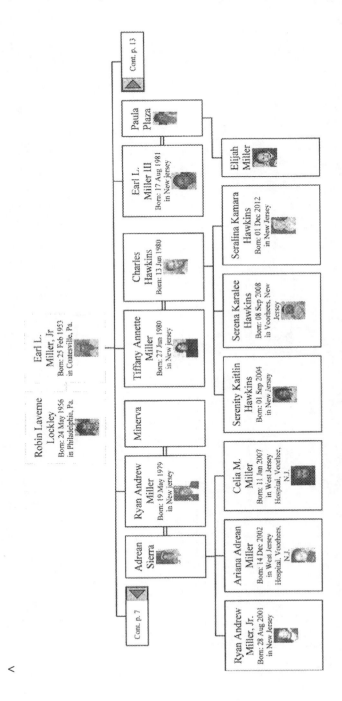

Descendants of Lorenzo D. Robinson

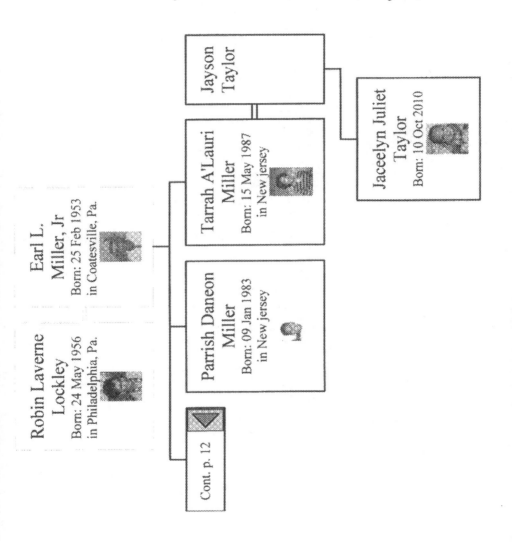

ARCHIBALD ROBINSON 1836

Archibald Robinson was the oldest child of Lorenzo Dow Robinson and his first wife Betty. He was first married to Marion Hodgess on December 24, 1857. No children were born of this union. When the 1860 Federal Census of King & Queen County was taken he was married to Maria Hudgins the sister of his father's second wife Martha Susan Hudgins. Sometime in 1861 during the Civil War he was taken from his home by a confederate enrolling officer and taken to work on the fortifications at Gloucester Point, Va. He stated that he did not return to King & Queen County until sometime in 1863. For his service he was paid 50 cents a day plus rations. In 1864 he was living on his 60 Acre farm near the Court House in King & Queen County, Va., with his wife Maria when Union Troops under the command of General Sheridan who were stationed in the area raided his farm for items needed for the troops. Under normal circumstances each military unite had a quartermaster who was responsible for securing supplies that were needed to sustain the troops. This Unit had none. An Act of Congress was passed on March 3, 1871 to set up a Commissioners of Claims to reimburse citizens who suffered these types of abuses during the Civil War.

Archibald Robinson filed his claim on June 26, 1872 for the following items taken from his farm: I horse, 25 bushels of corn, 150 pounds of Bacon and two Barrels of salted fish. When I read this claim I could not help but wonder if they left enough for the family to eat. His claim for $220.50 was reduced to $165.50 and approved on December 8 1873, no interest. On the back of his claim the following was written in ink, Good Union Man. (see appendix #2)

The 1870 and 1880 Agriculture Schedules for the County of King & Queen, Va. shows that Archie as he was know was still operating a small productive farm.

1870 Agriculture Schedule

County/State	King & Queen Co, VA
District	Stevensville
Page	
NARA M#	
Owner/Agent/Mgr	Archibald Robinson
Row #	

Description	Col	Value	Unit
Improved Land	2	30	Acres
Woodland	3	30	Acres
Other unimproved land	4		Acres
Present value	5	$300	
Farm implements/machinery value	6	$10	
Amt wages pd incl board	7	$50	
Horses	8		
Mules and Asses	9		
Milk cows	10	1	
Working cows	11	3	
Other cattle	12	3	
Sheep	13		
Swine	14	5	
Value all livestock	15	$150	
Spring wheat	16		Bu
Winter wheat	17	10	Bu
Rye	18	17	Bu
Indian corn	19	120	Bu
Oats	20		Bu
Barley	21		Bu
Buckwheat	22		Bu
Rice	23		Lbs
Tobacco	24		Lbs
Cotton (450# bales)	25		Bales
Wool	26		Lbs
Peas and beans	27		Bu
Irish potatoes	28		Bu
Sweet potatoes	29		Bu
Orchard products value	30	$	
Wine	31		Gals
Market Garden Produce	32	$	
Butter	33		Lbs
Cheese	34		Lbs
Milk sold	35		Gals
Hay	36		Tons
Clover seed	37		Bu
Grass seed	38		Bu
Hops	39		Lbs
Hemp	40		Tons
Flax	41		Lbs
Flax seed	42		Bu
Silk cocoons	43		Lbs
Maple sugar	44		Lbs
Cane sugar (1000 Lb Hhds)	45		Hhds
Molasses	46		Gals
Bees wax	47		Lbs
Honey	48		Lbs
Forest products	49	$	
Home manufactures	50	$	
Animals slaughtered/sold	51	$	
Value all farm production	52	$	

All rights reserved ©2007 J. Mark Lowe

1870 Agriculture Schedule - Archilbald Robinson

1880 Agriculture Schedule

County/State: King + Queen County, VA **District:** 39
Owner/Agent/Mgr: Archie Robinson

Description	Col	Value	Description	Col	Value	Description	Col	Value	Description	Col	Value
Owner	2	Acres	Other Cows	27		Barley – Crop	53	Bu	Maple Molasses	79	Gals
Rents for Fixed Money	3	Acres	Calves dropped	28		Buckwheat – Area	54	Acres	Pulse; Cow Peas	80	Bu
Rents for Share of Product	4	Acres	Cattle purchased	29		Buckwheat – Crop	55	Bu	Beans, Dry	81	Bu
Tilled, incl fallow & grass in rotation	5	Acres 55	Cattle sold living	30		Indian Corn – Area	56	Acres	Irish Potatoes – Area	82	Acres 1/2
Perm. Pastures, orchards, vineyards	6	Acres	Cattle slaughtered	31		Indian Corn – Crop	57	Bu	Irish Potatoes – Crop	83	Bu 50
Woodland & forest	7	Acres 7	Cattle died, strayed	32		Oats – Area	58	Acres	Sweet Potatoes – Area	84	Acres 1/4
Other unimproved	8	Acres	Milk sold or sent for Cheese	33	Lbs 50	Oats – Crop	59	Bu	Sweet Potatoes – Crop	85	Bu 20
Value, Farm, land, fences & buildings	9	$ 300	Butter produced on farm	34	Lbs	Rye – Area	60	Acres	Tobacco – Area	86	Acres
Farm implements & machinery value	10	$ 20	Cheese produced on farm	35	Gals 6	Rye – Crop	61	Bu	Tobacco – Crop	87	Lbs
Livestock value	11	$ 150	Sheep on hand June 1, 1880	36	6	Wheat – Area	62	Acres	Apples – Area	88	Acres
Bldg & repairs in 1879	12	$	Lambs dropped	37		Wheat – Crop	63	Bu	Apples- Trees	89	20
Fertilizer in 1879	13	$	Lambs purchased	38	1	Cotton – Area	64	Acres	Apples	90	Bu 20
Wages for farm labor incl board	14	$ 80	Lambs sold live	39	1	Cotton – Bales	65		Peach – Area	91	Acres
Weeks hired labor (White) & housewk	15		Sheep/lambs slaughtered	40		Flax – Area	66	Acres	Peach Trees	92	75
Weeks hired labor (Colored) & housewk	16	150	Sheep/lambs killed by dogs	41		Flaxseed	67	Bu	Peaches	93	Bu 75
Value, farm product sold, used & on hand	17		Sheep/lambs died of disease	42	2	Flax Straw	68	Tons	Value Orchard Products	94	$ 40
Grass lands, mown	18	Acres	Sheep/lambs d. of weather stress	43	6	Flax Fiber	69	Lbs	Nurseries – Area	95	Acres
Grass lands, not mown	19	Acres	No. of Fleeces	44	10	Hemp – Area	70	Acres	Value of Nursery Produce	96	$
Hay harvest in 1879	20	Tons	Weight of Fleece	45	Lbs	Hemp – Crop	71	Tons	Vineyards – Area	97	Acres
Clover seed	21	Bu	Swine on hand June 1, 1880	46	7	Cane Sugar – Area	72	Acres	Grapes sold	98	Lbs
Grass seed	22	Bu 1	Barnyard Poultry June 1, 1880	47	10	Cane Sugar	73	Hhds	Wine made 1879	99	Gals
Horses	23		Other Poultry on hand	48	30	Cane Molasses	74	Gals	Value Garden Product sold	100	$
Mules & Asses	24	1	Eggs	49	Doz	Sorghum – Area	75	Acres	Honey	101	Lbs
Oxen	25	1	Rice 1879 – Area	50	Acres	Sorghum Sugar	76	Lbs	Wax	102	Lbs
Milk Cows	26	1	Rice – Crop	51	Bu	Sorghum Molasses	77	Gals	Amt of wood cut 1879	103	Cords 10
			Barley – Area	52	Acres	Maple Sugar	78	Lbs	Value of forest product sold/used	104	$ 20

1880 Agriculture Schedule - Archilbald Robinson

Both of Archibald Robinson's sons were registered for the World War 1 Draft.

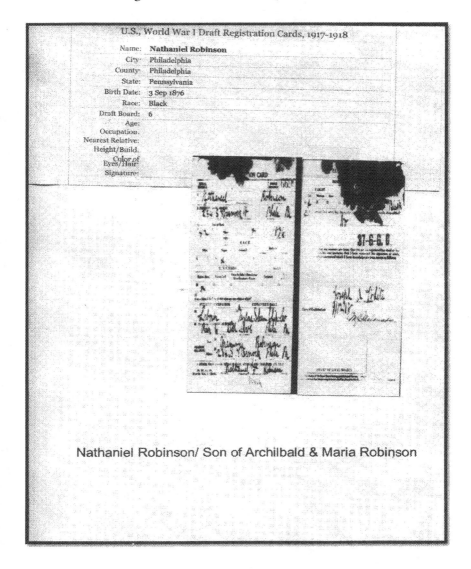

Nathaniel Robinson/ Son of Archilbald & Maria Robinson

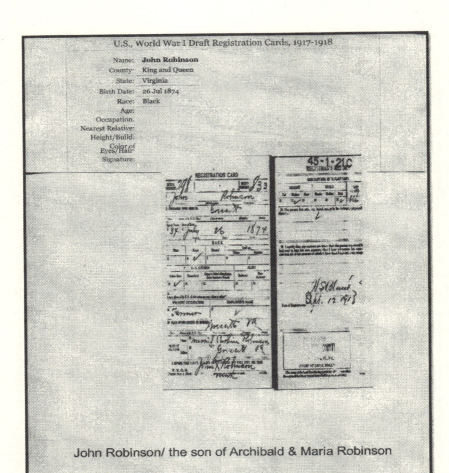

U.S., World War I Draft Registration Cards, 1917-1918

Name: **John Robinson**
County: King and Queen
State: Virginia
Birth Date: 26 Jul 1874
Race: Black
Age:
Occupation:
Nearest Relative:
Height/Build:
Color of Eyes/Hair:
Signature:

John Robinson/ the son of Archibald & Maria Robinson

VIRGINIA ROBINSON 1880 – 1951

Virginia Moved to Middlesex County, Virginia, where she married Robert Henry Lockley, on September 7, 1904. Robert purchased 6 Acres of land from his father on which he built the home for his family. By 1909 they had 3 children, Robert O. Lockley, Edith A. Lockley and Lorenzo C. Lockley. The 1910 Federal Census listed Virginia Lockley as a widow with 3 young children. Her husband died sometime before 1910.

During the early years when the Virginia Schools were segregated, most of the teachers were only required to take semi-normal courses. After completing the courses and the examination they were prepared for the classroom. This must have been the path that Virginia took to start her career as an educator.

Although the constitutional convention in 1867-68 did mandate free public schools the stipulation requiring integrated schools was deleted. The state never funded the schools adequately, and when money was appropriated, black schools got only a small portion of what was due them. In Middlesex and other rural counties across the state, no public funds were made available for black schools in the first few years after the Civil War. The same post-war groups of blacks who came together at crossroads communities to build churches and lodges also erected school houses. In some instances, the churches doubled as school houses, and the preachers were also the teachers.

My Ladys Bridge School

The first school that Virginia Robinson taught at was My Lady's Bridge School. This two room school was built on two acres of land purchased by Calvary Baptist Church. Other teachers were Alberta Harris, Daisey Perkins, Claudia Smith, Mary Duster and Rev. G.S. Russell. This school was destroyed by fire in 1926.

Continuing to move forward, in 1926, the patron of the Calvary community purchased three acres of land and built a three-room consolidated school. Funds for the school were raised by the community and matched by the Julius Rosenwald Fund, established by Sears, Roebuck and Company, to build schools for blacks in the south. This school was named Mill Road School. Some of their teachers were, Rev. O.M. Thomas, John Smith, Rev. Seebreeze, General Johnson, Edwardine Robinson, Thea Lockley Polson, Malissie Jackson, Christine Ferguson and Virginia Robinson Lockley Harris. This school also suffered the fate of the earlier school that was destroyed by fire. Virginia Robinson Lockley was no longer a widow; she had married Joseph Huck Harris on April 8, 1916. She had a young son, Bernard U. Harris.

The Pine Grove School was built on land donated by Thomas G. Jones in 1885. The school was located outside the town of Urbanna, Va. Originally a one room school, it was later became a two room school, and the school term was lengthened to cover the months of September to June. Teachers who taught at Pine Gove included Rosa Carter, Machie Kidd Rawley, Corneius Davis, Mr. Gallup, Hella Tabb, Butler Harris, Constance L. White, Otelia Payne, Gwendolyn Robinson, Mr. Seebreeze, Lucretia Carter Robinson, Rev. J Lewis, Julia Robinson, Naomi Harris, Sally Wood, Colby Rawley, Jerry Sutherlin, Wilma Jenkins Powell and Esther Morris. Pine Grove closed its doors as a school in 1950. This is the last school to employ Virginia Robinson Lockley Harris as a teacher.

ROBERT OCEOLA LOCKLEY 1905 – 1979

Robert was the oldest child of Virginia Robinson and Robert Henry Lockley. After the death of his father, his mother divided the 6 acres of land on which their home was located, equally between her three children. Since Robert was the only child who had children, he received that part of the land on which the home place was located. At the time of this division Robert was married to Marion Claurice Williams.

They had married on September 21, 1930 and were the parents of three sons.

In 1937 the home place needed some roof repairs, so Robert moved his young family to Philadelphia, Pa. The family stayed with one of his mothers older sisters (Mary Johnson) until he became employed.

He felt that he could earn money faster in Pennsylvania than he could in Middlesex County, Va. He got a job and moved his family to their own apartment. By the time he had saved enough money to repair the home place, his three sons were in school.

So the family decided that it was better to educate the children in the Philadelphia, Pa. public schools rather than the segregated schools of Virginia.

Claurice graduated from Cartier School of Beauty Culture in June, 1958. Becoming a licensed beautician, she also worked as Model for the Cromartie Modeling Guild, modeling for the Arlene Tooks Dress Shop and others in Philadelphia, Pa.

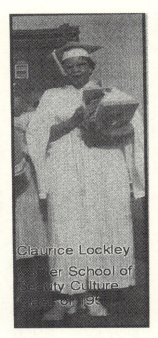

As time passed Robert and his wife decided to tear down the old house rather than repairing it and start building a new house that would be ready for their retirement. Working hard and putting the pieces together piece by piece they were able to build their new home and spend summers there during their vacations. During their retirement they enjoyed entertaining friends and family. Their home was a place everyone looked forward to visiting

This house was built by Robert Oceola Lockley to replace the old house that he inherited. It was ready for his retirement. Photo taken in 1958

Their three sons Robert Lorenzo Lockley, Reginald Elwood Lockley, and Harold Elwood Lockley would join them with their own families during the summer. Robert and his wife were able to accomplish their dream of returning to a place they loved so much in 1974. They were very proud of their sons; all three served their country by serving in the military during the 1950's, Robert & Reginald in the United States Air force, and Harold in the United States Army. After their military service they became honest hard working citizens.

They renewed their Christian commitment to Grafton Baptist Church, Hatfield, Va., during these years. Claurice sang on the choir and participated in many other church activities. Failing health began to become a fact of life. Claurice died in 1978 and Robert in 1979 almost a year to the day after his wife.

ROBERT LORENZO LOCKLEY 1931

Robert Lorenzo Lockley

After graduating from High School in June of 1950 I worked for a short time at a garment factory before joining the United States Air Force in May of 1951. After 8 weeks of basic training I was sent to North Dakota State School of Science, Wahpeton, North Dakota along with 49 other Airman to be trained as military clerks. This training included military correspondence, typing, morning reports, dewy decimal filing system, etc. After successfully completing the training I was sent to my permanent duty station, Chanute Air Force Base, Rantoul, Illinois. I joined the Air Force to see the world so after establishing myself as a clerk in the office of the base Provost Marshall I requested a transfer hoping to be sent to some nice duty station overseas.

As a result of this request I was sent to Elmendorf Air force Base, Anchorage, Alaska, as a youngster growing up in

Base Gym Elmendorf Air Force Base, Anchorage Alaska
Robert Lorenzo Lockley Scoring 2 of 32 against the Elks

Philadelphia I had become a skilled basketball player, playing in several amateur leagues around the city. Alaska didn't offer much for a young man to do during the short summers and long winter nights. So I joined the Elmendorf Commandos, the base basketball team. The team played in the Anchorage City-Military League. I became an outstanding player in the league and ended up with several college scholarship offers.

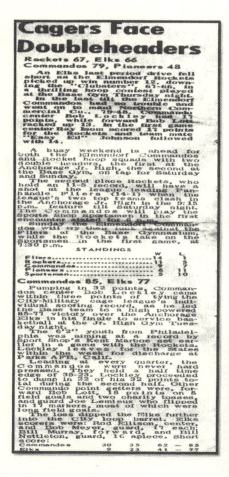

Rockets Take 2nd in City Loop
Commandos Succumb to Fliers

Sinking 29 points, forward "Easy Ed" Johnson led the Rockets to a 86-78 victory over the Sport Shop Sportsmen at the Base Gymnasium Thursday night, giving the Elmendorf team undisputed possession of second place in the City-Military League.

In the second tilt, the Commandos led the league leading Panhandle Fliers 43-39 briefly in the third stanza but ran out of gas during the final quarter as the Fliers picked up their 12th straight victory, winning 59-52.

City League Cage Schedule
Saturday, Dec. 19, Jr. High Gym—Elks vs. Panhandle, 9:15 p.m.
Tuesday, Dec. 22, Jr. High Gym—Northern Commercial vs. Sportsmen, 8 p.m.; Panhandle vs. Elks, 9:15 p.m.
Sunday, Dec. 27, Base Gym—Commandos vs. Rockets, 7:30 p.m.

Commandos 82, Sports Shop 68

Turning on a crushing fourth period drive, the Elmendorf Commandos played their best ball of the year in whipping the Sports Shop Sportsmen 82-68, in a City League hoop tilt played at the Base Gymnasium last Saturday night.

The Base team was dragging at the intermission but stamina in the last half, hot shooting of Cpl. Bob Lockley and appearance of Adie Jimerson, forward, and Joe Lemieux, guard, gave Elmendorf the victory.

For the Shop, Ken Norton, forward and Commander, with 22 points each, scoring combined with 17 defensive backboard work. Cpl. Lockley, the backboard of the half.

Lockley, a 6'2" flash from Texas, potted against Big Bill Nye, former University of Nine, Nine times during the last quarter alone, putting on the smooth offensive display.

Cpl. Cumming, former great Bob Loth, X'. Lewiston who gave the Commandos a hold for second place with their Nine point win over the Junior College Rockets, who lost to the Panhandle Fliers the very night Score:
Sports Shop   17 31 39 — 82

Commandos 78, Pioneers 74

Coming from behind, the Elmendorf Commandos nipped the N C Co. Pioneers, 78-74, in a thrilling hoop tilt played at the Anchorage Jr. High Gym Tuesday night.

Both quints played the fast break in a game that saw few shots miss their mark during the first half. Only one free throw was missed out of 13 attempts during the first two frames.

The Pioneers took the lead as the game opened and led the pair through most of the first tilt with the Elmendorf Cmdy in the up several times but never able to stay ahead.

They trailing 43-39, they went into a low dict when Jimerson, guard Joe Lemieux took the ball on a long pass down court, dribbled up under the basket and forged it in.

The second half also see-sawed, but this time the Pioneers were chasing the Commandos.

Bob Lockley, the Commandos push shot artist, led all scorers with 26 points. Center Bill Meyers led the Pioneers at the basket with 21 points.

Rockets 76, Elks 48

The Elmendorf Rockets cemented the Elks further in the City League cellar as they stomped the downtown aggregation 76-48 in a basketball game played at the Junior High Gym Tuesday evening.

Trailing 14-12 at the end of the first stanza, the Rockets opened up an eight point spread at halftime and went on to bury the Elks during the last two frames.

Center Charlie Klawicki, led the Rockets during the second half and wound up with 20 points, which most of the Rocket first five points on the farewell Ed Johnson and guard Bob Sneller each had 13 points apiece, and Bob McDonald, forward, had 12.

Rocket scoring was evenly distributed as the whole team got into the scoring column. Forward Gene Mullinax accounted for eight, Ray Lawrence, guard, six, and Ace Johnson-DeGrassi, guard, six, and newcomer Dick Mahar, two.

Larry Sundberg provided the lone needle for the Elks, racking up 18 points. Score:
Rockets   12 22 20 — 76
Elks

Front row: Maurice King, Blaine Hollinger, Mark Boxberger, Dallas Dobbs, John Parker, Ron Johnston, and Bob Lockley. Second row: Bill Brainard, Jim Toft, Lee Green, Dr. Allen, Lew Johnson, Gary Mowry, Al Hurst, Dick Borgen (manager) Third row: Dean Nesmith (trainer), Bob McMichael, John Flanagan, Jack Eskridge, Gene Elston, Harry Jett, Eddie Dater, and Dick Harp.

As fate would have it, the Korean War ended during my tour, creating a surplus in my career field. The Air Force decided to release 5 Airman in my career field from active duty to the inactive reserves. Those who applied for early release had to justify their request. Having a scholarship in hand must have been high on their list, because I was granted an early release. I was transferred to Parks Air Force Base, in Oakland California for my discharge in May 1954.

After I received my mustering out pay I stopped at at the University of Kansas Athletic Office to fill out the necessary papers, and made all the arrangement to enroll in the fall semester September 1954. Before I left Lawrence Kansas for my home in Philadelphia I honored the request of my coach in Anchorage by visiting with his family. His father was George Docking, Jr., President and owner of the Lawrence Kansas Bank. Mr. Docking had his son Robert Docking, Vice President.

Take me to his home for lunch then to Kansas City, Mo to catch my train to Philadelphia, Pa.

In order to stay busy until it was time to leave for school I took the Philadelphia City Clerk Typist examination. After passing the examination I was hired by the City of Philadelphia and assigned to work as a clerk Typist for the Social Work Department at Holmesburg Prison. I worked there from May 31, 1954 until it was time to leave for school; I think I resigned in mid August. Scholarship athletes were required to arrive early for registration.

During my freshman year the Big Eight conference didn't allow freshman to compete in athletics. We were supposed to take that first year to adjust to College life and concentrate on our academic goals. After completing my freshman year I returned to my Home in Philadelphia and started work at my summer job.

Before returning to school I decided to get married and take my new wife to Kansas with me. I married Patricia Ellis that august and arranged housing in Lawrence, Kansas near the campus. When my wife became pregnant I sent her back to Philadelphia to await the birth of our first child. I arrived in Philadelphia after completing my sophomore year to be greeted by my wife and new daughter, Robin Laverne Lockley.

Robert Lorenzo Lockley and 1st wife Patricia Ellis

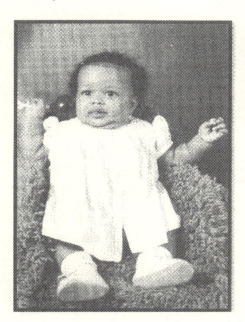

Now that I had a family to support I didn't return to Kansas for my junior year. The part time summer job became a permanent full time job.

Over the next four years I worked at the U S. Post Office where I played on their Basketball team, before becoming a licensed Insurance agent for North Carolina Mutual Insurance Company.

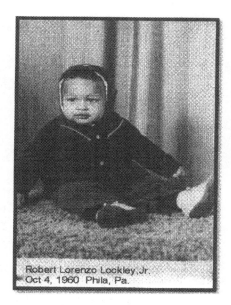

By this time my family had increased with the birth of my second child, born in 1960, Robert Lorenzo Lockley JR.

In 1960 my wife and I decided that another environment would be better for our relationship and that of our two children, so we moved to Los Angeles, California. I initially worked at the US Post Office in Los Angeles as a clerk before transferring to the US Immigration Department were I started as a clerk but later became Supervisor of the Visa Processing Unit. After some ups and downs in my personal life we moved back to Philadelphia in 1963.

I was able to transfer to the Veterans Administration Hospital, Philadelphia, Pa. initially as a Voucher Examiner/Agent Cashier. After promotions that involved stints as a payroll clerk, accounting technician and Assistant Supervisor Administrative Services. I started looking for a position that could be ideal before retirement would become a reality. My divorce from Patricia Ellis became final in 1968.

I set my sights on positions in the Washington, DC area where the headquarters of my then employer was located. I was hired in 1976 as a Systems and Procedures Analyst, in the Finance Service, Comptroller Veterans Administration. I was member of a staff of 8 other Analyst, who were replacing the old Audit teams that travelled the country performing audits at the 200 plus Hospitals and Regional offices thru out the country, Hawaii, Italy, Philippines and Puerto Rico.

Each Analyst on our staff was assigned a certain number of facilities. The financial records of all facilities were available to our staff thru various computer systems. If a problem is identified the supervisor determines who or how many Analyst are needed to resolve the problem. There were times when a Hospital Director would request that a member of our staff be sent to his facility to resolve a problem not identified in the finance records. The Veterans Administration Comptroller Office was also responsible for the Austin Texas Data Processing Center, where all payroll checks are processed and the Hines Data Processing Center, Hines, Ill where all veterans' benefits checks are processed. After years on the staff I witnessed the transition as new employees replaced the old. I was usually assigned the task of taking new employees on their first assignments to instruct them in proper protocol when visiting a facility.

I had been offered the position as Finance Officer at facilities I had helped, but turned down such offers until I was offered the position of Finance Officer of the Veterans Hospital and the Regional Office, San Juan, Puerto Rico. I was allowed to spend two weeks at the Hospital during the fiscal year closing (1983) before making up my mind. Although the finance operation for a Hospital and Regional Office are different I decided to accept the job. I called my girlfriend and told her of my decision. I married Raquel Coello on October 8, 1983 and reported to San Juan later that same month.

Robert Lorenzo Lockley and 2nd wife Raquel Coello

My wife was happy to be in Puerto Rico the country of her birth. We were able to spend weekends visiting her parents and her 7 siblings in Quebradillas, about 82 miles from San Juan.

Raquel, siblings & parents

Robert, Raquel, parents Manolo & Aleja

1762 Alcala Street
Colege Park
Rio Piedras, Puerto Rico

Robert harvesting Bananas from back yard of Alcala St. Home.

Robert Cleaning Pool at Alcala St. House, San Juan, Puerto Rico

To operate the Finance Office at both facilities I had a staff of 23 at the Hospital and 14 at the Regional Office, this included an Assistant Finance Officer at each facility.

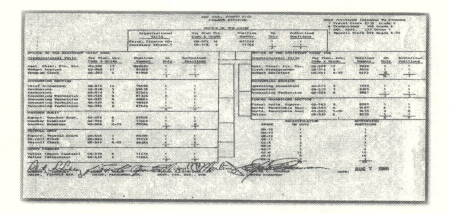

I was greeted with a warm reception by all members of the Finance Staff. I started my new job as Chief of the Finance Division with a great feeling of acceptance.

In each rating periods that I spent in this position I received an outstanding rating by the Hospital Director, Mr. Charles Freeman and the Director of the Regional Office, Mr. Angel S. Colazo.

As I was approaching the end of my 3 year tour of duty, my wife was expecting our first child. It became important that I received another assignment before her pregnancy reached the point that she could not fly. There were no other GS-14 Finance Officer positions available, so I requested reassignment to Veterans Administration Central Office, Office of Budget & Finance Washington, D.C. I was reassigned as Supervisory Administrative Officer on September 28, 1986 at the lower grade GS-13 with no lost in pay. My wife and I were elated about out good fortune.

We bought our new home and moved in, prior to the birth of our daughter Ashley Clarice Lockley born December 24, 1986.

Home in Upper Marlboro, Md.

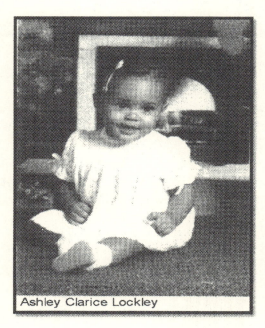

Ashley Clarice Lockley

About 7 or 8 months after my return to Finance Service, my new supervisor, Office of the Director, Myrta Sale was having some staffing problems and needed to move some staff around.

To assist in resolving the problem I agreed to relinquish the Administrative Officer Position and be reassigned to the Administrative Fiscal Policy Division on July 3, 1988, as a Systems and Procedures Analyst. It turned out to be a great job. I was involved in coordinating work with other agencies, interpretation of federal travel regulations, maintenance of division policy manuals and handbooks. As an ex-Finance Officer with Hospital Finance experience I was invited to participate in trips to Veterans Administration Hospitals and Regional Offices to conduct administrative reviews. The teams always wanted me to take care of the finance review. I worked in this capacity until I retired in December 1989.

Although my family had moved from Middlesex County Va., to Philadelphia, Pa., when I was 6 years old, we never spent a summer in Philadelphia. After the last day of school in June, my father always drove us to Middlesex County, Va., where we spent every summer. During the early years we spent the summer at my grandmother's home where my brothers and I were born.

This is the Home of my Grandmother Lucy Griffin-Williams. The birth place of Robert Lorenzo Lockley, Reginald Elwood Lockley and Harold Preston Lockley the sons of Rocert Oceola Lockley and Marian Claurica Williams-Lockley.

My mother didn't work when my brothers and I were young so she was always there with us. We were joined at the house by my mother's sister Eva and her two daughters Doris and Joline, from Baltimore, Md., and mother's brother Robert, his wife Gladys and their daughter Sarah, also from Baltimore. My father always left the car for our use during the summer. He would return and spend his vacation with us and return to Philadelphia. At the end of August was always a sad time, father always came to take us back to Philadelphia in time for the start of school.

During those summers we would sometimes use the car for shopping trips, however there were times when we used Uncle Robert's boat. In the area where we lived most of my relative made their living by farming, fishing, carrying fishing parties, Oystering in the winter and crabbing. Therefore just about every family owned a work boat. For all the children shopping by boat was one of the highlights of the summer. My grandmother's property was located on Whiting Creek so we had our own Warf where my uncle kept his boat. All the adults including my grandmother were loaded on the boat with the children, we then traveled out of the creek into the Rappahannock River, and then north to the Town of Urbanna, Va., while my uncle refueled the boat the rest of us walked up the hill to the shopping area.

Reginald Elwood Lockley and his mom Claurice Williams-Lockley on the boat of his uncle Robert Williams. This is the boat used for some shoping trips to Urbanna, Va & Lancaster County, Va.

On our return home we always anchored in the river for some fishing. During those years (1940's) we would catch a whole tub full of fish in less than an hour. By the time we arrived back at the Warf the adults would have cleaned the fish.

For my brothers and other youngsters who grew up in this type of environment, activities surrounding the water became like our playground. Everyone learned to swim, without a swimming coach. We were taught to respect the water, so in all my years spent in and around water no one was ever hurt and no one drowned.

Whiting Creek, Middlesex County, Va. Left to Right, John Davenport (Cousin), Robert Lorenzo Lockley, Reginald Elwood Lockley, Harold Preston Lockley. This was our swimming Pool every summer

It became my dream as a youngster to own my own boat. I made that childhood dream come true when I purchased my boat in 1982.

A 1981, 25 foot Viking Fly bridge Cruiser, Fiberglass, 260 Mercury Inboard, and Fuel Capacity: 75 main/15 reserve, Water Capacity: 30 Gallons, Am/Fm Stereo throughout, Depth Finder and many other extras. I named her Princess, my nickname for Raquel, who was with me when I picked up the boat at the middle river marina near Baltimore, Md. We left middle river and traveled down the Chesapeake Bay, under the Chesapeake Bay Bridge to Breezy Point Marina where we docked at my boat slip that I had already rented in anticipation of our trip.

Lockley's Marina, Rappahannock River, Chesapeake Bay, Breezy Point, Md

During my Assignment to Puerto Rico I stored the boat at the Edgewater Marina, Edgewater, Md. When I returned in 1986 I moved the boat to the Urbanna Yachting Center, Urbanna, Va. Urbanna is close to my home in Middlesex, County just off the Rappahannock River, in familiar surroundings. Before making the permanent move we made several week end trips to our Virginia home, sometime spending a night or two on the boat at the Lockley's Marina.

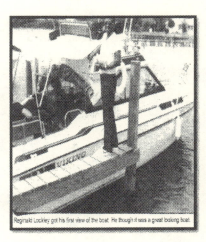

Reginald Lockley got his first view of the boat. He though it was a great looking boat.

Raquel & Anthony wave to well wishers on shore as we leave Lockleys Marina, Va. Returning to home port of breezy Point, Md. Capt Robert Lockley, Raquel Coello, Anthony and Charlene Coello.

My children are now grown with families of their own. I have 9 grandchildren and 11 great-grandchildren. Life has been good to me; I have been retired 25 years.

Robin Lockley-Miller daughter of Robert Lorenzo Lockley and her family. Left to Right: Tiffany, Ryan, Earl Jr., Parish and Tarah.

son of Robert Lorenzo Lockley and his family. Left to Right: Robert Lorenzo Lockey Jr., Robert III, Ava, Sheryl

Daughter of Robert Lorenzo Lockley and her family. Left to Right: Kevin Hall holding Manolo, Cheyanne and Ashley.

My wife and I enjoyed spending time in the summer at our Virginia home.

Home in Locust Hill, Va

We always enjoyed cruising to the Caribbean, making sure that Puerto Rico is on the schedule so that my wife could visit with her family.

Grandeur of the Seas, at San Juan

Robert & Raquel at dinner

Robert on deck

Robert & Raquel

Robert & Raquel in Haiti

Descendants of Robert Lorenzo Lockley (1 of 5)

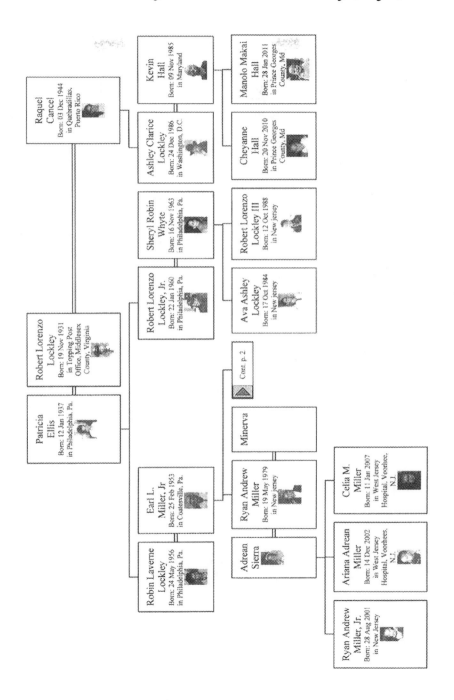

Descendants of Robert Lorenzo Lockley (2 of 5)

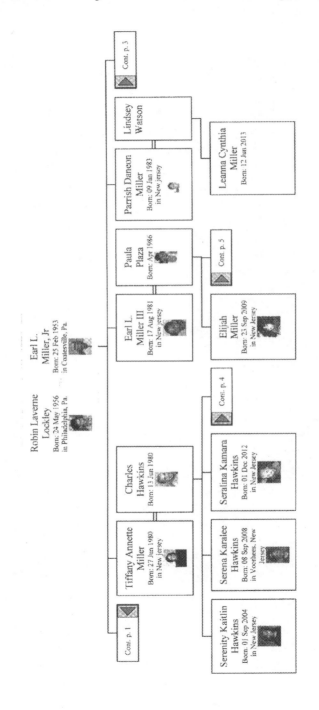

Descendants of Robert Lorenzo Lockley (3 of 5)

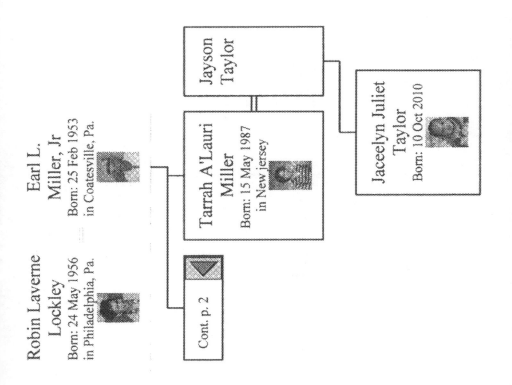

Descendants of Robert Lorenzo Lockley (4 of 5)

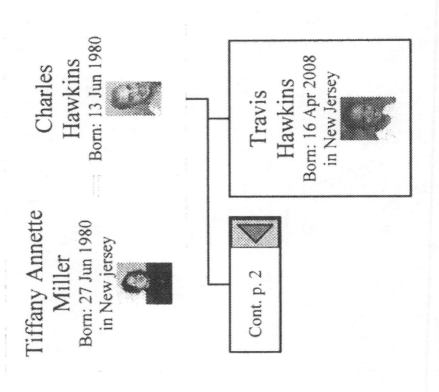

Descendants of Robert Lorenzo Lockley (5 of 5)

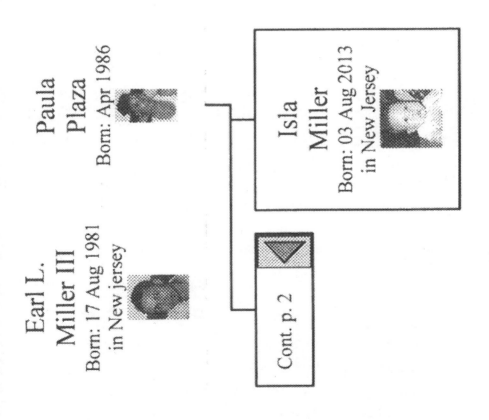

REGINALD ELWOOD LOCKLEY
1933 – 1989

Reginald Left High School and joined the United States Air Force December 11, 1951. After completing his basic training at Samson Air Force Base, New York, he was sent to Amarillo Air Force Base, Texas from July 1952 to October 1952 for technical training as an Aircraft Maintenance Mechanic.

Upon successfully completing his training he was sent to his permanent duty station, Tyndall, Air Force Base, Jacksonville, Florida. There he was assigned to 3631st Flight Line Maintance Squadron as an A&E Mechanic.

Records indicate that he was an outstanding Aircraft Mechanic. He Remained at Tyndall Air Force Base until completion of his four year enlistment. He received an Honorable release from active service December 10, 1955. After serving the required four additional years in the Air Force Reserves, he received his Honorable Discharge on December 10, 1959.

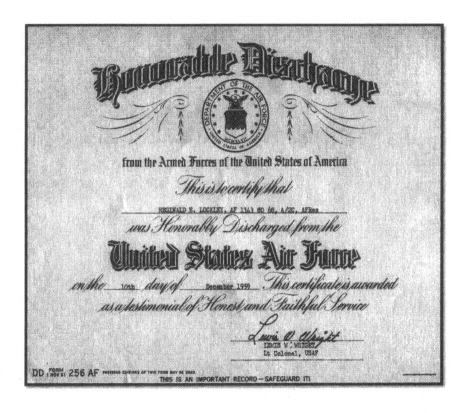

Reginald was an avid fight fan. He could tell you who the best fighters in every weight class were. He and several of his friends attended fights on a regular basis at the Horizon and Philadelphia Arena. These were Philadelphia's answer to New York's Madison Square Garden. Unlike his brothers Robert and Harold who were involved in basketball as participants. Reginald would only attend games as a fan. He loved to participate in Bowling. He was a member of at least 2 bowling teams. His favorite team was the VPA Club team. Because of his popularity with  the VPA Club membership committee I (Robert) received a lifetime membership to the club at no cost.

Reginald took the Post Office examination and started working as a Clerk shortly after his discharge from the Air Force. After passing all the Philadelphia city schemes required by the Post Office, he became a unit clerk working the night shift. He always said that working this shift allowed you to do your job with little interference for supervisors. During the day shift there were as many supervisors as regular employees.

Reginald was never married so in the mid 1980's when there was a recurrence of a health issue that was terminal he called to ask me to help him get his affairs in order. At the time I was residing in Maryland and he was in New Jersey. At his request I filed all the necessary documents with the Post Office for his retirement, had an attorney prepare his will and Power of Attorney. Unfortunately he didn't live long enough to receive any of his retirement benefits. With the years he spent in the Air force and his Post Office Years he had over 33 years of Federal Service.

Before he became ill Reginald had selected the plans for a house he planned to build in Virginia. His plan was to sell his house in Sicklerville, N.J. and use the proceeds for his dream house. Virginia, where he was born was where he had hoped to spend his retired years fishing; crabbing and visiting with the many relatives we had living in the area. Unfortunately some of the best plans made by man are never realized.

Home of Reginald Elwood Lockley at the time of his death Sicklerville, N.J.

Back of Sicklerville, N.J. Home

As he had requested I buried him in the family plot at Grafton Baptist Church, Hartfield, Va. the church were our ancestors had attended for generations. He is near his mother, father and our youngest brother Harold Preston Lockley along with many other family members. Although he was never married he is survived by four children.

Charosangina Morrow, Daughter of Reginald Elwood Lockley

[caption illegible], Daughter of Reginald Elwood Lockley

Kyle Richardson Son of Reginald Elwood Lockley

Rhonda Glover daughter of Reginald Elwood Lockley

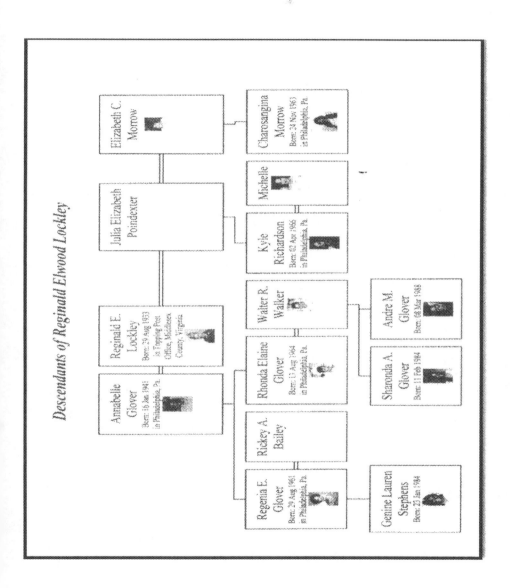
Descendants of Reginald Elwood Lockley

HAROLD PRESTON LOCKLEY 1937 – 1970

He Graduated from Simon Gratz High School in 1955.

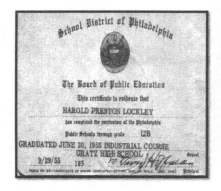

Harold Preston Lockley - High School Prom

Harold was drafted into the United States Army. After completing his basic training in South Carolina he was reassigned with his unit to Orleans, France. Since no war was going on during his tour of duty, most of his units time was spent training, cleaning equipment and participating in war games.

Harold Preston Lockley on the Army Post, Orleans, France

During his spare time during the winter months he played basket in the Garrison Basketball League for USAG, Company, and his military unit team. This gave him an opportunity to travel to Norway, Switzerland and several other European countries.

USAG Basketball League, Orleans, France. Pfc Ron Shirley of the 439th Company on the left goes up with Pvt. Harold Lockley of USAG Company. Tipoff opening game of season. The contest was won by 439th, 56-53.

Being so close to Paris made it possible to visit the Scenic sights of Paris and enjoy the night life that he said was second to none. According to Harold, French women made life in France a great experience.

He returned to the United States after completing his tour of duty and received an Honorable Discharge from the United States Army. He was reemployed at the factory where he worked as a Floor Supervisor prior to being drafted.

With employment secured he married in 1958 and settled into civilian life.

1958 wedding of Harold Preston Lockley & Maxine Norton, Robert Lorenzo Lockley, best man, Claurice Williams-Lockley, mother.

His family was saddened when he suddenly became Ill and died at age 33 in 1970.

He only had one son from his marriage, Harold Preston Lockley Jr. He had two other children, Sandra Saugling and Derrick A. Dickens.

Sandra Saugling Daughter of Harold Preston Lockley

Harold Preston Lockley Jr.

Derrick Dickens Son of Harold Preston Lockley

Descendants of Harold Preston Lockley

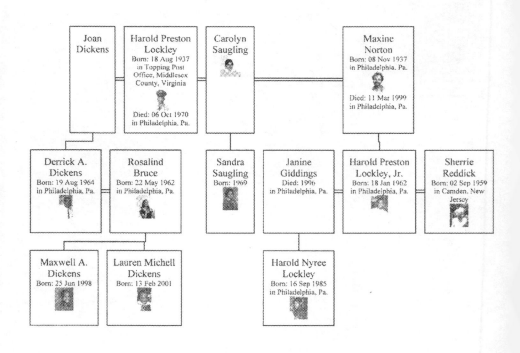

EDITH ALYCE LOCKLEY 1907 – 1976

Edith was the only daughter of Virginia Robinson and Robert Henry Lockley. Although, she was born in Middlesex County, Va., the records do not indicate that she ever attended public school there. Instead, she attended the public schools in Philadelphia, Pa. graduating from Joseph Hill School in 1924 and Roosevelt Junior High School in 1925. She completed her high school education at Hartshorn Memorial College High School, Richmond, Va., on June 5, 1928.

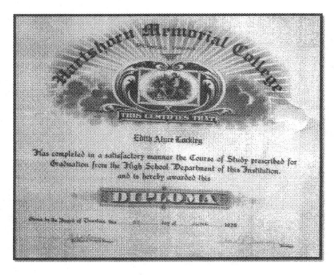

Edith's college career was as follows:

New York University N.Y. N.Y.	1928 - 1930 Transferred
Virginia Union University Richmond, Va.	1931 - 1933 Bachelor of Arts Degree
Fisk University Nashville Tenn.	1934 - 1935 Master (Sociology) *
University of Chicago, Chicago IL	1940 – 1942 Master (Social Work) *

These two degrees were earned on National Fellowships *

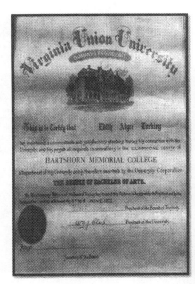
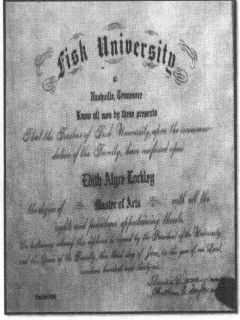

Although she was well educated she was some-what of a reformer. Therefore she sometimes met with resistance with some of her progressive ideas. Edith was also a pioneer in many respects being the first black female to be hired by some agencies. According to her records she was the first Medical Psychiatric Social Worker, at the Workers Compensation Bureau, New York Department of Labor. Edith spent 3 years as Social Worker (First Negro) at the New York State Department of Mental Hygiene, Albany, New York., (Rockland State Hospital, and Orangeburg, New York).

In addition to the positions identified in the above paragraph, Edith held a variety of other positions in the field of social work. Some listed in her resume were. Brooklyn Bureau of Social Service, Brooklyn Children's Aid Society, Brooklyn Training School & Home for girls, Pennsylvania Department of Public Assistance, Philadelphia, Pa. She ended her career with thirteen and 1/2 years with the State-Wide Family Court, as a Probation Officer, Office of Probation, New York City, N.Y. At the time of her death in 1976 she was certified by the University of the State of New York to practice Social Work independently as a profession.

Although both of her marriages ended in divorce Aunt Edith didn't have any children, so her attention was turned to her 3 nephews, my brothers Reginald Lockley, Harold Lockley and yours truly. She always said that we were different, and a lot was expected of us. She never gave us toys for Christmas; we could always expect the usual books.

Edith had her thesis written for her Master's Degree at Fisk University published by Vantage Press, Inc. The publication was dedicated to those who had made a difference in her life. The publication was titled Spiritualist Sect in Nashville.

This work is dedicated with gratitude, to the memory of those great, inspiring, and perceptive leaders and teachers who enriched my life by freeing my mind to share its exciting lessons constructively with my fellowman, especially:
My Mother: Mrs. Virginia Robinson Lockley Harris, Elementary School Principal and Teacher.
My Aunt: Mrs. Mary E. "Kitt" Robinson, Teacher, founder of the Home for Working Girls, Gtn., Philadelphia, and the first appointed church Social worker of that city.

Spiritualist Sect In Nashville

EDITH A. WHITE

It is noted that Dr. Robert E. Park, sociologist, author and professor in the Graduate School of Sociology at the University of Chicago, for his examination of the material and referring to her handling of the subject matter as the most brilliant witnessed by him in 20 years at the masters level.

At the time of her death in 1976 Edith had retired and was enjoying life at her home in Philadelphia, Pa.

Home of Edith in 1976
3526 Baring St
Phila, Pa.

According to her will, the Baring Street property was inherited by her nephew, Robert Lorenzo Lockley and his son Robert Jr, and daughter Robin.

LORENZA C. LOCKLEY 1909 - 1966

Lorenzo C. Lockley was one of three children born to Robert Henry Lockley and Virginia Robinson. His father died when he and his siblings were very young. His mother remarried and they moved into the home of her new husband, Joseph Huck Harris.

He always said that he was very unhappy living in the Harris home so he left home after the 7th grade and settled in Philadelphia, Pa. My father said that he told him that even after his death he never wanted to be buried in Virginia. He never visited his home in Virginia for the rest of his life, even thou his mother continued to live there and teach school. His older brother Robert O. Lockley married and lived there with his wife's family and sister Edith was sent to Philadelphia to live with her mother's sister Lillie Robinson Gordon. His mother had their original property which consisted of 5 Acres divided equally between the three siblings. The part of the property on which the house was situated went to Robert O. Lockley because he was the only child with children. Lorenzo and Edith were given the rest. Lorenzo never married or had children so he told his brother Robert that he could have his part of the land. Lorenzo and Edith preceded Robert O. Lockley in death, so Robert O's family ended up with the entire property.

When my father Robert O. moved his family to Philadelphia in 1937 we saw a lot of Uncle Lorenzo over the years. I remember him as being a very happy pleasant man, who was always very proud of his 3 nephews. We were always happy to see our uncle Lo as we called him. He worked in what they called in those days, Private Family as a Chauffeur, so he was always well dressed.

On July 5, 1943 he was drafted into the United States Army at Ft. Meade, Md. After his basic training he served in New Guinea and Luzon in the Philippine Islands. As a result of his military service he earned the Asia Pacific Service Medal with 2 bronze stars, Good conduct medal, Philippines Liberation Ribbon With 1 bronze star and the Victory Medal. As part of the demobilization he returned from overseas on December 8, 1945 and was given his Honorable Discharge on December 22, 1945.

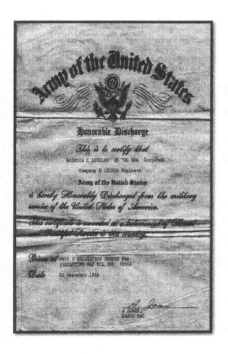
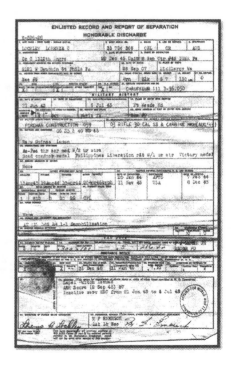

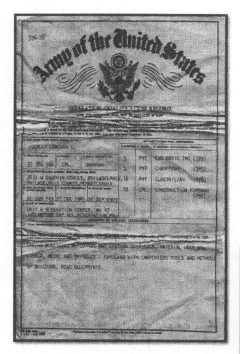
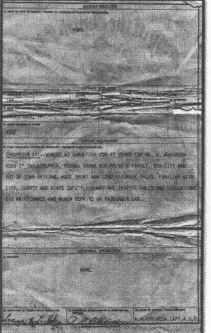

In his return Lorenzo worked as a Chauffeur for the rest of his working years.

Lorenzo C. Lockley   Chauffeur

He died at the Veterans Administration Hospital, Philadelphia, Pa. in 1966. At the time I was an employee there working in the Finance Department, which made it possible for me to spend time with him each day during his final days?

CHAPTER 6

ROSETTA ROBINSON 1815

Descendants of Rosetta Robinson

Generation 1

1. **Rosetta[1] Robinson** was born in 1815 in King & Queen County, Va.. She married **Benjamin A. Harris**. He was born in King & Queen County, Va.. She married **James Bluefoot**. He was born in 1822 in King & Queen County, Va.. She married **James Gatewood**.

   Benjamin A. Harris and Rosetta Robinson had the following children:

       i.   **Quitta[2] Harris** was born in 1847 in King & Queen County, Va.

       ii.   **Margarett Harris** was born in 1842 in King & Queen County, Va..

       iii.   **Calvert Harris** was born in 1841 in King & Queen County, Va..

James Bluefoot and Rosetta Robinson had the following children:

2.   i.   POLLY ANN^2 BLUEFOOT was born on 07 Apr 1853 in King & Queen County, Va.. She died on 12 Oct 1927 in King & Queen County, Va.. She married John Robert Jordan, son of George Jordan and Frances Williams on 26 Dec 1876 in Mt. Olivet Church, King & Queen County, Va.. He was born on 01 Feb 1853 in King & Queen County, Va.. He died on 26 Jun 1916 in King & Queen County, Va..

    ii.   ISIAH BLUEFOOT was born in 1857 in King & Queen County, Va.. He died in 1943 in King & Queen County, Va..

Generation 2

2. **Polly Ann[2] Bluefoot**(Rosetta[1] Robinson) was born on 07 Apr 1853 in King & Queen County, Va.. She died on 12 Oct 1927 in King & Queen County, Va.. She married John Robert Jordan, son of George Jordan and Frances Williams on 26 Dec 1876 in Mt. Olivet Church, King & Queen County, Va.. He was born on 01 Feb 1853 in King & Queen County, Va.. He died on 26 Jun 1916 in King & Queen County, Va..

Notes for Polly Ann Bluefoot:

Polly Ann Bluefoot used the surname of her step father James Gatewood on her marriage certificate for her marriage to John R. Jordan on Dec 26, 1876. I found no record of an adoption.

John Robert Jordan and Polly Ann Bluefoot had the following children:

3. i. **Rosie Jane[3] Jordan** was born on 10 Jan 1878 in King & Queen County, Va.. She died on 19 Jun 1936 in Little Plymouth, Va.. She married John Thomas Davenport, son of Joshua Davenport and Mary F. Kauffman on 15 Nov 1900 in King & Queen County, Va.. He was born in 1872 in King & Queen County, Va.. He died on 07 Nov 1933 in Little Plymouth, Va..

4. ii. **George Franklin Jordan** was born in Feb 1883 in King & Queen County, Va.. He died in Oct 1950 in Little Plymouth, Va.. He married (1) Sarah Collins, daughter of James Collins and Maggie Wyatt on 24 Apr 1913 in King & Queen County, Va.. She was born in 1893 in King & Queen County, Va.. He married Bertha Jackson Collins. She died in 1953 in King & Queen County, Va..

5.   iii.   JOHN KELLY JORDAN was born on 18 Feb 1885 in King & Queen County, Va.. He died in Apr 1963 in Stormont, Va.. He married Eva S. Morris, daughter of Noah Morris and Catherine in Sep 1914. She was born in 1894 in Middlesex County, Va.. She died in Mar 1972 in Middlesex County, Va..

6.   iv.   SAMUEL ISIAH JORDAN was born on 22 Feb 1891 in King & Queen County, Va.. He died on 09 Sep 1971 in Tappahannock, Va.. He married Elizabeth Miles, daughter of William Miles and Elnora Campbell on 20 Mar 1913 in King & Queen County, Va.. She was born on 22 Oct 1891 in Middlesex County, Va.. She died on 04 Jan 1993 in Tappahannock, Va..

7.   v.   ETHAN ALLEN JORDAN was born on 14 May 1896 in King & Queen County, Va.. He died on 22 Dec 1980 in King & Queen County, Va.. He married RUTH HOLMES. She died in 1964.

     vi.   JAMES ELIJAH JORDAN was born in 1880 in King & Queen County, Va.. He died on 25 Dec 1944 in Little Plymouth, Va.. He married Sarah Louise Collins, daughter of Leonidas Collins and Lucy Robinson on 04 Jun 1909 in King & Queen County, Va.. She was born in 1884 in King & Queen County, Va..

8.   vii.   WILLIAM THOMAS JORDAN was born on 15 May 1882 in King & Queen County, Va.. He died in Dec 1971 in Little Plymouth, Va.. He married Maude Allen, daughter of Williams Elias Allen and Eliza Byrd on 16 Apr 1908 in King & Queen County, Va.. She was born in 1891. She died in May 1977 in King & Queen County, Va..

Generation 3

3. **Rosie Jane**[3] **Jordan** (Polly Ann[2] Bluefoot, Rosetta[1] Robinson) was born on 10 Jan 1878 in King & Queen County, Va.. She died on 19 Jun 1936 in Little Plymouth, Va.. She married John Thomas Davenport, son of Joshua Davenport and Mary F. Kauffman on 15 Nov 1900 in King & Queen County, Va.. He was born in 1872 in King & Queen County, Va.. He died on 07 Nov 1933 in Little Plymouth, Va..

Notes for Rosie Jane Jordan:

Four of her children died as infants: Helen M, Hattie B., Hyburnies N., and John J.,

John Thomas Davenport and Rosie Jane Jordan had the following children:

      i.   Luvenia Ann[4] Davenport was born on 16 Jun 1902 in King & Queen County, Va.. She died on 01 Jan 1984 in Baltimore, Md.. She married Frank Wilson. He died on 19 Aug 1975 in Baltimore, Md..

     ii.   Ella Bertha Davenport was born on 21 Jun 1903 in King & Queen County, Va.. She married Oliver Campbell, son of Joseph Campbell and Susan on 28 Dec 1924 in King & Queen County, Va.. He was born in 1903 in Middlesex County, Va.. He died in Feb 1983.

9.   iii.   Pearl Jane Davenport was born on 26 Jan 1908 in King & Queen County, Va.. She died on 20 Jul 1984. She married Perry W. Reed, son of Abe Reed and Lili on 31 Jul 1930 in King & Queen County, Va.. He was born in Oct 1895 in Middlesex County, Va.. He died in Mar 1940.

     iv.   Robert L.T. Davenport was born on 31 Mar 1910 in King & Queen County, Va.. He died on 02 Mar 1989.

	v.	Etha Irene Davenport was born on 07 Jan 1912 in King & Queen County, Va.. She died in Sep 2001. She married Walter Richardson, son of Richard Richardson and Grace on 07 Jan 1933 in King & Queen County, Va.. He was born in 1903 in Gloucester County, Va..
10.	vi.	Mary Frances Davenport was born on 18 Aug 1916 in King & Queen County, Va.. She married Roger Wormley. He was born on 05 Dec 1910.
11.	vii.	Elijah Davenport was born on 25 Jun 1917 in King & Queen County, Va.. He married Doshie Stewart. She was born on 08 Aug 1919. She died on 16 Aug 1995.
12.	viii.	Lillian E. Davenport was born on 20 May 1919 in King & Queen County, Va.. She married Benjamin Guest. He was born on 27 Nov 1916. He died on 02 Mar 1991 in Baltimore, Md..
13.	ix.	Missouri Olivia Davenport was born on 08 Aug 1921 in King & Queen County, Va.. She married Boyce Barton Sr.. He was born on 15 Dec 1899. He died on 01 May 1994.
14.	x.	George Moses Davenport was born on 10 Sep 1913 in King & Queen County, Va.. He died on 18 Jan 1990 in Rockville, Maryland. He married (1) Virginia Fitchett, daughter of Oscar Leroy Fitchett and Susie West on 12 Jun 1935 in Mddlesex county, Va.. She was born on 07 Sep 1919 in Middlesex County, Va.. She died on 30 Oct 2004 in Middlesex County, Va.. He married Ludie Hilda Williams. She was born on 31 Dec 1921. She died on 28 Jan 1969.
	xi.	Helen M. Davenport was born in Apr 1901. She died in In Infancy.
	xii.	Hattie B. Davenport was born on 21 Aug 1904.
	xiii.	Hyburnies N. Davenport was born on 05 Nov 1906.

4. **George Franklin[3] Jordan** (Polly Ann[2] Bluefoot, Rosetta[1] Robinson) was born in Feb 1883 in King & Queen County, Va.. He died in Oct 1950 in Little Plymouth, Va.. He married (1) Sarah Collins, daughter of James Collins and Maggie Wyatt on 24 Apr 1913 in King & Queen County, Va.. She was born in 1893 in King & Queen County, Va.. He married **Bertha Jackson Collins**. She died in 1953 in King & Queen County, Va..

George Franklin Jordan and Sarah Collins had the following children:

    i.   Ida B.[4] Jordan was born in Oct 1913 in King & Queen County, Va.. She died in 1929 in Died at age 15..

    ii.   Catherine Jordan was born on 12 Nov 1915.

15.   iii.   Sarah Beatrice Jordan was born on 13 Jul 1918. She married Raymond Roye. He was born on 17 Jul 1914. He died in 1981.

    iv.   Viola Jordan was born in 1921. She died about 1922 in Died in infancy.

5. **John Kelly[3] Jordan** (Polly Ann[2] Bluefoot, Rosetta[1] Robinson) was born on 18 Feb 1885 in King & Queen County, Va.. He died in Apr 1963 in Stormont, Va.. He married Eva S. Morris, daughter of Noah Morris and Catherine in Sep 1914. She was born in 1894 in Middlesex County, Va.. She died in Mar 1972 in Middlesex County, Va..

John Kelly Jordan and Eva S. Morris had the following children:

16.   i.   Thelma[4] T. Jordan was born on 05 Apr 1915 in Middlesex County, Va.. She died on 20 Mar 2000 in Middlesex County, Va.. She married (1) Jehu W. Thornton in 1936. He was born in Middlesex County, Va.. He died in 1947 in Middlesex County, Va.. She married (2) Earl Lockley, son of Thomas Lockley and Bessie Ann Banks in 1955. He was born on 03 Dec 1911 in Middlesex County, Va.. He died on 02 Feb 1973.

17. ii. JOHN HOLLIS JORDAN was born on 08 Mar 1917 in Middlesex County, Va.. He died on 08 Oct 1984 in Middlesex County, Va.. He married ROSA SUTHERLIN. She was born on 02 Feb 1917. She died on 24 Jul 2001 in Middlesex County, Va..

18. iii. THOMAS A. JORDAN was born on 06 Sep 1918 in Middlesex County, Va.. He married LILY BELL MINOR. She was born on 16 Apr 1916. She died on 14 Oct 1980. He married YVONNE GILMORE. She was born on 05 Feb 1939.

iv. CATHERINE JORDAN was born in 1919 in Middlesex County, Va..

19. v. DOROTHY NADINE JORDAN was born on 05 Jan 1920 in Middlesex County, Va.. She died on 23 Sep 1977. She married MOSES HELM.

20. vi. GEORGE WILBUR JORDAN was born on 18 Mar 1921 in Middlesex County, Va.. He died on 21 Oct 1986 in Middlesex County, Va.. He married SADIE BALL. She was born on 17 Sep 1920. She died on 24 Apr 1976.

21. vii. EVELYN RUTH JORDAN was born on 14 Jul 1924 in Middlesex County, Va.. She married LLOYD BAYLOR. He was born on 22 Apr 1922.

viii. LILLIAN JUANITA JORDAN was born on 16 Jan 1923 in Middlesex County, Va.. She died in Died at age 7 of Diptheria.

22. ix. HERBERT NATHANIEL JORDAN was born on 03 Jun 1928 in Middlesex County, Va.. He married CHARLETTA PAYNE. She was born on 06 May 1929.

23. x. BERTHA EDNA JORDAN was born on 24 Apr 1931 in Middlesex County, Va.. She married NATHANIEL TAYLOR. He was born on 31 Oct 1929.

24. xi. ELIZABETH MAURICE JORDAN was born on 05 Feb 1936 in Middlesex County, Va.. She married Jr Thomas Milton Ward on 15 Jun 1968 in Mathews, Va.. He was born on 11 Nov 1934 in Mathews, Va..

25. xii. MARY CELESTINE JORDAN was born on 01 Jan 1939 in Middlesex County, Va.. She married SR EDWARD S. THORNTON. He was born on 14 Sep 1931. He died on 30 Mar 1974 in Middlesex County, Va..

6. **SAMUEL ISIAH**^{3} **JORDAN** (Polly Ann^2 Bluefoot, Rosetta^1 Robinson) was born on 22 Feb 1891 in King & Queen County, Va.. He died on 09 Sep 1971 in Tappahannock, Va.. He married Elizabeth Miles, daughter of William Miles and Elnora Campbell on 20 Mar 1913 in King & Queen County, Va.. She was born on 22 Oct 1891 in Middlesex County, Va.. She died on 04 Jan 1993 in Tappahannock, Va..

Samuel Isiah Jordan and Elizabeth Miles had the following children:

26. i. WILLIAM PRESTON^4 JORDAN was born on 22 May 1914 in King & Queen County, Va.. He died on 17 Sep 1994. He married Julia A. Garnett, daughter of Paul Garnett and Martha Jones on 01 Sep 1939 in King & Queen County, Va.. She was born on 29 Aug 1919 in King & Queen County, Va.. She died on 16 Apr 1995.

27. ii. ROSCOE SAMUEL JORDAN was born on 15 Jun 1916 in King & Queen County, Va.. He died on 13 Feb 1992 in Richmond, Va.. He married Gladys Johnson, daughter of Leu Johnson and Ella Graves on 24 Dec 1939 in King & Queen County, Va.. She was born on 26 Jul 1918 in King & Queen County, Va..

iii. HERBERT LEE JORDAN was born in King & Queen County, Va.. He died in Died as an infant.

28.	iv.	JOHN MARK JORDAN was born on 04 Jul 1920 in King & Queen County, Va.. He died on 26 Jan 1995 in Anchorage, Alaska. He married JOCELYN.
29.	v.	HENRY CLAY JORDAN was born on 31 Jul 1923 in King & Queen County, Va.. He died on 17 Oct 1977 in Bryn Marw, Pa.. He married FLOSSIE STEWART. She was born on 25 Aug 1933 in South Carolina.
	vi.	CRESSA ERLENE JORDAN was born in King & Queen County, Va.. She died in Died as an infant.
30.	vii.	ROBERT NATHAN JORDAN was born on 04 Jan 1926 in King & Queen County, Va.. He died on 28 Aug 2000. He married ALEATHA ADKINS. She was born on 14 Nov 1924 in Middlesex County, Va.. She died on 06 Jul 2000 in West Point, Va..
31.	viii.	OLIVIA ELIZABETH JORDAN was born on 18 Jan 1928 in King & Queen County, Va.. She died on 09 Mar 1986 in Silver Spring, Md.. She married GEORGE LEWIS. He was born on 06 Feb 1925 in Illinois. He died on 06 Jun 1989.
32.	ix.	MORVITZ SINCLAIR JORDAN was born on 14 Mar 1930 in King & Queen County, Va.. He married Dolly Lee Robinson, daughter of Elizabeth Miles on 14 Mar 1950 in King & Queen County, Va.. She was born on 26 Jun 1930 in King & Queen County, Va..

7. **ETHAN ALLEN[3] JORDAN** (Polly Ann[2] Bluefoot, Rosetta[1] Robinson) was born on 14 May 1896 in King & Queen County, Va.. He died on 22 Dec 1980 in King & Queen County, Va.. He married **RUTH HOLMES**. She died in 1964.

Notes for Ethan Allen Jordan:

Ethan Allen Jordan, better known as 'BUNKS'

Ethan Allen Jordan and Ruth Holmes had the following child:

    i.   LARRY[4] JORDAN.

8. **WILLIAM THOMAS**[3] **JORDAN** (Polly Ann[2] Bluefoot, Rosetta[1] Robinson) was born on 15 May 1882 in King & Queen County, Va.. He died in Dec 1971 in Little Plymouth, Va.. He married Maude Allen, daughter of William Elias Allen and Eliza Byrd on 16 Apr 1908 in King & Queen County, Va.. She was born in 1891. She died in May 1977 in King & Queen County, Va..

William Thomas Jordan and Maude Allen had the following children:

    i.   OLIVER WENDELL[4] JORDAN was born in 1908 in King & Queen County, Va.. He died in 1975. He married ILA.

33. ii. FLORENTINE MELANIE JORDAN was born on 24 Jun 1909 in King & Queen County, Va.. She died on 12 Dec 1993 in Mattaponi, Va.. She married Albert Clinton White, son of Lilbon White and Bessie Montague on 02 Jun 1942 in King & Queen County, Va.. He was born on 14 Sep 1909 in King & Queen County, Va..

    iii. RUTH ESTHER JORDAN was born on 11 Apr 1913 in King & Queen County, Va.. She died on 30 Sep 1996 in King & Queen County, Va..

    iv. WILLIAM ROBERT JORDAN was born on 14 Sep 1914 in King & Queen County, Va.. He married LENORA.

34. v. REXFORD JORDAN was born on 28 Mar 1917 in King & Queen County, Va.. He died about 1997. He married Priscilla Haskins, daughter of Henry Haskins and Mattie Osborne on 05 Mar 1938 in King & Queen County, Va.. She was born in 1917 in King & Queen County, Va..

	vi.	AUSTIN DOUGLAS JORDAN was born on 13 Sep 1913 in King & Queen County, Va.. He died on 14 Nov 1988.
35.	vii.	BURNETT ALLEN JORDAN was born on 01 Nov 1921 in King & Queen County, Va.. He died on 24 Dec 1999. He married CONSTANCY LACY. She was born on 08 Jul 1923. She died on 22 Sep 1998.
36.	viii.	FANNIE VERNELL JORDAN was born on 16 Dec 1923 in King & Queen County, Va.. She died on 26 Apr 1986 in King & Queen County, Va.. She married ALFRED TERRY.
37.	ix.	JAMES THOMAS JORDAN was born on 24 Feb 1926 in King & Queen County, Va.. He married FRANCIS EDWARDS. She was born on 31 Dec 1928 in West Point, Va..
38.	x.	DOXIE ALFONZA JORDAN was born on 27 Jul 1932 in King & Queen County, Va.. He married (1) GLADYS MARIE SATTERWHITE, daughter of Willie Samuel Satterwhite on 06 Sep 1966 in King & Queen County, Va.. She was born on 19 Nov 1942 in King & Queen County, Va.. He married BARBARA HOLMES.

Generation 4

9. **Pearl Jane[4] Davenport** (Rosie Jane[3] Jordan, Polly Ann[2] Bluefoot, Rosetta[1] Robinson) was born on 26 Jan 1908 in King & Queen County, Va.. She died on 20 Jul 1984. She married Perry W. Reed, son of Abe Reed and Lili on 31 Jul 1930 in King & Queen County, Va.. He was born in Oct 1895 in Middlesex County, Va.. He died in Mar 1940.

Perry W. Reed and Pearl Jane Davenport had the following children:

   i. Rosetta[5] Reed was born on 30 Mar 1931.

   ii. Walter Perry Reed was born on 02 Mar 1939.

   iii. Mary Reed was born on 29 Nov 1936.

10. **Mary Frances[4] Davenport** (Rosie Jane[3] Jordan, Polly Ann[2] Bluefoot, Rosetta[1] Robinson) was born on 18 Aug 1916 in King & Queen County, Va.. She married **Roger Wormley**. He was born on 05 Dec 1910.

Roger Wormley and Mary Frances Davenport had the following children:

   i. Allen[5] Wormley was born on 28 Jul 1939.

   ii. Joan Wormley was born on 27 Feb 1941.

11. **Elijah[4] Davenport** (Rosie Jane[3] Jordan, Polly Ann[2] Bluefoot, Rosetta[1] Robinson) was born on 25 Jun 1917 in King & Queen County, Va.. He married **Doshie Stewart**. She was born on 08 Aug 1919. She died on 16 Aug 1995.

Elijah Davenport and Doshie Stewart had the following child:

   i. Shirley[5] Davenport was born on 06 Dec 1940.

12. **Lillian E.**[4] **Davenport** (Rosie Jane[3] Jordan, Polly Ann[2] Bluefoot, Rosetta[1] Robinson) was born on 20 May 1919 in King & Queen County, Va.. She married Benjamin Guest. He was born on 27 Nov 1916. He died on 02 Mar 1991 in Baltimore, Md..

Benjamin Guest and Lillian E. Davenport had the following children:

    i.   George[5] Guest was born on 19 Sep 1941. He died on 17 Apr 1996.

    ii.   Jerome Guest was born on 11 Sep 1942.

    iii.   Cecil Guest was born on 27 Sep 1946. He died in Jul 1981.

    iv.   Deborah Guest was born on 28 May 1948.

    v.   Diane Guest was born on 03 May 1950.

13. **Missouri Olivia**[4] **Davenport** (Rosie Jane[3] Jordan, Polly Ann[2] Bluefoot, Rosetta[1] Robinson) was born on 08 Aug 1921 in King & Queen County, Va.. She married **Boyce Barton Sr.**. He was born on 15 Dec 1899. He died on 01 May 1994.

Boyce Barton Sr. and Missouri Olivia Davenport had the following child:

    i.   James[5] Davenport was born on 05 Mar 1943.

14. **George Moses**[4] **Davenport** (Rosie Jane[3] Jordan, Polly Ann[2] Bluefoot, Rosetta[1] Robinson) was born on 10 Sep 1913 in King & Queen County, Va.. He died on 18 Jan 1990 in Rockville, Maryland. He married (1) **Virginia Fitchett**, daughter of Oscar Leroy Fitchett and Susie West on 12 Jun 1935 in Mddlesex county, Va.. She was born on 07 Sep 1919 in Middlesex County, Va.. She died on 30 Oct 2004 in Middlesex County, Va.. He married **Ludie Hilda Williams**. She was born on 31 Dec 1921. She died on 28 Jan 1969.

George Moses Davenport and Virginia Fitchett had the following child:

39. i. JOHN^5 DAVENPORT was born on 02 May 1937 in Pennsylvania. He married Priscilla Price, daughter of John Price and Bertha A. Mars on 08 Dec 1956 in New York City, N.Y.. She was born on 10 Jun 1941 in New York, New York.

George Moses Davenport and Ludie Hilda Williams had the following children:

ii. CHERYL DAVENPORT was born on 10 Dec 1953.

iii. CYNTHIA DAVENPORT was born on 25 Jul 1957.

iv. PHILBERT DAVENPORT was born on 26 Aug 1952.

15. **SARAH BEATRICE^4 JORDAN** (George Franklin^3, Polly Ann^2 Bluefoot, Rosetta^1 Robinson) was born on 13 Jul 1918. She married **RAYMOND ROYE**. He was born on 17 Jul 1914. He died in 1981.

Raymond Roye and Sarah Beatrice Jordan had the following child:

i. JOYCE^5 ROYE was born on 04 Jul 1947.

16. **THELMA^4 T. JORDAN** (John Kelly^3 Jordan, Polly Ann^2 Bluefoot, Rosetta^1 Robinson) was born on 05 Apr 1915 in Middlesex County, Va.. She died on 20 Mar 2000 in Middlesex County, Va.. She married (1) **JEHU W. THORNTON** in 1936. He was born in Middlesex County, Va.. He died in 1947 in Middlesex County, Va.. She married (2) **EARL LOCKLEY**, son of Thomas Lockley and Bessie Ann Banks in 1955. He was born on 03 Dec 1911 in Middlesex County, Va.. He died on 02 Feb 1973.

Jehu W. Thornton and Thelma T. Jordan had the following children:

    i.   JOHN R.[5] THORNTON was born on 30 Jan 1937. He died on 04 Feb 1995.

    ii.   THELMA J. THORNTON was born on 02 Jan 1938.

    iii.   WILLIAM B. THORNTON was born on 07 Jan 1939. He died on 20 Oct 1996.

    iv.   CAROL MAXANN THORNTON was born on 28 Dec 1941.

    v.   THOMAS M. THORNTON was born on 02 Jul 1945. He died on 08 Aug 1967 in Japan.

17. **JOHN HOLLIS[4] JORDAN** (John Kelly[3], Polly Ann[2] Bluefoot, Rosetta[1] Robinson) was born on 08 Mar 1917 in Middlesex County, Va.. He died on 08 Oct 1984 in Middlesex County, Va.. He married **ROSA SUTHERLIN**. She was born on 02 Feb 1917. She died on 24 Jul 2001 in Middlesex County, Va..

John Hollis Jordan and Rosa Sutherlin had the following children:

    i.   CYNTHIA R.[5] JORDAN was born on 11 Jan 1945.

    ii.   JR JOHN H. JORDAN was born on 01 Jul 1946.

    iii.   ROBERT M. JORDAN was born on 03 Sep 1952.

18. **THOMAS A.[4] JORDAN** (John Kelly[3], Polly Ann[2] Bluefoot, Rosetta[1] Robinson) was born on 06 Sep 1918 in Middlesex County, Va.. He married **LILY BELL MINOR**. She was born on 16 Apr 1916. She died on 14 Oct 1980. He married **YVONNE GILMORE**. She was born on 05 Feb 1939.

Thomas A. Jordan and Lily Bell Minor had the following children:

    i.   THOMAS[5] JORDAN. He died in In Infancy.

ii.   Franklin N. Jordan was born on 22 Nov 1939.

19. **Dorothy Nadine**[4] **Jordan** (John Kelly[3], Polly Ann[2] Bluefoot, Rosetta[1] Robinson) was born on 05 Jan 1920 in Middlesex County, Va.. She died on 23 Sep 1977. She married **Moses Helm**.

Moses Helm and Dorothy Nadine Jordan had the following child:

i.   Cappie[5] Helm was born in 1955. He died in Mar 2002.

20. **George Wilbur**[4] **Jordan** (John Kelly[3], Polly Ann[2] Bluefoot, Rosetta[1] Robinson) was born on 18 Mar 1921 in Middlesex County, Va.. He died on 21 Oct 1986 in Middlesex County, Va.. He married **Sadie Ball**. She was born on 17 Sep 1920. She died on 24 Apr 1976.

George Wilbur Jordan and Sadie Ball had the following children:

i.   Joyce A.[5] Jordan was born on 13 Oct 1942. She died on 28 May 1998.

ii. Eva P. Jordan was born on 10 Jan 1944.

iii. Barbara Jordan was born on 15 Jul 1945.

iv. George W. Jordan was born on 16 Oct 1963.

21. **Evelyn Ruth**[4] **Jordan** (John Kelly[3], Polly Ann[2] Bluefoot, Rosetta[1] Robinson) was born on 14 Jul 1924 in Middlesex County, Va.. She married **Lloyd Baylor**. He was born on 22 Apr 1922.

Lloyd Baylor and Evelyn Ruth Jordan had the following children:

i.   Ruthie B.[5] Baylor was born on 08 Aug 1949.

ii. Joan B. Baylor was born on 13 Jul 1950.

iii. Gordon Baylor was born on 02 Jul 1951.

iv. Linda Baylor was born on 07 Jul 1952.

v. TIMOTHY BAYLOR was born on 23 May 1954.

vi. KATHY BAYLOR was born on 18 Mar 1961.

22. **HERBERT NATHANIEL**^{4} **JORDAN** (John Kelly^3, Polly Ann^2 Bluefoot, Rosetta^1 Robinson) was born on 03 Jun 1928 in Middlesex County, Va.. He married **CHARLETTA PAYNE**. She was born on 06 May 1929.

Herbert Nathaniel Jordan and Charletta Payne had the following children:

i. KEITH^5 JORDAN was born on 31 Jan 1953.

ii. LARRY JORDAN was born on 30 Sep 1955.

iii. ANTHONY JORDAN was born on 11 Nov 1966. He died on 22 Feb 1991.

23. **BERTHA EDNA**^{4} **JORDAN** (John Kelly^3, Polly Ann^2 Bluefoot, Rosetta^1 Robinson) was born on 24 Apr 1931 in Middlesex County, Va.. She married **NATHANIEL TAYLOR**. He was born on 31 Oct 1929.

Nathaniel Taylor and Bertha Edna Jordan had the following children:

i. SILVIA^5 JORDAN was born on 08 Apr 1952.

ii. TONEY BROKENBOROUGH was born on 02 Oct 1953.

iii. JR NATHANIEL TAYLOR was born on 28 Apr 1957.

iv. CHERYL TAYLOR was born on 30 Apr 1958.

v. WELFORD TAYLOR was born on 19 Mar 1959.

vi. WILLIAM TAYLOR was born on 19 Mar 1959.

vii. MARILYN TAYLOR was born on 06 Aug 1960.

24. **ELIZABETH MAURICE**^{4} **JORDAN** (John Kelly^3, Polly Ann^2 Bluefoot, Rosetta^1 Robinson) was born on 05 Feb 1936 in Middlesex County,

Va.. She married Jr Thomas Milton Ward on 15 Jun 1968 in Mathews, Va.. He was born on 11 Nov 1934 in Mathews, Va..

Jr Thomas Milton Ward and Elizabeth Maurice Jordan had the following children:

    i.   ALETA M.[5] WARD was born on 03 Dec 1957.

    ii.   JOSEPH T. WARD was born on 22 Aug 1963.

    iii.   RENE WARD was born on 24 Aug 1965.

    iv.   DUANE M. WARD was born on 14 Jul 1966.

    v.   JUAN G. WARD was born on 20 Nov 1968.

25. **MARY CELESTINE**[4] **JORDAN** (John Kelly[3], Polly Ann[2] Bluefoot, Rosetta[1] Robinson) was born on 01 Jan 1939 in Middlesex County, Va.. She married **SR EDWARD S. THORNTON**. He was born on 14 Sep 1931. He died on 30 Mar 1974 in Middlesex County, Va..

Sr Edward S. Thornton and Mary Celestine Jordan had the following children:

    i.   EDWARD S.[5] THORNTON was born on 20 Nov 1969.

    ii.   BRIAN ETHAN THORNTON was born on 25 Oct 1974.

26. **WILLIAM PRESTON**[4] **JORDAN** (Samuel Isiah[3], Polly Ann[2] Bluefoot, Rosetta[1] Robinson) was born on 22 May 1914 in King & Queen County, Va.. He died on 17 Sep 1994. He married Julia A. Garnett, daughter of Paul Garnett and Martha Jones on 01 Sep 1939 in King & Queen County, Va.. She was born on 29 Aug 1919 in King & Queen County, Va.. She died on 16 Apr 1995.

William Preston Jordan and Julia A. Garnett had the following children:

i. Bryant Clifton[5] Jordan was born on 16 Nov 1959 in King & Queen County, Va.. He married Marlene Alethia Jones, daughter of Jeter B. Jones and Virginia Yates on 16 Nov 1977 in King & Queen County, Va.. She was born in 1958 in King & Queen County, Va..

ii. W. Franklin Jordan was born on 03 Feb 1941 in Shacklefords, Va..

iii. Samuel T. Jordan was born on 15 Feb 1942 in Shacklefords, Va..

iv. Preston Garest Jordan was born on 15 Jul 1943 in Shacklefords, Va.. He died in In Fancy.

v. Julia Pauline Jordan was born on 05 Nov 1944 in Shacklefords, Va..

vi. Garry Maxwell Jordan was born in Shacklefords, Va.. He died in In Infancy.

vii. Lawrence D. Jordan was born on 07 Jul 1953 in Shacklefords, Va.. He died on 15 Jul 1972.

27. **Roscoe Samuel[4] Jordan** (Samuel Isiah[3], Polly Ann[2] Bluefoot, Rosetta[1] Robinson) was born on 15 Jun 1916 in King & Queen County, Va.. He died on 13 Feb 1992 in Richmond, Va.. He married Gladys Johnson, daughter of Leu Johnson and Ella Graves on 24 Dec 1939 in King & Queen County, Va.. She was born on 26 Jul 1918 in King & Queen County, Va..

Roscoe Samuel Jordan and Gladys Johnson had the following child:

40. i. Laverne[5] Jordan was born on 12 Nov 1942. She died on 26 Oct 1990 in Beaufort, South Carolina. She married Richard Scott.

28. **John Mark[4] Jordan** (Samuel Isiah[3], Polly Ann[2] Bluefoot, Rosetta[1] Robinson) was born on 04 Jul 1920 in King & Queen County, Va.. He died on 26 Jan 1995 in Anchorage, Alaska. He married **Jocelyn**.

John Mark Jordan and Jocelyn had the following child:

    i.   DAYMON^5 JORDAN.

29. **HENRY CLAY^4 JORDAN** (Samuel Isiah^3, Polly Ann^2 Bluefoot, Rosetta^1 Robinson) was born on 31 Jul 1923 in King & Queen County, Va.. He died on 17 Oct 1977 in Bryn Marw, Pa.. He married FLOSSIE STEWART. She was born on 25 Aug 1933 in South Carolina.

Henry Clay Jordan and Flossie Stewart had the following child:

    i.   DOROTHY LEE^5 JORDAN was born on 27 Sep 1952.

30. **ROBERT NATHAN^4 JORDAN** (Samuel Isiah^3, Polly Ann^2 Bluefoot, Rosetta^1 Robinson) was born on 04 Jan 1926 in King & Queen County, Va.. He died on 28 Aug 2000. He married **ALEATHA ADKINS**. She was born on 14 Nov 1924 in Middlesex County, Va.. She died on 06 Jul 2000 in West Point, Va..

Robert Nathan Jordan and Aleatha Adkins had the following children:

    i.   BARBARA O.^{5} JORDAN was born on 26 May 1945 in Richmond, Va..

    ii.   LASANDRA C. JORDAN was born on 16 Jul 1948 in Richmond, Va..

    iii.   ERIC N. JORDAN was born on 08 Jul 1950 in Richmond, Va..

31. **OLIVIA ELIZABETH^4 JORDAN** (Samuel Isiah^3, Polly Ann^2 Bluefoot, Rosetta^1 Robinson) was born on 18 Jan 1928 in King & Queen County, Va.. She died on 09 Mar 1986 in Silver Spring, Md.. She married GEORGE LEWIS. He was born on 06 Feb 1925 in Illinois. He died on 06 Jun 1989.

George Lewis and Olivia Elizabeth Jordan had the following children:

      i.   DONNA W.[5] LEWIS was born on 02 Feb 1949.

      ii.   DON KENRICK LEWIS was born on 28 Jul 1951.

32. **MORVITZ SINCLAIR**[4] **JORDAN** (Samuel Isiah[3], Polly Ann[2] Bluefoot, Rosetta[1] Robinson) was born on 14 Mar 1930 in King & Queen County, Va.. He married Dolly Lee Robinson, daughter of Elizabeth Miles on 14 Mar 1950 in King & Queen County, Va.. She was born on 26 Jun 1930 in King & Queen County, Va..

Morvitz Sinclair Jordan and Dolly Lee Robinson had the following children:

      i.   JR MORVITZ S.[5] JORDAN was born on 05 Feb 1950.

      ii.   LEON G. JORDAN was born on 08 May 1951. He died on 13 Mar 1998 in Little Plymouth, Va..

      iii.   A. CASSELL JORDAN was born on 14 Jun 1953.

      iv.   DEBORAH A. JORDAN was born on 08 Apr 1955.

      v.   GLYNIS L. JORDAN was born on 31 Jan 1957.

      vi.   ROWENA K. JORDAN was born on 14 Mar 1958.

      vii.   Keith Vincent Jordan WAS BORN ON 09 JUL 1960.

      viii. STEPHANIE A. JORDAN was born on 11 Feb 1962.

      ix.   AVERY MILES JORDAN was born on 08 Dec 1963.

      x.   MORVIKA D. JORDAN was born on 27 Aug 1970.

33. **FLORENTINE MELANIE**[4] **JORDAN** (William Thomas[3], Polly Ann[2] Bluefoot, Rosetta[1] Robinson) was born on 24 Jun 1909 in King & Queen County, Va.. She died on 12 Dec 1993 in Mattaponi, Va.. She married Albert Clinton White, son of Lilbon White and Bessie Montague on 02 Jun 1942 in King & Queen County, Va.. He was born on 14 Sep 1909 in King & Queen County, Va..

Albert Clinton White and Florentine Melanie Jordan had the following child:

    i.   VERDELL[5] WHITE was born on 05 Nov 1949.

34. **REXFORD**[4] **JORDAN** (William Thomas[3], Polly Ann[2] Bluefoot, Rosetta[1] Robinson) was born on 28 Mar 1917 in King & Queen County, Va.. He died about 1997. He married Priscilla Haskins, daughter of Henry Haskins and Mattie Osborne on 05 Mar 1938 in King & Queen County, Va.. She was born in 1917 in King & Queen County, Va..

Rexford Jordan and Priscilla Haskins had the following children:

    i.   ARLENA[5] JORDAN.

    ii.   ALBERETTA JORDAN.

    iii.   Carl Jordan.

35. **BURNETT ALLEN**[4] **JORDAN** (William Thomas[3], Polly Ann[2] Bluefoot, Rosetta[1] Robinson) was born on 01 Nov 1921 in King & Queen County, Va.. He died on 24 Dec 1999. He married CONSTANCY LACY. She was born on 08 Jul 1923. She died on 22 Sep 1998.

Burnett Allen Jordan and Constancy Lacy had the following child:

    i.   BRENDA[5] JORDAN.

36. **FANNIE VERNELL**[4] **JORDAN** (William Thomas[3], Polly Ann[2] Bluefoot, Rosetta[1] Robinson) was born on 16 Dec 1923 in King & Queen County, Va.. She died on 26 Apr 1986 in King & Queen County, Va.. She married ALFRED TERRY.

Alfred Terry and Fannie Vernell Jordan had the following child:

    i.   MICHAEL[5] TERRY.

37. **James Thomas[4] Jordan** (William Thomas[3], Polly Ann[2] Bluefoot, Rosetta[1] Robinson) was born on 24 Feb 1926 in King & Queen County, Va.. He married Francis Edwards. She was born on 31 Dec 1928 in West Point, Va..

James Thomas Jordan and Francis Edwards had the following children:

    i.   Arlette[5] Jordan was born on 18 Dec 1951.

    ii.   Regena Jordan was born on 07 Jul 1953.

38. **Doxie Alfonza[4] Jordan** (William Thomas[3], Polly Ann[2] Bluefoot, Rosetta[1] Robinson) was born on 27 Jul 1932 in King & Queen County, Va.. He married (1) **Gladys Marie Satterwhite**, daughter of Willie Samuel Satterwhite on 06 Sep 1966 in King & Queen County, Va.. She was born on 19 Nov 1942 in King & Queen County, Va.. He married **Barbara Holmes**.

Doxie Alfonza Jordan and Gladys Marie Satterwhite had the following children:

    i.   Jr Doxie A.[5] Jordan was born on 27 Jun 1969.

    ii.   Deotis Jordan was born on 27 Jul 1974.

Doxie Alfonza Jordan and Barbara Holmes had the following children:

    iii.   Wanda Jordan.

    iv.   Montez Jordan.

    v.   Vincent Jordan.

Generation 5

39. **John**[5] **Davenport** (George Moses[4], Rosie Jane[3] Jordan, Polly Ann[2] Bluefoot, Rosetta[1] Robinson) was born on 02 May 1937 in Pennsylvania. He married Priscilla Price, daughter of John Price and Bertha A. Mars on 08 Dec 1956 in New York City, N.Y.. She was born on 10 Jun 1941 in New York, New York.

John Davenport and Priscilla Price had the following children:

- 41. i. John Patrick[6] Davenport was born on 10 Dec 1956 in New York, New York. He married Arletha Bias.
- 42. ii. Wayne Davenport was born on 16 Sep 1958 in New York, New York. He died on 03 Jan 2012 in Virginia. He married Wanda Petty. She was born on 01 Jan 1955.

40. **Laverne**[5] **Jordan** (Roscoe Samuel[4], Samuel Isiah[3], Polly Ann[2] Bluefoot, Rosetta[1] Robinson) was born on 12 Nov 1942. She died on 26 Oct 1990 in Beaufort, South Carolina. She married **Richard Scott**.

Richard Scott and Laverne Jordan had the following child:

- i. Jr Richard[6] Scott was born on 08 Jul 1968.

Generation 6

41. **JOHN PATRICK**[6] **DAVENPORT** (John[5], George Moses[4], Rosie Jane[3] Jordan, Polly Ann[2] Bluefoot, Rosetta[1] Robinson) was born on 10 Dec 1956 in New York, New York. He married **ARLETHA BIAS**.

John Patrick Davenport and Arletha Bias had the following child:

    i.   LAURA[7] DAVENPORT was born in 1986 in New York, NY..

42. **WAYNE**[6] **DAVENPORT** (John[5], George Moses[4], Rosie Jane[3] Jordan, Polly Ann[2] Bluefoot, Rosetta[1] Robinson) was born on 16 Sep 1958 in New York, New York. He died on 03 Jan 2012 in Virginia. He married **WANDA PETTY**. She was born on 01 Jan 1955.

Wayne Davenport and Wanda Petty had the following children:

    i.   CALEB[7] DAVENPORT was born in 1984.

    ii.   JOSHUA DAVENPORT was born in 1986.

    iii.   DANIEL DAVENPORT was born in 1988.

    iv.   MICAH DAVENPORT was born in 1990.

Descendants of Rosetta Robinson (1 of 22)

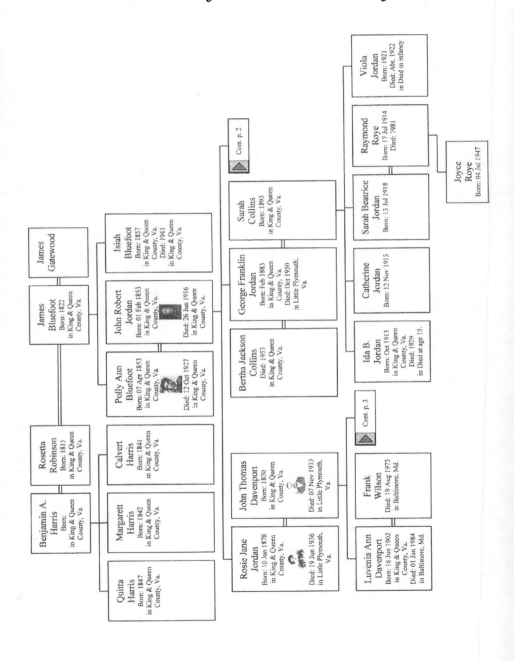

Descendants of Rosetta Robinson

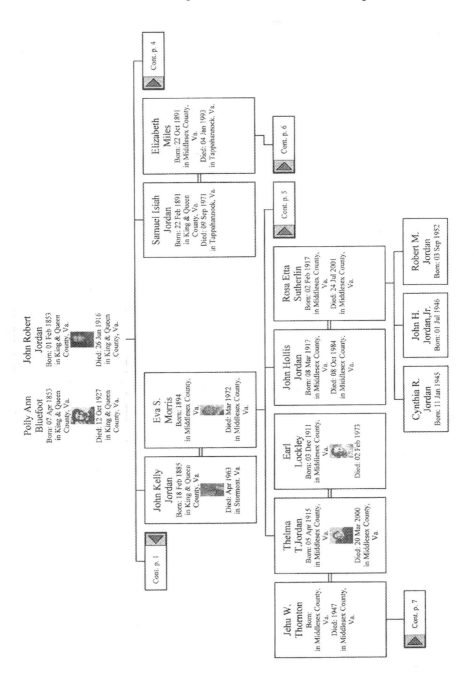

Descendants of Rosetta Robinson (3 of 22)

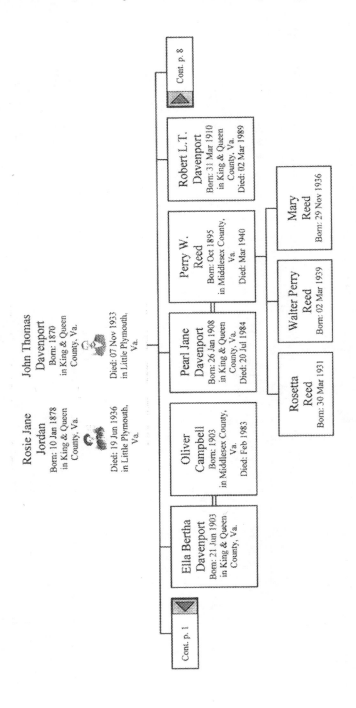

Descendants of Rosetta Robinson

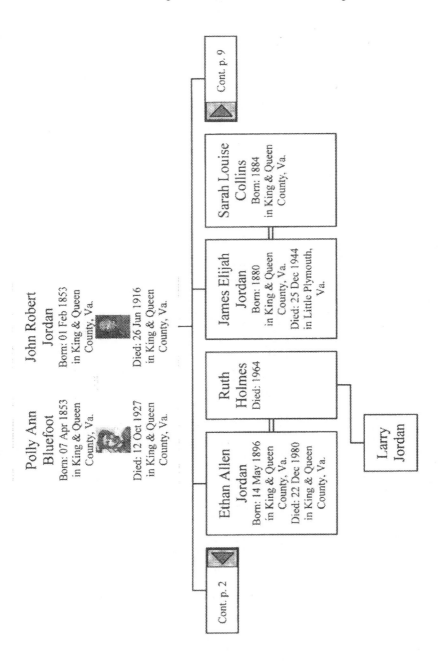

Descendants of Rosetta Robinson

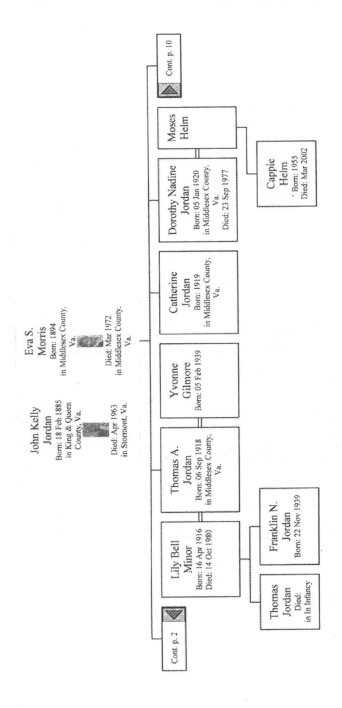

Descendants of Rosetta Robinson (6 of 22)

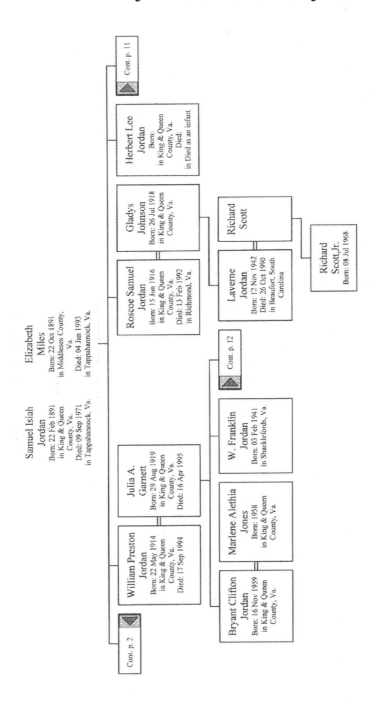

Descendants of Rosetta Robinson

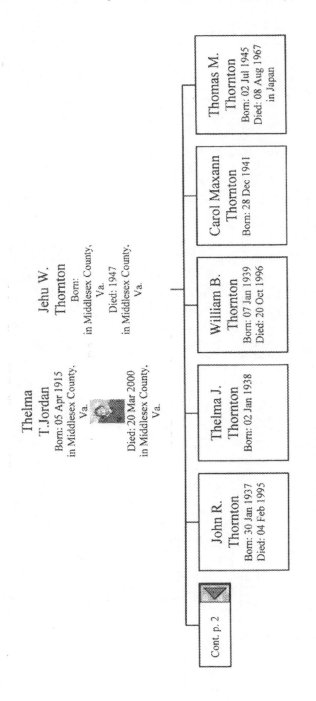

Descendants of Rosetta Robinson

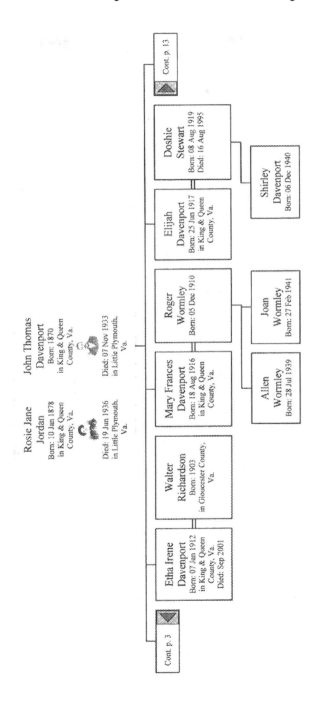

Descendants of Rosetta Robinson

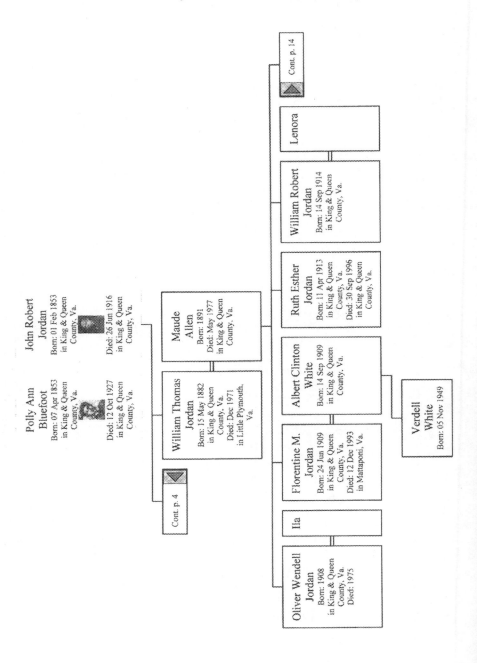

Descendants of Rosetta Robinson (10 of 22)

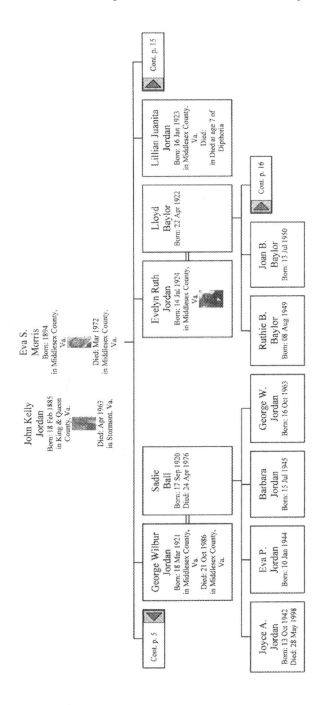

Descendants of Rosetta Robinson

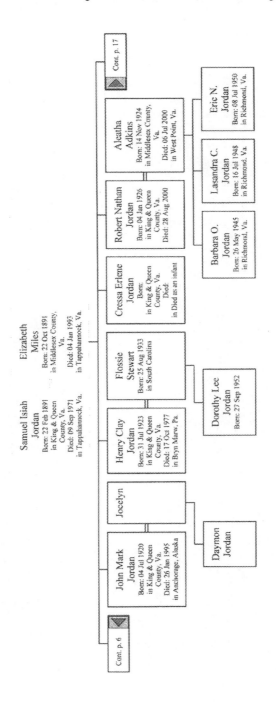

Descendants of Rosetta Robinson

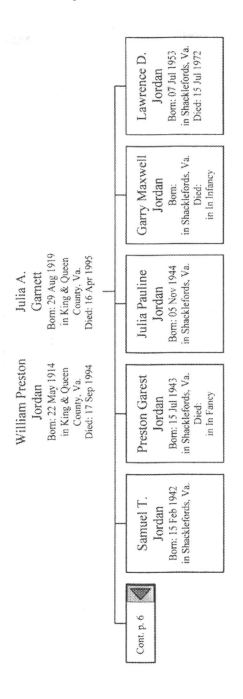

Descendants of Rosetta Robinson

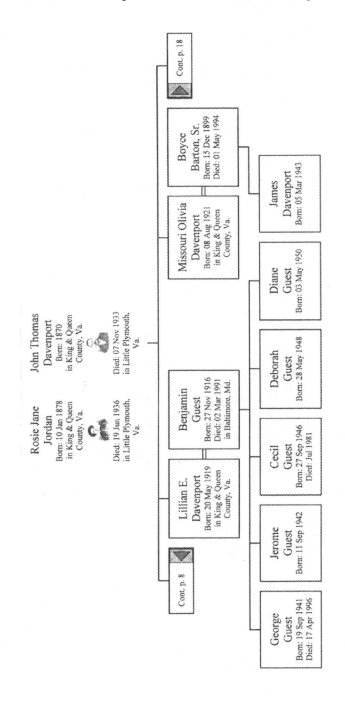

Descendants of Rosetta Robinson (14 of 22)

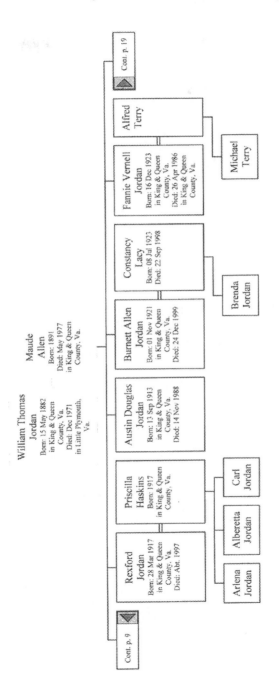

Descendants of Rosetta Robinson (15 of 22)

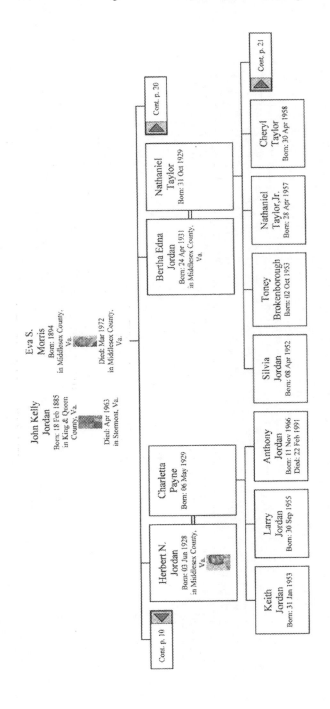

Descendants of Rosetta Robinson

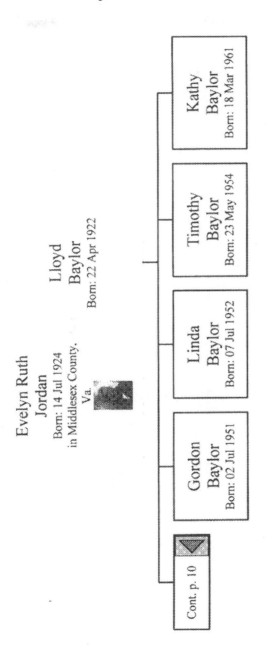

Descendants of Rosetta Robinson

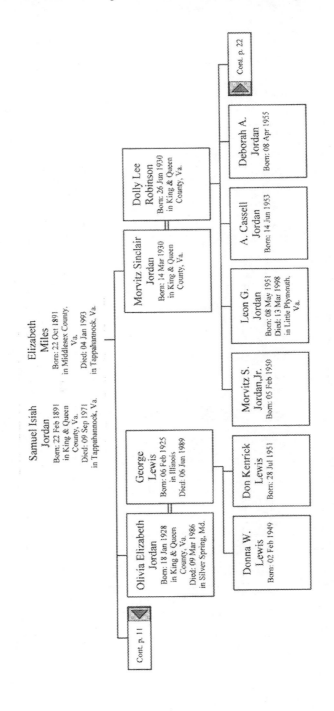

Descendants of Rosetta Robinson (18 of 22)

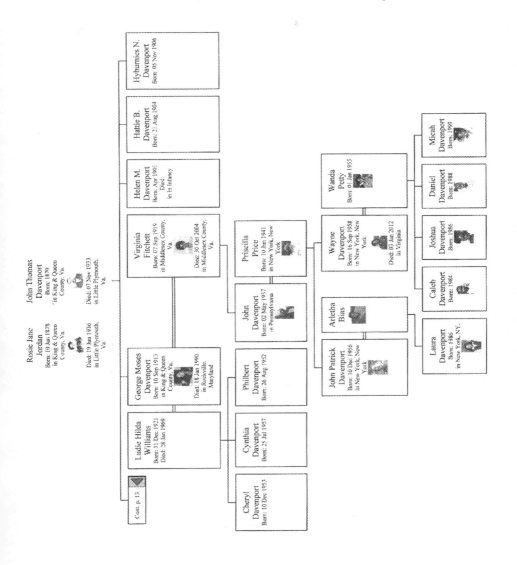

Descendants of Rosetta Robinson

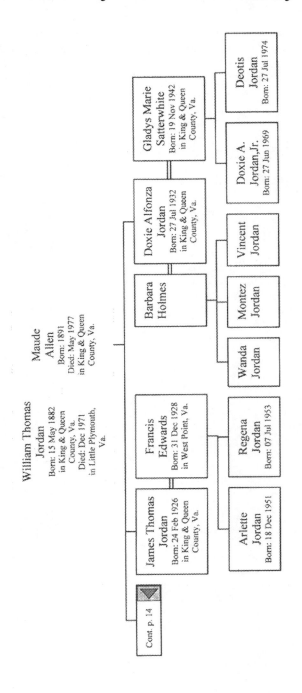

Descendants of Rosetta Robinson (20 of 22)

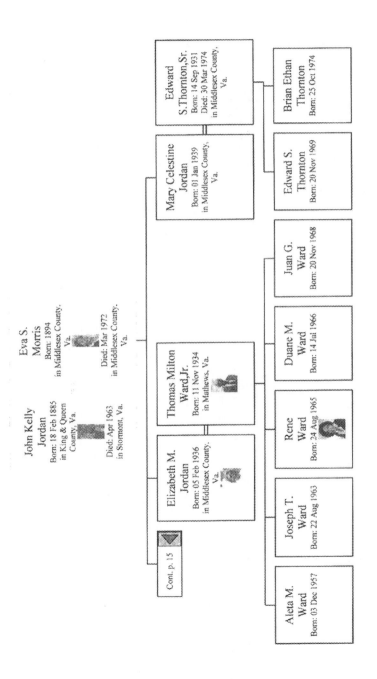

Descendants of Rosetta Robinson

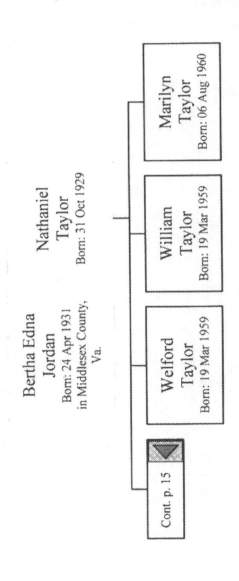

Descendants of Rosetta Robinson

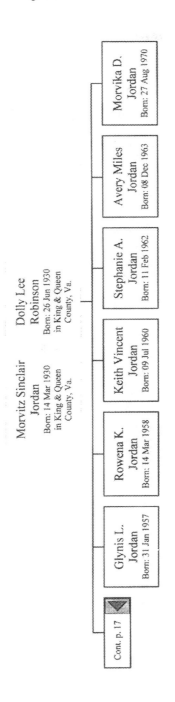

ROSIE JANE JORDAN
1/10/1878 – 6/19/1936

Rosie Jane, the firstborn and only daughter of Polly Ann Bluefoot, was named Rosie after her grandmother Rosetta Robinson. She married John Thomas Davenport of King and Queen County, Va., a successful farmer and businessman. They settled on a farm near the Second Mount Olive Church, in the Little Plymouth area with their children. Rosie was deaconess and missionary, her husband John was deacon. Their family consisted of fourteen children. John Thomas Davenport died 11/7/1933.

Descendants of Rosie Jane Jordan

Generation No. 1

1. Rosie Jane^3 Jordan (John Robert^2, George^1) was born 10 Jan 1878 in King & Queen County, Va., and died 19 Jun 1936 in Little Plymouth, Va.. She married John Thomas Davenport 15 Nov 1900 in King & Queen County, Va., son of JOSHUA DAVENPORT and MARY KAUFFMAN. He was born 1870 in King & Queen County, Va., and died 07 Nov 1933 in Little Plymouth, Va..

Notes for ROSIE JANE JORDAN:

Four of her children died as infants: Helen M, Hattie B., Hyburnies N., and John J.,

More About ROSIE JANE JORDAN:

Caste: Mulatto

Children of ROSIE JORDAN and JOHN DAVENPORT are:

    i.   LUVENIA ANN^4 DAVENPORT, b. 16 Jun 1902, King & Queen County, Va.; d. 01 Jan 1984, Baltimore, Md.; m. FRANK WILSON; d. 19 Aug 1975, Baltimore, Md..

More About LUVENIA ANN DAVENPORT:

Caste: Mulatto

    ii.   ELLA BERTHA DAVENPORT, b. 21 Jun 1903, King & Queen County, Va.; m. OLIVER CAMPBELL, 28 Dec 1924, King & Queen County, Va.; b. 1903, Middlesex County, Va.; d. Feb 1983.

More About ELLA BERTHA DAVENPORT:

Caste: Mulatto

  iii. PEARL JANE DAVENPORT, b. 26 Jan 1908, King & Queen County, Va.; d. 20 Jul 1984; m. PERRY W. REED, 31 Jul 1930, King & Queen County, Va.; b. Oct 1895, Middlesex County, Va.; d. Mar 1940.

More About PEARL JANE DAVENPORT:

Caste: Mulatto

  iv. ROBERT L.T. DAVENPORT, b. 31 Mar 1910, King & Queen County, Va.; d. 02 Mar 1989.

More About ROBERT L.T. DAVENPORT:

Caste: Mulatto

  v. ETHA IRENE DAVENPORT, b. 07 Jan 1912, King & Queen County, Va.; d. Sep 2001; m. WALTER RICHARDSON, 07 Jan 1933, King & Queen County, Va.; b. 1903, Gloucester County, Va..

More About ETHA IRENE DAVENPORT:

Caste: Mulatto

  vi. MARY FRANCES DAVENPORT, b. 18 Aug 1916, King & Queen County, Va.; m. ROGER WORMLEY; b. 05 Dec 1910.

More About MARY FRANCES DAVENPORT:

Caste: Mulatto

  vii. ELIJAH DAVENPORT, b. 25 Jun 1917, King & Queen County, Va.; m. DOSHIE STEWART; b. 08 Aug 1919; d. 16 Aug 1995.

More About ELIJAH DAVENPORT:

Caste: Mulatto

    viii.   LILLIAN E. DAVENPORT, b. 20 May 1919, King & Queen County, Va.; m. BENJAMIN GUEST; b. 27 Nov 1916; d. 02 Mar 1991, Baltimore, Md..

More About LILLIAN E. DAVENPORT:

Caste: Mulatto

    ix.   MISSOURI OLIVIA DAVENPORT, b. 08 Aug 1921, King & Queen County, Va.; m. BOYCE BARTON, SR.; b. 15 Dec 1899; d. 01 May 1994.

More About MISSOURI OLIVIA DAVENPORT:

Caste: Mulatto

    x.   GEORGE MOSES DAVENPORT, b. 10 Sep 1913, King & Queen County, Va.; d. 18 Jan 1990, Rockville, Maryland; m. (1) LUDIE HILDA WILLIAMS; b. 31 Dec 1921; d. 28 Jan 1969; m. (2) VIRGINIA FITCHETT, 12 Jun 1935, Mddlesex county, Va.; b. 07 Sep 1919, Middlesex County, Va.; d. 30 Oct 2004, Middlesex County, Va..

More About GEORGE MOSES DAVENPORT:

Burial: Columbus, Georgia

Caste: Mulatto

More About VIRGINIA FITCHETT:

Burial: 07 Nov 2004, Grafton Baptist Church, Hartfield Virginia

    xi.   HELEN M. DAVENPORT, b. Apr 1901; d. In Infancy.

    xii.   HATTIE B. DAVENPORT, b. 21 Aug 1904.

    xiii.   HYBURNIES N. DAVENPORT, b. 05 Nov 1906.

GEORGE MOSES DAVENPORT
9/10/1913 – 1/18/1990

The first wife of George was Virginia, Fitchett. They were married June 12, 1935 in Middlesex County, Va. One son, John Davenport was born to this union in 1937.

Descendants of George Moses Davenport

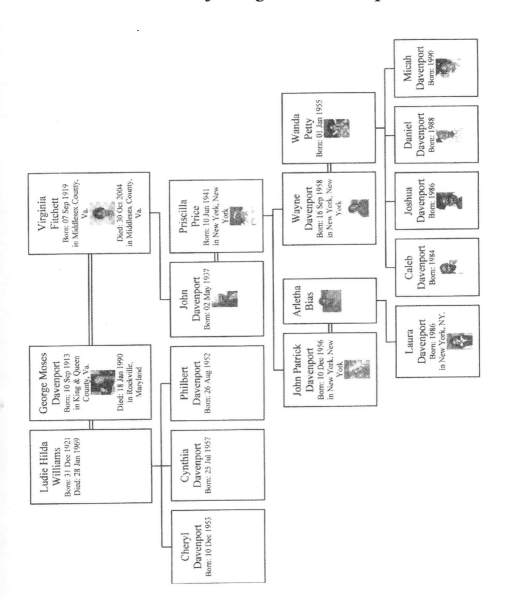

JOHN DAVENPORT 5/2/1937

John or Johnny as he was known to his friends and family was born in Pennsylvania and raised in New York City. However each summer he could be found at the home of His great uncle and his wife, Jack & Adel Fitchett in Middlesex County, Va.

John Married Priscilla Price in 1956 they raised their two sons, John Patrick Davenport and Wayne Davenport in New York City where John worked for the New York City Transit Authority.

It was the custom of relatives who left for cities such as New York, Philadelphia, Baltimore and New Jersey for better jobs and non segregated schools to educate their children to send their children to the safe environment of Middlesex County every summer where they could spend time fishing, swimming, boating and establishing relationships with other relatives that also returned each summer.

Whiting Creek, Middlesex County, Va. Left to Right, John Davenport (Cousin), Robert Lorenzo Lockley, Reginald Elwood Lockley, Harold Preston Lockley. This was our swimming Pool every summer

At the time of his retirement his sons were both married and raising their own families. John and Priscilla moved to the home he had inherited from his late Uncle and Aunt, Jack and Adel Fitchett in Middlesex County, Va. John did a little farming, bough himself a little boat for fishing wish kept him busy while Priscilla took a job working in the Middlesex County Court House as a clerk. She did an outstanding job and became so popular with fellow workers and members of the community that she ran for and was elected Commissioner of Revenue for Middlesex County, Virginia. As of January 2014 she still serves in that position.

Descendants of John Davenport

Generation No. 1

1. JOHN[5] DAVENPORT *(GEORGE MOSES[4], JOHN THOMAS[3], JACKSON[2], THOMAS[1])* was born 02 May 1937 in Pennsylvania. He married PRISCILLA PRICE 08 Dec 1956 in New York, NY, daughter of JOHN PRICE and BERTHA MARS. She was born 10 Jun 1941 in New York, New York.

    Children of JOHN DAVENPORT and PRISCILLA PRICE are:

    2. i. JOHN PATRICK[6] DAVENPORT, b. 10 Dec 1956, New York, New York.
    3. ii. WAYNE DAVENPORT, b. 16 Sep 1958, New York, New York; d. 03 Jan 2012, Virginia.

Generation No. 2

2. JOHN PATRICK[6] DAVENPORT *(JOHN[5], GEORGE MOSES[4], JOHN THOMAS[3], JACKSON[2], THOMAS[1])* was born 10 Dec 1956 in New York, New York. He married ARLETHA BIAS.

Child of JOHN DAVENPORT and ARLETHA BIAS is:

    i.   LAURA[7] DAVENPORT, b. 1986, New York, NY..

3. WAYNE[6] DAVENPORT *(JOHN[5], GEORGE MOSES[4], JOHN THOMAS[3], JACKSON[2], THOMAS[1])* was born 16 Sep 1958 in New York, New York, and died 03 Jan 2012 in Virginia. He married WANDA PETTY. She was born 01 Jan 1955.

Children of WAYNE DAVENPORT and WANDA PETTY are:

    i.   CALEB[7] DAVENPORT, b. 1984.

    ii.   JOSHUA DAVENPORT, b. 1986.

    iii.   DANIEL DAVENPORT, b. 1988.

    iv.   MICAH DAVENPORT, b. 1990.

Descendants of John Davenport

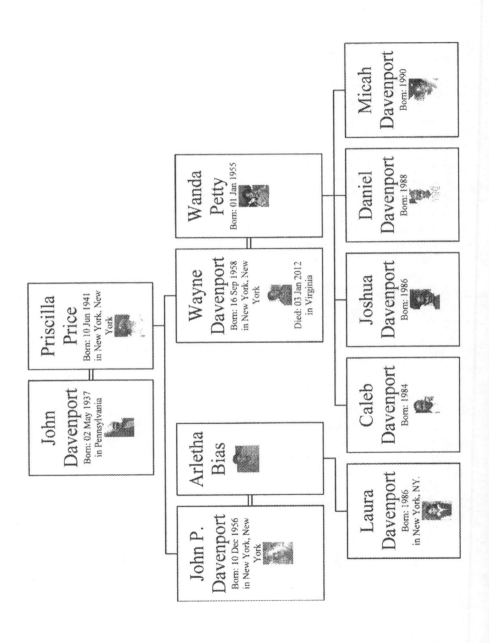

CHAPTER 7

MARGARETT ROBINSON 1820

Descendants of Margaret Robinson

Generation 1

1. **MARGARET[1] ROBINSON** was born in 1820 in King & Queen County, Virginia. She died on 01 May 1888 in King & Queen County, Va.. She married **ALEXANDER GILMORE**. He was born in 1799 in King & Queen County, Va.. She married **GEORGE JORDAN**. He was born in 1814 in King & Queen County, Va..

Alexander Gilmore and Margaret Robinson had the following children:

    i.   FANNY ELLEN[2] GILMORE was born in 1843.

    ii.   Lucy Ann Gilmore WAS BORN IN 1845.

    iii.   HARRIETT T GILMORE was born in 1847.

    iv.   SARAH JANE GILMORE was born in 1849.

George Jordan and Margaret Robinson had the following children:

    i.   LUCY[2] JORDAN was born in 1845 in King & Queen County, Va..

2. ii.   SARAH J. JORDAN was born in 1849 in King & Queen County, Va.. She married Dabney Robinson, son of John Robinson and Mary Harris on 26 Dec 1875 in King & Queen County, Va.. He was born in 1835 in King & Queen County, Va..

3. iii. MARIA IRENA JORDAN was born in 1851 in King & Queen County, Va.. She married (1) WILLIAM B. COLLINS, son of Mason Collins and Susan Dungy on 27 Jan 1869 in King & Queen County, Va.. He was born in 1840 in King & Queen County, Va.. She married (2) GEORGE W. HENDERSON, son of Peter Henderson and Elizabeth Tuppence on 02 Apr 1891 in King & Queen County, Va.. He was born in 1830 in King & Queen County, Virginia.

4. iv.   PRISCILLA JORDAN was born in 1852 in King & Queen County, Va.. She married (2) Livi LEE on 13 Dec 1888 in King & Queen County, Va.. He was born in 1846 in King & Queen County, Va..

Generation 2

2. **SARAH J.² JORDAN** (Margaret¹ Robinson) was born in 1849 in King & Queen County, Va.. She married Dabney Robinson, son of John Robinson and Mary Harris on 26 Dec 1875 in King & Queen County, Va.. He was born in 1835 in King & Queen County, Va..

Notes for Sarah J. Jordan:

Sarah J. Jordan took the sirname of her step father. Her father was Alexander Gilmore the first husband of her mother.

Notes for Dabney Robinson:

The 1875 Marriage to Sarah Jordan was performed by his uncle Lorenzo Robinson

Dabney Robinson and Sarah J. Jordan had the following children:

	i.	HARRIET³ ROBINSON was born in 1879.
	ii.	MARGARET ROBINSON was born in 1882. She married O. KADEMY.
5.	iii.	FANNIE E. ROBINSON was born in 1885. She married O. MCDONALD.
6.	iv.	JULIE A. ROBINSON was born in 1886. She married JOHN H. PATTERSON. He was born in 1877.
	v.	ALFRED G. ROBINSON was born in 1888. He married LOMIE.

3. **MARIA IRENA² JORDAN** (Margaret¹ Robinson) was born in 1851 in King & Queen County, Va.. She married (1) **WILLIAM B. COLLINS**, son of Mason Collins and Susan Dungy on 27 Jan 1869 in King & Queen County, Va.. He was born in 1840 in King & Queen County, Va.. She married (2) **GEORGE W. HENDERSON**, son of Peter Henderson and Elizabeth Tuppence on 02 Apr 1891 in King & Queen County, Va.. He was born in 1830 in King & Queen County, Virginia.

Notes for Maria Irena Jordan:

Identified as a Mulatto in the 1870 K&Q county census.

Notes for William B. Collins:

Identified as a Mulatto in the 1870 K&Q county census.

William B. Collins and Maria Irena Jordan had the following children:

    i.   MARY ALICE[3] COLLINS was born in 1869 in King & Queen County, Va..

Notes for Mary Alice Collins:

Identified as a Mulatto in the 1870 K&Q county census

    ii.   MARTHA J. COLLINS was born in 1871 in King & Queen County, Va..

    iii.   GEORGE MASON COLLINS was born in 1876 in King & Queen County, Va..

    iv.   SARAH C. COLLINS was born in 1876 in King & Queen County, Va..

Notes for Sarah C. Collins:

Identified as a Mulatto in the 1870 K&Q county census.

    v.   WILLIAM ARCHIE COLLINS was born in 1878 in King & Queen County, Va..

George W. Henderson and Maria Irena Jordan had the following child:

    i.   HENRY[3] HENDERSON.

4. **Priscilla² Jordan** (Margaret¹ Robinson) was born in 1852 in King & Queen County, Va.. She married (2) **Livi Lee** on 13 Dec 1888 in King & Queen County, Va.. He was born in 1846 in King & Queen County, Va..

Notes for Priscilla Jordan:

Identified as a Mulatto in the 1870 K&Q county census

Priscilla Jordan had the following children:

       i.   James Albert³ Jordan was born in 1871.

      ii.   Lucy Jordan was born in 1878.

Livi Lee and Priscilla Jordan had the following children:

       i.   Lillian³ Lee.

      ii.   James Lee.

     iii.   Daisy Lee.

Generation 3

5. **FANNIE E.[3] ROBINSON** (Sarah J.[2] Jordan, Margaret[1]) was born in 1885. She married **O. MCDONALD**.

    O. McDonald and Fannie E. Robinson had the following child:

    i. ROBERT[4] MCDONALD was born in 1911.

6. **JULIE A.[3] ROBINSON** (Sarah J.[2] Jordan, Margaret[1]) was born in 1886. She married **JOHN H. PATTERSON**. He was born in 1877.

    John H. Patterson and Julie A. Robinson had the following children:

    i. JOHN A.[4] PATTERSON was born in 1908.
    ii. JAMES H. PATTERSON was born in 1910.
    iii. ETHEL PATTERSON was born in 1912.
    iv. SARAH PATTERSON was born in 1914.
    v. WILLIAM PATTERSON was born in 1919.

CHAPTER 8

GEORGE ROBINSON 1828

Descendants of George Robinson

Generation 1

1. **GEORGE[1] ROBINSON** was born in 1828 in King & Queen County, Va.. He married **JUDITH**. She was born in 1831.

Notes for Judith:

Mulatto Per 1870 Census

George Robinson and Judith had the following children:

- 2. i. CLARENCE[2] ROBINSON was born in 1858 in King & Queen County, Va.. He married ETTA. She was born in 1869 in King & Queen County, Va..
  - ii. LEWIS J. ROBINSON was born in 1860 in King & Queen County, Va..
  - iii. MARY A. ROBINSON was born in 1864 in King & Queen County, Va..
- 3. iv. WILLIAM ROBINSON was born in 1865 in King & Queen County, Va.. He married FANNY. She was born in 1873.
  - v. GEORGIANA ROBINSON was born in 1867 in King & Queen County, Va..

vi. ROBERTA ROBINSON was born in 1869 in King & Queen County, Va..

vii. CHARLEY ROBINSON was born in 1871 in King & Queen County, Va..

4. viii. MOSES ROBINSON was born in 1872 in King & Queen County, Va.. He married ANNA. She was born in 1874.

ix. LEAH ROBINSON was born in 1875 in King & Queen County, Va..

x. LUCY J. ROBINSON was born in 1880 in King & Queen County, Va..

Generation 2

2. **CLARENCE² ROBINSON** (George¹) was born in 1858 in King & Queen County, Va.. He married **ETTA**. She was born in 1869 in King & Queen County, Va..

Clarence Robinson and Etta had the following children:

- 5. i. MABEL³ HOLMES was born in 1896 in King & Queen County, Va.. She married William Robinson in 1920 in King & Queen County, Va..
  - ii. LIDA W. ROBINSON was born in 1898 in King & Queen County, Va..
  - iii. JOHN ROBINSON was born in 1901 in King & Queen County, Va..

3. **WILLIAM² ROBINSON** (George¹) was born in 1865 in King & Queen County, Va.. He married **FANNY**. She was born in 1873.

William Robinson and Fanny had the following children:

- 6. i. LEBURTA³ ROBINSON was born in 1896 in King & Queen County, Va.. She married JAMES L. KIDD. He was born in 1896 in King & Queen County, Va..
  - ii. TRESSIE J. ROBINSON was born in 1896 in King & Queen County, Virginia.
  - iii. VIRGINIA ROBINSON was born in 1898 in King & Queen County, Va..
  - iv. GEORGE T. ROBINSON was born in 1902 in King & Queen County, Va..
  - v. HELEN ROBINSON was born in 1904 in King & Queen County, Va..
  - vi. OTHENA ROBINSON was born in 1906 in King & Queen County, Va..

       vii.   STANLEY ROBINSON was born in 1908 in King & Queen County, Va..

      viii.   JOSEPH ROBINSON was born in 1910 in King & Queen County, Va..

       ix.   JULIA ROBINSON was born in 1913 in King & Queen County, Va..

4. **MOSES² ROBINSON** (George¹) was born in 1872 in King & Queen County, Va.. He married **ANNA**. She was born in 1874.

Moses Robinson and Anna had the following children:

7.   i.   MARIAN³ ROBINSON was born in 1901 in King & Queen County, Va.. She married James L. Brown, son of Edward Brown and Fannie on 27 Jul 1921 in King & Queen County, Va.. He was born in 1882 in King & Queen County, Va..

8.   ii.   ANNIE MAY ROBINSON was born in 1903 in King & Queen County, Va.. She married Doney Green, son of Philip Green and Florence on 10 Dec 1930 in King & Queen County, Va.. He was born in 1882 in Essex County, Va..

       iii.   JR MOSES ROBINSON was born in 1905.

       iv.   SAM ROBINSON was born in 1907.

       v.   WILLIAM ROBINSON was born in 1907.

       vi.   JAMES E. ROBINSON was born in 1909.

       vii.   ROBERT S. ROBINSON was born in 1912.

      viii. BROWN ROBINSON was born in 1915.

       ix.   JOSEPHINE ROBINSON was born in 1917.

Generation 3

5. **Mabel**[3] **Holmes** (Clarence[2] Robinson, George[1] Robinson) was born in 1896 in King & Queen County, Va.. She married William Robinson in 1920 in King & Queen County, Va..

   William Robinson and Mabel Holmes had the following children:

       i.   Gladys M.[4] Robinson was born in 1916 in King & Queen County, Va..

       ii.   Orrin Blide Robinson was born in 1916 in King & Queen County, Va..

6. **Leburta**[3] **Robinson** (William[2], George[1]) was born in 1896 in King & Queen County, Va.. She married **James L. Kidd**. He was born in 1896 in King & Queen County, Va..

   James L. Kidd and Leburta Robinson had the following child:

       i.   Lizzie[4] Kidd was born in 1916 in King & Queen County, Va..

7. **Marian**[3] **Robinson** (Moses[2], George[1]) was born in 1901 in King & Queen County, Va.. She married James L. Brown, son of Edward Brown and Fannie on 27 Jul 1921 in King & Queen County, Va.. He was born in 1882 in King & Queen County, Va..

   James L. Brown and Marian Robinson had the following children:

       i.   Lillian[4] Brown was born in 1923 in King & Queen County, Va..

       ii.   Lelia Brown was born in 1924 in King & Queen County, Va..

       iii.   Elenora M. Brown was born in 1925 in King & Queen County, Va..

iv. BERTHA BROWN was born in 1928 in King & Queen County, Va..

v. JAMES E. BROWN was born in 1931 in King & Queen County, Va..

vi. CONSTANCE BROWN was born in 1934 in King & Queen County, Va..

vii. ROGER BROWN was born in 1938 in King & Queen County, Va..

8. **ANNIE MAY**^{3} **ROBINSON** (Moses^2, George^1) was born in 1903 in King & Queen County, Va.. She married Doney Green, son of Philip Green and Florence on 10 Dec 1930 in King & Queen County, Va.. He was born in 1882 in Essex County, Va..

Doney Green and Annie May Robinson had the following children:

i. RUSSELL^4 GREEN was born in 1924 in King & Queen County, Va..

ii. EVELYN GREEN was born in 1933 in King & Queen County, Va..

iii. MOSES GREEN was born in 1935 in King & Queen County, Va..

iv. EDNA GREEN was born in 1937 in King & Queen County, Va..

BIBLIOGRAPHY

Tracts of Land, 1865, King & Queen County, VA

King & Queen County Land Book 1837 - 1842

"Commissioner Records King & Queen County, VA". "A Listing of Free Negroes and Mulattoes, - 1833".

Claims Filed in King & Queen County, Va. Under Act of Congress of March 3, 1871

United States Census Record; 1830 thru 1940

Agriculture Census Records for King & Queen County, Va. 1850 – 1880

Agriculture Census Records for Middlesex County, Va. 1850

Photo of Gloucester Point Water Battery (Courtesy of the Library of Congress) taken in Early May 1861.

Arlingtoncemetery.net Photo of General Philip Sheridan

King & Queen County, Va. Chancery Order Books

King & Queen County, Va. Order Books

King & Queen County, Va. Marriage Registers

King & Queen County, Va. Deed Books

King & Queen County, Va. Wills

Jordan Chronicles 1820-2002 LaSandra Jordan Murray. Family Historian

U.S., World War 1 Draft Registration Cards, 1917-1918

Vital Statistic Records – Richmond, Va. Library and Ancestry Program

APPENDIX

Appendix I

Marriages performed by Lorenzo Dow Robinson – 1860'S & 70's.

Appendix 2

U.S. Southern Claims Commission, Allowed Claims 1871-1888. Property Removed from private property during the civil war.

Lorenzo Dow Robinson – June 18, 1864

Archie Robinson – June 18, 1864

Roll 25

Target 3

KING AND QUEEN COUNTY, VIRGINIA
Robinson, Archie

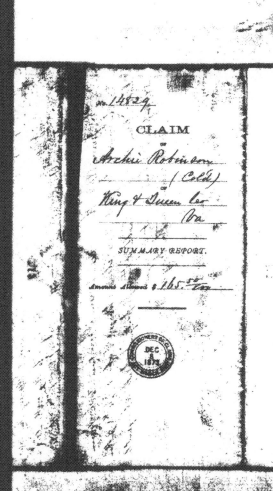

NARA 122

No. 14529.

The Claim of Archie Robinson (Col'd), of King & Queen Co., in the State of Virginia

	No. of Item	NATURE OF CLAIM	AMOUNT CLAIMED Dollars	Cts.	AMOUNT ALLOWED Dollars	Cts.	AMOUNT DISALLOWED Dollars	Cts.
1864 June	1	One Horse	150		100		50	
	2	25 Bushels Corn	25		25			
	3	150 pounds of Bacon	25	50	25	50		
	4	Two Barrels salted fish	20		15		5	
			$220	50	$165	50	$55	00

REMARKS

The claimant is a free born colored man & owned a farm of about 60 acres on which he resided during the war. We think he was a Union man in sympathy with the Union cause & an adherent to the cause & [illegible] of the United States during the [illegible] [illegible].

In June 1864, the forces of Gen. Sheridan took from the claimant the first three items charged & about 3/4ths of the last item and considerable other property, probably chargeable as supplies which is not charged.

We recommend the payment of $165.50

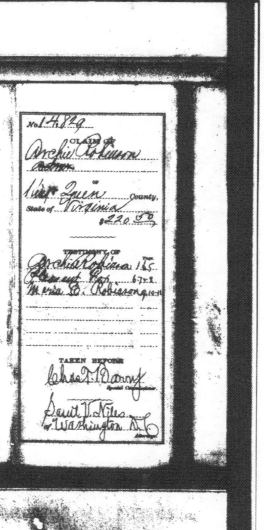

NARA 124

[FIRST PAGE]

Before the Commissioners of Claims.
ACT OF CONGRESS, MARCH 3, 1871.

Case of *Archie Robinson (Colored)*
No. *14,884*

It is hereby certified, that on the *5th* day of *October* 187*8*, at *King & Queen Court House* in the county of *King & Queen* and State of *Virginia* personally came before me the following persons, viz:

Archie Robinson .... Claimant,
Alfred Pollard, Richland .... Council, or Attorney,
and *Clement Fox, Nancy E. Robinson, wife* ....
.... Claimant's Witnesses,

for the purpose of a hearing in the above entitled claim.

Each and every deponent, previous to his or her examination, was properly and duly sworn or affirmed by me to tell the truth, the whole truth, and nothing but the truth, concerning the matters under examination; and the testimony of each deponent was written out by me, or in my presence, and as given before me, and subsequently read over to said deponent, by whom it was also subscribed in my presence.

Witness my hand and seal this *5th* day of *October* 187*8*.

[signature]
Special Commissioner of Claims.

Deposition of *Claimant*

In answer to the First General Interrogatory, deponent says:

My name is *Archie Robinson*, my age *31* years; my residence *King & Queen Court House*, in the State of *Virginia*, and my occupation is *Farmer, Archie ( )*
I am *the related to the* claimant,
and have *no* beneficial interest in *the claim*.

[Note: The Claimant should always (if he can read and write) write out his own deposition.]

To question 2. He says from April 1" 1861 to June 1 1865 — I lived about 3 miles from this Court House in King and Queen County, Virginia, on my own lands a farm of sixty acres, about 8 acres cultivated & the rest woodland & cut-land, farming — neither changed my residence —

To question 3, 4, 5. He says, By pressure I have. In 1861 I was taken from my home near here, and carried to Gloucester Point and made to work on fortifications for about 1 hour, got off there on a weeks furlough & started home on foot (it is about 40 miles) arrived home safely. In 1863 the Confederate enrolling officer took me and carried me to Stevensville, kept until noon next day, then discharged me to come home and house Buxton Robinsons sack of corn which they carried away, he was my brother in law, & I never was troubled after that —

To question 7 to 20 inclusive, He says No Sir

" 24. He says only as before described —
I never took any oath to get released, never arrested by the U.S. Government

" 25. He says, the Confederates took some fodder, that is all, did not pay me for it.

" 26 to 39 inclusive, He says No Sir

40. He says. At the beginning of the Rebellion I sympathized with the Union Cause — my feelings & sympathies were in favor of the Union Cause all through — I had no relative, ally or associate who enlisted I wished a success to Union cause —

41. He says I am a loyalty seeking that

beginning & end of hostilities my sympathies
were constantly with the cause of the Union. That
I never did of my own free will and accord do
anything against said cause and was always
willing to do all in my power for said cause.

13 He says He says Am free Bought the
House of Eliz H. Garrett in 1863. paid 15 a
worked in the Country about 6 months earning the
money. Bought the farm 60 acres at six dollars
an acre in 1862 my father worked farming & cutting
wood. did not pay for it when I bought
it. I owe some on the farm yet. owe on
the farm yet yes No one has any interest
in this claim but myself

At the taking of the first testy

To question 1 He says I was present

2 He says. I saw the Horse & Bacon — fresh
flour — corn — Clothes — meal — Beans —
When my claim was made out I did not
remember all these items

3 He says. The Horse was in the lot near
my house. they were union soldiers came and
put a halter and led him away. The Bacon
was taken same time by Union Soldiers. They took
6 hams, the pieces would weigh hams
would average, I think 25 lbs per
 the corn was taken at same time

4.

out of crib, 5 Barrels. (25 Bushels) 4 Bbls ...... in the crib. the other Bbl was in ...... the Cart — afton. 1/2 Bbl. — 1 Bushel meal + 5 Bags taken at same time — They [the] soldiers said they was going to carry these articles away, and that it would make one a better citizen

" " 4/ He says from my farm. 1864. June 17, by Union Soldiers. should think there was 4 or 5 taking the property & 40 or 50 around the house. They were engaged about 1/4 of an hour

" 5 He says nobody but my wife & myself..
" 6. He says I did not recognize any officers..
" 7 He says. the horses & corn put in bags. Bacon in bags. flour & meal in bags.
" 8 He says by Union Soldier in Hancock..
" 9 He says. I don't know they started in direction of Camp. all ..... I did not follow it

" " 10 He says. Myself some of the ..... the other I know nothing of

" " 11 He says. I complained to the soldiers they said I was a rebel and they would take my property and make me a better man

" " 12 He says. None I did not ....
" " 13 He says. ....
" " 14 He says. About 20 ....

NARA 128

hing they came there on the 17th day of June
and left on the 8th day of Nov 1864
I knew none of the Officers

Question 15 Heros — The Corn was ripe in the out on the
Oct. The Horse was 4 Year old small good
condition worth about $150 – 1 bushel of
meal good condition Bacon good condition
smoked —

Question 16 Heresay Measured the Corn had 5 barrels
5 bushels to the barrel. had 8 pieces of bacon
weight 175 lbs. het and 2 of these there was
Lackey & was just from the mill the full barrell
of fish marshed mew worth about 13 per
hundred the 1/4 barrell was being worth about
$4.50 & sail all the property taken.

Question 17 Heresay Not applicable

Circular Jany 20th 1872

I have never received pay for anything
furnished the Government a Ration

Archie Robinson

Claim of Archie Robinson

Deposition of Pleasant Ross (Colored)

My name is Pleasant Ross, my age is 64 years old. My residence is Henry & Green County Va. My occupation is a Farmer. I am not related to the claimant and have no interest in this claim.

Question 1. Ans. I was present
Question 2. Ans. I saw the Horse, Pork & bacon taken
Question 3. Ans. I saw Union Soldiers take off the Horses. I saw the bacon carried away. I saw one barrel of Pork carried away

Question 4. Ans. About 3 miles from the Court House on James Mitchell's farm of which claimant was Tenant, In 1864 on the 17th of June. I saw some 10 or 12 Soldiers engaged in the taking. I think they were cavalry about 34 of an hour.

Question 5. Ans. There was nobody else with me
Question 6. Ans. I don't know
Question 7. Ans. The Soldiers came and took the property and went off.
Question 8. Ans. By Soldiers on their horses
Question 9. Ans. They carried it to their Camps about 1/2 mile from claimant's farm. I went with them, they took me along.
Question 10. Ans. I don't know myself, but believe that they used it themselves

NARA 130

To Inter 11 Harvey I don't know
To Inter 12 Harvey I don't know
To Inter 13 Harvey Yes In the daytime openly
To Inter 14 Harvey The Lewis Army passed through there on a raid they rec this about one day

To Inter 15 Harvey One Sorrel Horse about 5 years old gait with about 750 —. I did not see the bacon weighed there was 6 pieces in all shoulders hams, & sides. I don't know as to the value of the Fish.

To Inter 16 Harvey I never think bought the horse and see him taken away. I don't know as to the quantity of Bacon as was on barrel of Fish don't know how many pounds

To Inter 17 & 18 Harvey Not applicable

Questions as to loyalty

I have known the Claimant for 14 years I was intimate with him during the war I lived about 1/4 of a mile from him. he always expressed his sentiments in favor of the Union Cause. I was an adherent of the Union cause and the Claimant is regarded to me. I always conversed with him

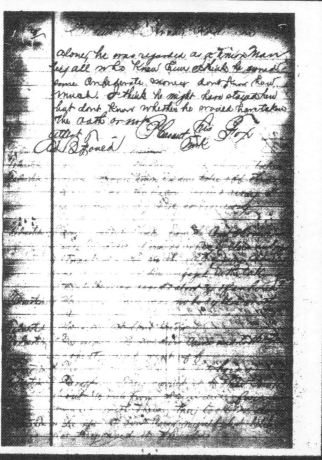

14829

Claim of Archie Robinson

Deposition of Maria E Robinson (colored)

My name is Maria E Robinson, my age is 34 years, my residence is near King & Queen Court House Va. my occupation a housewife. I am the claimant's wife, and have a beneficial interest in this claim.

To Question 1st — He says I own ?????

" " 2 I saw the Horse, Meat & Corn taken also the flour and meal & fish

" " 3 All these things were taken at one time by Soldiers of Genl Sheridans Army

" " 4 Things — On our Farm situated about 2½ miles from King & Queen Court House. The Horse was from the pasture adjoining the house. The meat was taken from the Smoke house, the fish was taken out of the Smoke House, the Corn was taken out of the Crib, the flour and Meal from our dwelling. It happened the year before the war ended in June on a Saturday, by Soldiers belonging to Genl Sheridans Army, there was a large number present perhaps 30 or more. I saw ? go into the Smokehouse.

" " 5 Theare myself & my Husband only

" " 6 Theare I dont know

" " 7 of the use The Horse was led off. part of the Corn was fed to their Horses and part carried off in bags on horseback, the probability being the ??? in bags including the fish

The Bacon flour and Meat were put in
bags slung across the horse's back and
carried off in that manner.
10 Question 9 She says I don't know Sir.
"   " 11 She says I saved some of the Corn fed to the
Horses on the lot, the rest of the property
Suppose was taken for the use of the Soldiers
but don't know.
"   " She says, I do Sir
"   " 12 She says No Sir I did not ask to be remunerated
"   " 13 She says In the daytime about 2 or 3 o'clock
in the afternoon none taken secretly
"   " 14 She says There was an encampment about ½
mile above ours 1½ miles from our houses
they came Saturday evening and left next day no
battle around, there.
"   4 15 She says, The Horse was right young and in
good condition my husband told me he gave 150 –
for her – The bacon consisted of Hams shoulders
and Midlings – The Corn was on the Cob and in
the Crib – The Fish were in a barrel in good condition – The flour and meal was in a barrel
don't know what they were worth.
"   " 16 She says Because the wine taken – Saw Corn
taken don't know how much, I saw 6 pieces
of bacon taken – I had part of a barrel of fish
and part of a barrel of Cherry and they took

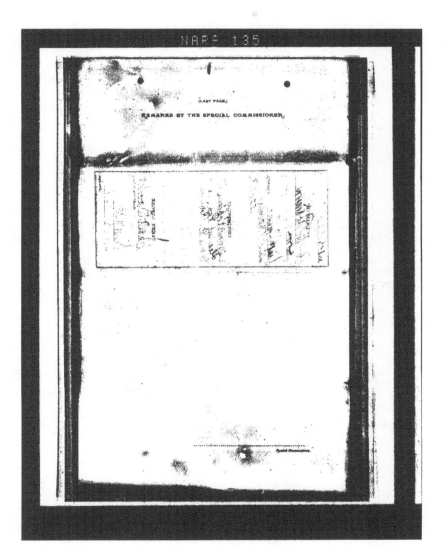

14829

OFFICE OF THE
Commissioners of Claims.

Washington, D.C., Aug 21, 1873.

MEMORANDUM:

Archie Robinson
King & Queen Co
Va.

Good Union man

Mr Hasley Collector
of Customs at West Point
and Hereford Anderson
Informants —

Report of Spl Agent Geo
Tucker —

"Y"

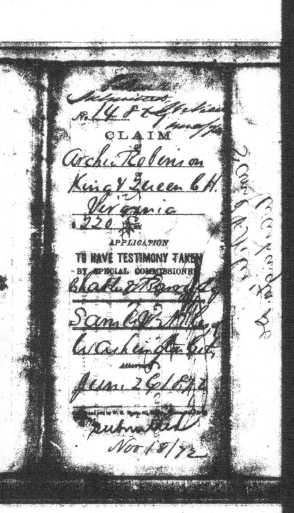

Before the Commissioners of Claims.
Under Act of Congress of March 3, 1871.

In the matter of the Claim of Archie Robinson, col'd

Comes now the Claimant Charles F. T. Racey, Esq. Special Commissioner for the State of Virginia

1	One horse	100	00
2	25 bushels of corn	25	00
3	750 pounds of bacon		
4	two barrels of salted fish		

$220.50

That, as stated in the Petition aforesaid, the property in question was taken from claimant, Archie Robinson of King &
Queen Co Va in Va for the use of a portion
of the army of the United States, to-wit (3) Cavalry &c
and commanded by Gen Phil Sheridan and that
the persons who took or received the property, or who authorized or directed it to be taken or furnished, were the following:

Names	Regiments, Corps, or Station
Phil Sheridan	May Gene Co &c not known

That the property was removed to Camp Stony
and used for or by (5) U S troops
all this on or about the
day of June in the year 186 4 as appears by the petition presented to the
Commissioners

Pleasant Fox — King & Queen C H Va
Lorenzo D Robinson — do

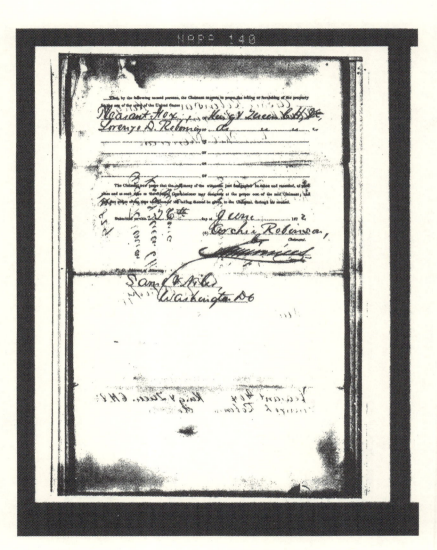

14829 June 27

PETITION
of
Archie Robinson
(Colored)

TO THE
COMMISSIONERS OF CLAIMS.

Residence of Claimant _Kingsdown_
County of Henrico, Va.

Nature of Claim _for prop-_
erty taken for
use of Army

Amount claimed, $ 220.50

FILED BY
Saml. V. Niles
Washington D.C.
June 26/87

PETITION.

To the Honorable Commissioners of Claims,
Under the Act of Congress of March 3, 1871, Washington, D. C.

The Petition of (1) Archie Robinson

respectfully represents:

That he is a citizen of the United States, and reside at present at or near King & Queen Court House, Virginia, and that he resided when this claim accrued at or near King & Queen Court House, in King & Queen County, Virginia.

That he has a claim against the United States for property taken for the use of the army of the United States during the late rebellion at (or near) King & Queen Court House, in the County of King & Queen, and State of Virginia.

That the said claim, stated by items, and excluding any and all items of damage, destruction, and loss, (and not one,) of property, of unauthorized or unnecessary depredations by bodies of other persons upon property, or of trust or compensation for the use or occupation of buildings, grounds, or other real estate, is as follows:

	QUANTITIES AND ARTICLES.	VALUE.	
		20 00	
		25 00	
		20 00	
	Total	$220 50	

NARA 143

... That the property in question was taken or furnished by the army of the United States, known as the _____ army corps that _____ and commanded by Generals Philip Sheridan and that the persons who took or received the property, or who authorized or directed it to be taken or furnished, were the following:

No.	NAME	CO.	Regiment, Corps or Station
	Philip Sheridan		

... That the property was removed to a neighboring _____ and used for or by said troops for military purposes all this on or about the eighteenth day of June in the year 1864.

That no voucher, receipt, or other writing was given for the property

That your petitioner verily believe that the property described was taken under the following circumstances, or one or more of such circumstances, viz:

1. For the actual use of the army, and not for the mere gratification of individual officers or soldiers already provided by the Government with such imitation to their necessity as people who share or hire.
2. In consequence of the failure of the troops of the United States to receive from the Government in due regularity supplies, or to have in such proportion as the time, the articles and supplies necessary for them, of which they were entitled to receive and have.
3. In consequence of some necessity for the articles taken, or similar articles, which necessity justified the officers or soldiers taking them.
4. The same purpose to necessity, could, beneficial or practicable to the stores of the Government to pay for it.
5. Under threats or authority of some officer, or other person concerned with the army, whose rank, effective duties or other circumstance at the time constrained, compelled, or justified him in taking or receiving it, or putting it to the uses received.

That _____ your Petitioner _____ of the original owner of said claim; and that he is _____ the present owner of the same _____ and that no other person has any beneficial interest in the claim

... That your petitioner remained loyally adherent to the cause and the Government of the United States during the war, and was so loyal before and at the time of the taking _____ of the property for which this claim is made, and he solemnly declares that, from the beginning of hostilities against the United States to the end thereof, his sympathies were constantly with the cause of the United States; that he never, of his own free will and accord, did anything, or offered, or sought, or attempted to do anything, by word or deed, to injure said cause or favor the cause; and that he was at all times ready and willing, when called upon, to aid and assist the cause of the Union, or its supporters, so far as his means and power, and the circumstances of the case, permitted.

Note to Deputies: Who requisitions are fully and particularly explainable.
1. Division will be sent to fields this yard to which subsequently was surveyed.
2. State as fully and accurately as possible, the particular persons or commands, using the property, and to whose particular pass it was applied to founded to be applied.
3. If any documents or writings papers were given, annex the originals or copies, or make where the originals are to be found and give the substance of them.
4. "Taken" or "furnished."
5. The loyalty of the owner of the property when taken or furnished, and of all persons having a pecuniary interest therein to the claim, must be established by proof.
6. If any other persons than the original person now own or have an interest in the claim, state how such ownership or interest was acquired.

NARA 144

Roll 25

Target 4

KING AND QUEEN COUNTY, VIRGINIA
Robinson, Lorenzo D.

#14828

CLAIM

Lorenzo D. Robinson
(Cold)

King & Queen Co
Va

SUMMARY REPORT.

$305

No. 14525

The Claim of Lorenzo D. Robinson (Cold), of King & Queen Co., in the State of Virginia

		NATURE OF CLAIM	AMOUNT CLAIMED		AMOUNT ALLOWED		AMOUNT DISALLOWED	REMARKS
1864	1	Two horses	300	00	200	00	100	He is a freeborn Colored man sixty years of age. He o[wns] a farm of 270 acres about half a mile from King & Queen C[ourt] Ho. on which he resided throughout the war. He was a l[oy]al Union man in full sympathy with the Union cause. [?] the above people they were always believers [of the?] Union failed & few of it surrender –
June	2	One new Saddle	10	00	10			
"	3	100 Bushels of Chain Corn	100	00	25		75	
"	4	3 cr tb. Bacon @ 15¢	45	00	45			
"	5	One Bbl. Salt fish	10	00	10			
"	6	25 sacks (bags)	10	00	10			
"	7	½ Bbl flour	7	50	5		2	50
			482	50	305	00	177	50

His property was taken from his farm in June 1864 [by] Gen. Sheridans forces – It is doubtful whether more than [half?] fourth the quantity of Corn charged was taken – the other ite[ms] are exceedingly well proven –

We recommend the payment of $305.00

No. 14,828

CLAIM OF

Lorenzo D. Robinson

of

King & Queen County,
State of Virginia

$482.50

TESTIMONY OF

Lorenzo D. Robinson	1 & 5
Martha Robinson	6 & 9
Mathilda N. Robinson	10 & 12
Dunbar Robinson	13 & 14

TAKEN BEFORE

Chas. T. Dorsey

Saml. P. Files
of Washington D.C.

[FRONT PAGE.]

Before the Commissioners of Claims.

ACT OF CONGRESS, MARCH 3, 1871.

Case *Lorenzo Robinson*
No. 14,828

It is hereby certified that on the 7th day of October 1872, at _King & Queen C.H._, in the county of _King & Queen_ and State of _Virginia_, personally came before me the following persons, viz:

Lorenzo Robinson .... Claimant,
Robert G. Saint & Miles .... Council, or Attorney,
and _Martha Robinson, Matilda A. Robinson & Gustavus Robinson_ .... CLAIMANT'S WITNESSES,

for the purpose of a hearing in the above entitled cause.

Each and every deponent, previous to his or her examination, was properly and duly sworn or affirmed by me to tell the truth, the whole truth, and nothing but the truth, concerning the matters under examination; and the testimony of each deponent was written out by me, or in my presence, and as given before me, and subsequently read over to said deponent, by whom it was also subscribed in my presence.

Witness my hand and seal this 7 day of October, 1872.

[SEAL]

Chas. F. Davis
Special Commissioner of the Commissioners of Claims.

Deposition of _Lorenzo Robinson_

In answer to the First General Interrogatory, the Deponent says:

My name is _Lorenzo Robinson_, my age _60_ years, my residence in _King & Queen Co._, in the State of _Virginia_, and my occupation a _Farmer_; I am _related to the Claimant_, and have _a beneficial_ interest in the claim.

14828

Answers to 1st set of Questions

Ans. 2 Answer. I lived on my farm about 2½ miles from King & Queen Court House Virginia. My farm contains about 270 acres, about 90 acres were cultivated the balance was woodland and my occupation was Farming

Question 3 to 29 inclusive Re pays No sir

3 Answer. My Son Archie was carried to Gloucester Point Virginia by the Confederates to work on the fortifications, he did not stay more than half an hour I did not furnish him with anything whatever

30 to 39 inclusive the pays No Sir

40 Answer. At the beginning of the War I was in favor of the Union and remained so throughout the War. I thought the Union was the Colored Mans Salvation

41 Answer. I do most solemnly declare that from the beginning of hostilities to the end thereof my sympathies were constantly with the cause of the United States, and I never did anything against the Union but always tried to assist them all in my power. — I was far from my farm Apl me altogether about two _____ at _____ the _____

Answer to 2 set of Question

Answer 1. Answer. I was not present at first, but saw some of the property taken

Question Answer. I saw the Corn, flour, Bacon, Fish & saddle this is all that was taken in my presence

" 2 Answ. The property was all taken during 1 day, by soldiers belonging to Genl Sheridans Command, they stated that they had orders to take the property

" 4 Answ. From my farm situated about 2½ miles from King & Queen Court House Virginia on the 10th day of June AD 1864, by soldiers belonging to Genl Sheridans Command. I saw about 75 or 80 engaged in the taking of the property; they were engaged from 12 M. until sundown

" 5 Answ. Myself wife and daughter were present
" 6 Answ. I saw no officer present
" 7 Answ. The soldiers took the saddle and carried it away — the Corn was taken in bags & in a cart. the bacon was taken in bags and put on their horse backs — the Fish was taken in bags same as bacon — they used the bags to put in the fish & bacon, the flour was put in a bag same as bacon & fish

To Intert 9 Answ. I believe to their Camp about 2 miles from my house

" 10 Answ. The Soldiers ordered my wife to bake some bread for them out some of the flour, they said they took it for their own use

NARA 152

Q. 11 Ansp. No Sir
" 12 Ansp. No Sir I did not know that I could
at one. I had a conversation with one of
the officers the day after the property was taken
he stated to me that they had been on a raid
and that they were short of food and they
were ordered to take the property
" 13 Ansp. The property was taken in the day time
and openly from about 12 o'clock noon
until sunset
" 14 Ansp. The command of Genl Sheridan army
encamped about ½ mile from my farm when
the property was taken, the came there Saturday
morning and left on Sunday morning
" 15 Ansp. Two gray horses one of them was about
4 years old and worth about $150 in greenbacks
one was 10 years old and worth the same.
the saddle was new I paid $40 in greenbacks
for it The corn was piled in the barn ripe it
was worth about $5 per barrel. The bacon was
new and worth between 17 & 20 cts per pound
the fish were worth 12½ cts each. The best seals
were worth about 5 cts a each. The flour was
worth about 7.50 at that time
" 16 Ansp. I owned the 2 horses I seen them
the saddle and taken in my presence, I merely estimate
the quantity of corn. There were 2 pieces of bacon
taken consisting of Shoulder middling
I saw the fish taken I have another

14828

Claim of Loring Robinson Colored

Testimony of Martha Robinson Colored wife of Claimant

My name is Martha Robinson my age is about 33 years my residence near King & Queen Court House, my occupation Housekeeper. I am wife of the Claimant and I have a beneficial interest in the Claim.

As to the taking of the property

To question 1. She says. I was present.

" 2 . . . . I saw two horses, Corn, meat flour, salt fish, Bags, & one saddle.

" 3 She says. All these articles taken in one day. Taken by Sheridans Soldiers during the raid through this section. They came onto our lot and took all the property named and left.

4 She says. from our farm near here. In June the year before the end of the war I think, by private soldiers of Sheridans Command. There was a quantity of soldiers engaged in taking our property. Should think there were a hundred. They were there at my place from about 2 o'clock P.M. till sundown

5 She ... Myself & Madison Robinson (son ... that) were only one present at ... before they left. Loring the Claimant ...

6 She says. No officers were present

7. She says the horses were led away, one was taken from the pasture & one from the stable. The saddle taken from the Barn. Corn was taken out of the Barn in bags. The Hams [Bacon?] & Bacon were taken out of the Smoke House. The soldiers said they were ordered to take the property, said the Generals ordered it done.

8. The Horses led away, the saddle was put on the horses back, put the corn in bags and carried on horseback, some carried [it] in bags & some in Buckets. The Bacon and flour was carried off in some manner.

9. She says they started in the direction of Bull Creek but I don't know where they went.

10. She says, I don't know the use for which the property was taken but from the nature of the property I think for the use of the Army.

11. She says No complaint that I know of. We didn't know where the officers was, don't know as we would have known enough to do it anyway.

12. She says no receipts was asked for or given, we did not know it was of any use.

13. She says none taken in the night or secretly.

NARF 156

To question 14   She says, yes sir there were an incampments
about one mile from our house. Shermans
Command or part of it. just come there
that day and left there the next
day. Sunday. no cattle around there. I
knew none of the Quartermasters. or officers

15   She says. One was an old horse, but a
good working horse. the other was a young
Colt not broken. just been saddle broken
The Saddle was an old fashioned plain saddle
dont know its value. or of the horses
The Corn was ripe in the Crib on bacon
on the Cob. it was good. Bacon salted
Salt fish in good Condition & rice flour,
and bag were some in good Condition &
some not.

16   She says. I saw both horses taken. one
saddle. I dont know how much corn there
was taken. There was one. one horse wagon
load taken and the rest in bags. I cant
say how much was taken. I saw 23 or
24 pieces of Bacon taken. they gave me
one piece back after they had taken it
all. it was Hams Shoulders & side pieces
we did not weigh it. Hay took one
whole bbl of Salt & had out most of a
half bbl which we had in the smoke house
There was three Bushels of flour in one bag
which they took. it was measured and was

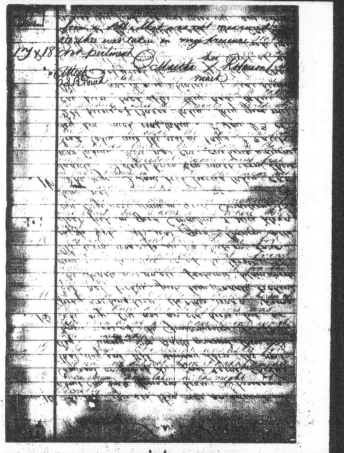

NARA 158

14828 Claim of Lorenzo Robinson

Testimony of Matilda West colored
daughter of Claimant.

My name is Matilda West, my age is
26 years, my residence near Troy & Green
Court House, Virginia, my occupation
Housekeeper. I am daughter of the
Claimant.

As to the taking of the property

To question 1. She says Yes sir I was present

2. She says I saw two Horses, 23 pieces
of Bacon, about one Bbl of fish salted,
about 15 or 20 Bbls of Corn, about one
Bbl flour, about 12 or 13 Bags —

3. She says There were all taken in one day
by soldiers of Genl Sheridans during his
raid down through this section. There
was no officer present, they said they were
ordered to take the property, and that they
were in need of it for their eating and
for their horses &c

4. She says from my fathers farm near here
It was about a year before the war closed
in the month of June, on Saturday
by soldiers of the Union Army under
Genl Sheridan. I do not know how many
but there was a good many of them. I
think there was a hundred all helped
to take the property.

She says My master Master Bo—

and my father the Claimant came just before they left. these were the only ones present.

6. She says. There was no officer I recollect that I know of.

7. She says. one of the horses was taken from the Stable & one from the pasture & led off. The saddle was placed on one of them. The corn was put in Bags & in a small Jersey wagon. the Bacon taken as it was in pieces. the fish were some on strings & some in bags. the Bags were used to put the corn, flour & ▓▓▓ & fish in.

8. She says. by Soldiers on horseback and in a small Jersey wagon.

9. She says. I saw them start towards Camp, but did not see or follow them clear there. as their Camp was out of sight.

10. She says. I only know the use for which it was taken, by what the Soldiers said. they told one they were on a raid and were in need of supplies &c

11. She says she complaint was made that day. the next day he went to complain about it. and he said it was wrong to take all that we had. but that the soldiers needed provisions & such like & had to take all they could get.

Levy Robinson

12 She says No receipts was asked for or given. I don't know why.

13 She says all the property was taken openly in the daytime, afternoon.

14 She says There was camp at Mitchells Hill. About one mile from our place they came there to catch Saturday about 12 M. and Staid until Sunday. No Battle near that I knew of. I did'nt know the Quartermaster or other officer.

15 She says One of the Horses was right Young and one I expect was 9 years old. I don't know the age of either exactly. Just commenced breaking the youngest. the other was a white horse and good work horse. I dont know what their respective value was.

16 She says I saw the 2 Horses & the saddle taken. I saw the Corn taken but dont know how much there was only by hearsay. I think I saw at least 15 Barrels taken at least. this is guessing. I counted 23 pieces of Bacon taken — they were not weighed. I Judge they would average about 20 lbs apiece. one Bbl of Salt Shal, I saw & counted 13 Bags and about one Bbl of flour.

17 & 18 Not pertinent

Matilda L. West
her mark

11828
13

Claim of Lorenzo Robinson

Testimony of Dunbar Robinson Colo
My name is Lorenzo Robinson my age
is 37 my residence near King & Queen Court
House Virginia my occupation farming
I am a Nephew of the Claimant
but have no beneficial interest in the
Claim

I have known Lorenzo Robinson all my
life I was intimate with him during
the war. I lived within one mile of him
all the war, except when I was carried
into the Confederate army (about 6 or 7 months
in all) — I saw him at least 3 or 4
times a week. I often talked with him
about the war. I was a union man of
Course, all colored men wanted to be free
& was if they had any sense union men.
& Lorenzo knew I was a united States
man, and he was in favor of the Union
Cause. and always said so. when I
talked with him alone and in presence
of others. he told the colored peoples
they would be always slaves if the
Union Cause should fail but they was
to be free if it succeeded. all colored
men was looked upon as union men
& inside, about, abroad, and Lorenzo
was same. I don't think Lorenzo
any thing to give but he was in

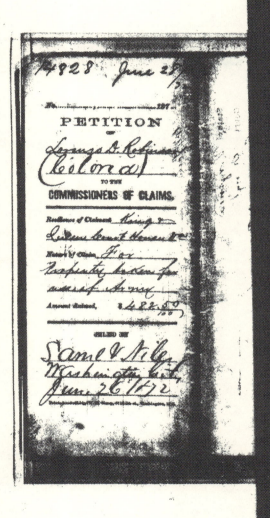

PETITION.

To the Honorable Commissioners of Claims,
Under the Act of Congress of March 3, 1871, Washington, D. C.

The Petition of (1) *Lorenzo Dow Robinson*

respectfully represents:

That he is a citizen of the United States, and reside at present at or near *King & Queen Court House, Virginia*

and that he resided when this claim accrued at or near (2) *King & Queen Court House in the County of King & Queen Va.*

That he has a claim against the United States for property (4) *taken* for the use of the army of the United States during the late rebellion at (or near) *the place where he now resides*

in the County of *King & Queen* and State of *Virginia*

That the said claim, stated by items, and excluding any and all items of damage, destruction, and loss, (and not use,) of property; of unauthorized or unnecessary depredations by troops and other persons upon property, or of rent or compensation for the use or occupation of buildings, grounds, or other real estate, is as follows:

Date.	Quantities and Articles.	Value.	
[illegible]	To two horses pressed into service and used as cavalry horses @ $150 each	300	00
" "	To one new saddle used do do	20	00
" "	To 50 bushels of indian corn used to feed cavalry horses @ $2 per bus	100	00
" "	To 302 lbs of bacon @ 15 per lb.	45	[illegible]
" "	To 1 bbl of salt fish	10	00
" "	To 25 [illegible] bags used to carry off corn in	[illegible]	[illegible]
" "	To 1/2 bbl of flour @ $15 per bbl.	7	50
	Total.	$482	50

Note 1. State full names of all the petitioners.
2. Give the residence of each petitioner.
3. Give the former residence of each petitioner.
4. "Taken," or "furnished."

NARA 166

That said claim has not before been presented to the _____ on account of the inquity for [illegible] _____

And _Samuel H. Liles_ hereby authorized and empowered to act as Attorney for the prosecution of this claim.

Wherefore your petitioner pray for such action of your Honorable Commission in the premises as may be deemed just and proper.

Witness:
L. H. Pai
[illegible]

[S] _George D. Robinson_

State of _Virginia_
County of _King & Queen_

[15] _Lorenzo D. Robinson_

being duly sworn [15] _____

deposes and says, that he is _____ the petitioner named in the foregoing petition, and who signed the same; that the matters therein stated are true, of the deponent's own knowledge, except as to those matters which are stated on information and belief, and as to those matters he believes them to be true; and deponent further says that he did not voluntarily serve in the Confederate army or navy, either as an officer, soldier, or sailor, or in any other capacity, at any time during the late rebellion; that he never voluntarily furnished any stores, supplies, or other material aid to said Confederate army or navy, or to the Confederate government, or to any officer, department or adherent of the same in support thereof, and that he never voluntarily accepted or exercised the functions of any office whatsoever under, or yielded voluntary support to, the said Confederate government.

Witnesses:
E. B. Montague   _George D. Robinson_
Thos. M. Garrett

Sworn and subscribed in my presence, the _ninth_ day of _May_ 1872
B. G. Taylor, Clerk of King [L. S.]
[illegible] County Court

Names and residences of witnesses who will be relied upon to prove loyalty:
Hickie Robinson   King & Queen Co Va
Dunbar Robinson   "   "   "

Names and residences of witnesses who will be relied upon to prove [illegible] in the foregoing petition:
Hickie Robinson
Dunbar Robinson

Post office address of claimant: _King & Queen [illegible]_
Post office address of attorney: _Walker[illegible]_

Rule 11. If the claim has heretofore been presented to any branch of the government, state when, and what action was taken upon it.
14. Claimants sign here.
15. Give the name of all the petitioners.
16. If more than one petitioner, insert the words "each for himself," [illegible] insert "one of" in the proper blanks.

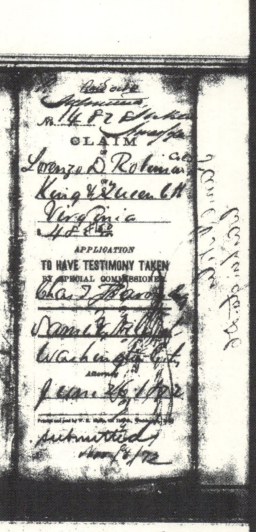

NARA 169

Before the Commissioners of Claims,
Under Act of Congress of March 3, 1871.

In the matter of the claim of *James D. Robinson* ...
... ...
and State of *Virginia* ...

Comes now the Claimant *Charles F. Parry*, Esq., Special Commissioner for the State of *Virginia* ..., and represents that he has heretofore filed with the above-named Commissioners a Petition for the allowance of a claim for property (?) *taken* ... for the use of the army of the United States, which claim, as stated below, arose and accrued the sum of *five thousand dollars*.

That the said claim, stated by items and embracing therefrom all such items as refer to the DAMAGE, DESTRUCTION and LOSS, also to the USE, of property; to accounts for unnecessary DEPREDATIONS of troops and other persons upon the property, or to RENT or compensation for the occupation of buildings, grounds or other real estate, is as follows:

No.	Description and Explanation	Amount	Value
1	Two (2) horses		300.00
2	One new saddle		10.00
3	10 bush. l. of corn		
4	700 pound of bacon		45.00
5	One barrel of extra fish		10.00
6	28 with a pig		10.00
7	One half (½) barrel of flour		7.50
		$	482.50

NARA 170

That aforesaid in the Petition referred to, the property in question was taken from said **Lorenzo D Robinson**, _Knight_ **Tazewell** in the State of **Virginia**, for the use of a portion of the army of the United States, known as (3) **Cavalry**, and commanded by **Gene Phil Sheridan**, and that the persons who took or received the property, or who authorized or directed it to be taken or furnished, were the following:

Name	Rank	Regiment, Corps or Station
Phil Sheridan	Maj Gen	6th Cavalry Division

That the property was removed to (4) **Camp** _____ and used by (5) _and troops_ ; all this on or about the ____ day of **June**, in the year 186_4_, as appears by the petition presented to the _Ct (Claims)_.

That by the following named persons, the claimant ____ loyal ____ against the United States in the said ____, his sympathies were constantly with the cause of the United States ____ he did ____ own will and accord, ____ ____ ____ to injure said cause or retard its success, and did ____ ____ willing to ____ ____ of United upon, in aid and assist the cause of the Union, its supporters, so as to ____ and ____ by any ____ of the ____

Archie Robinson _Knight Tazewell, 6th Q_
Dunlap Robinson ____

14828 **Office of the**
Commissioners of Claims.

Washington, D.C., Aug 31, 1872.

MEMORANDUM:

Lorenzo Robinson
King & Queen Co
Va

Good Union Man

Mr. Massey Collector
of Customs at West Point
and Hansford Anderson
Informants —

Report of Spl Agent
Geo Tucker

"J"

MARRIAGE LICENSE.

VIRGINIA, King William County to wit:

To any Person Licensed to Celebrate Marriages.

You are hereby authorized to join together in the Holy State of Matrimony, according to the rites and ceremonies of your Church, or religious denomination, and the laws of the Commonwealth of Virginia, James Campbell and Octavia Bingham (colored persons).

Given under my hand, as Clerk of the County Court of King William this 24 day of December 1867.

_____ CLERK.

CERTIFICATE TO OBTAIN A MARRIAGE LICENSE.
To be annexed to the License, required by Act passed 15th March, 1861.

Time of Marriage, 1867 Decem 25
Place of Marriage, Centreville
Full names of Parties Married, James Campbell & Octavia Bingham
Age of Husband, 45
Age of Wife, 25
Condition of Husband, (widowed or single,) Single
Condition of Wife, (widowed or single,) Single
Place of Husband's Birth, King William
Place of Wife's Birth, do
Place of Husband's Residence, do
Place of Wife's Residence, do
Names of Husband's Parents, _____
Names of Wife's Parents, Stephen Bingham
Occupation of Husband, Farmer

Given under my hand this 24 day of December 1867.

_____ CLERK.

MINISTER'S RETURN OF MARRIAGE.

I certify, that on the 25 day of December, 1867, at 8 o'clock, I united in marriage the above named and described parties, under authority of the annexed License. Lorenzy Robinson

☞ The Minister celebrating a Marriage is required, within ten days thereafter, to return the License to the Office of the Clerk who issued the same, with an endorsement thereon of the FACT of such marriage, and of the TIME and PLACE of celebrating the same.

MARRIAGE LICENSE.

VIRGINIA, King and Queen County, to wit:

To any Person Licensed to Celebrate Marriages:

You are hereby authorized to join together in the Holy State of Matrimony, according to the rites and ceremonies of your Church, or religious denomination, and the laws of the Commonwealth of Virginia, Charles Brown and Leah Robinson free persons.

Given under my hand, as Clerk of the County Court of King and Queen this 7th day of December, 1867.

Robert Pollard, Clerk.

CERTIFICATE TO OBTAIN A MARRIAGE LICENSE,

To be annexed to the License, required by Act passed 18th March, 1861.

Time of Marriage, 1867 December 7th
Place of Marriage, at the late residence of Thos. E. Edgell
Full names of Parties Married, Charles Brown & Leah Robinson
Age of Husband, 24 years
Age of Wife, 19
Condition of Husband, (widowed or single,) single
Condition of Wife, (widowed or single,) single
Place of Husband's Birth, Lancaster County Va
Place of Wife's Birth, King and Queen
Place of Husband's Residence, King and Queen
Place of Wife's Residence, King and Queen
Names of Husband's Parents,
Names of Wife's Parents,
Occupation of Husband, Farmer

Given under my hand this 7 day of December, 1867.

Robert Pollard, Clerk.

MINISTER'S RETURN OF MARRIAGE.

I certify, that on the 7 day of December, 1867, at Baraugh's, I united in marriage the above named and described parties, under authority of the annexed License.

Lorenzo Robinson

The Minister celebrating a Marriage is required, within ten days thereafter, to return the License to the Office of the Clerk who issued the same, with an endorsement thereon of the fact of such marriage, and of the time and place of celebrating the same.

MARRIAGE LICENSE.

VIRGINIA, King & Queen County to wit:

To any Person Licensed to Celebrate Marriages

You are hereby authorized to join together in the Holy State of Matrimony, according to the rites and ceremonies of your Church, or religious denomination, and the laws of the Commonwealth of Virginia, James Campbell and Octavia Brashear Brashear

Given under my hand, as Clerk of the County Court of King & Queen this 24 day of December 1867.

_____ CLERK.

CERTIFICATE TO OBTAIN A MARRIAGE LICENSE,
To be annexed to the License, required by Act passed 15th March, 1861.

Time of Marriage, 1867 December 25
Place of Marriage, Taylorsville
Full names of Parties Married, James Campbell & Octavia Brashear
Age of Husband, 65
Age of Wife, 25
Condition of Husband, (widowed or single,) Single
Condition of Wife, (widowed or single,) Single
Place of Husband's Birth, King & Queen
Place of Wife's Birth, do
Place of Husband's Residence, do
Place of Wife's Residence, do
Names of Husband's Parents,
Names of Wife's Parents, Stephen Brashear
Occupation of Husband, Farmer

Given under my hand this 24 day of December 1867.

_____ CLERK.

MINISTER'S RETURN OF MARRIAGE.

I certify, that on 25 day of December 1867, at 8 P.M., I united in marriage the above named and described parties, under authority of the annexed License. Lorenzo Robinson

The Minister celebrating a Marriage is required, within ten days thereafter, to return the License to the Office of the Clerk who issued the same, with an endorsement thereon of the FACT of such marriage, and of the TIME and PLACE of celebrating the same.

MARRIAGE LICENSE.

VIRGINIA, King and Queen County to wit:

To any Person Licensed to Celebrate Marriages:

You are hereby authorized to join together in the Holy State of Matrimony, according to the rites and ceremonies of your Church, or religious denomination, and the laws of the Commonwealth of Virginia, Charles Brown and Sarah Robinson free persons

Given under my hand, as Clerk of the County Court of King and Queen this 7th day of December, 1867.

Robert D. Ellett, CLERK.

CERTIFICATE TO OBTAIN A MARRIAGE LICENSE,
To be annexed to the License, required by Act passed 15th March, 1861.

Time of Marriage, 1867 December 7th
Place of Marriage, at the late residence of Rev'd E. Wyatt
Full names of Parties Married, Charles Brown & Sarah Robinson
Age of Husband, 24 years
Age of Wife, 19
Condition of Husband, (widowed or single,) single
Condition of Wife, (widowed or single,) single
Place of Husband's Birth, Lancaster County Va
Place of Wife's Birth, King and Queen
Place of Husband's Residence, King and Queen
Place of Wife's Residence, King and Queen
Names of Husband's Parents,
Names of Wife's Parents,
Occupation of Husband, Farmer

Given under my hand this 7 day of December, 1867.

Robert D. Ellett, CLERK.

MINISTER'S RETURN OF MARRIAGE.

I CERTIFY, That on the 7 day of December, 1867, at Baptist I united in marriage the above named and described parties, under authority of the annexed License. Lorenzo Robinson

MARRIAGE LICENSE.

VIRGINIA, King & Queen County, to wit:

To any Person Licensed to Celebrate Marriages:

You are hereby authorized to join together in the Holy State of Matrimony, according to the rites and ceremonies of your Church, or religious denomination, and the laws of the Commonwealth of Virginia. Mr. George W. Henderson and Miss Elizabeth Robinson.

Given under my hand, as Clerk of the .... County .... Court of King & Queen this 21st day of December, 1871.

L. A. Tyler, dep'ty, CLERK.

CERTIFICATE TO OBTAIN A MARRIAGE LICENSE.

To be annexed to the License, required by Act passed 15th March, 1861.

Time of Marriage, 1871 Decr. 21st
Place of Marriage, King & Queen County
Full names of Parties Married, Geo. W. Henderson & Elizabeth Robinson
Age of Husband, 41 years
Age of Wife, 24 Do
Condition of Husband (widowed or single), Widower
Condition of Wife (widowed or single), Single
Place of Husband's Birth, King & Queen County
Place of Wife's Birth, Do Do
Place of Husband's Residence, Do Do
Place of Wife's Residence, Do Do
Names of Husband's Parents, Peter Henderson & Elizabeth
Names of Wife's Parents, John Robinson & Mary
Occupation of Husband, Farmer & mechanic

Given under my hand this 21st day of December, 1871.

L. A. Tyler, dep'ty, CLERK.

MINISTER'S RETURN OF MARRIAGE.

I CERTIFY, that on the 21 day of December, 1871, at Gregers, I united in Marriage the above named and described parties, under authority of the annexed License. Lorenzo G. Robinson

The minister celebrating a marriage is required, within ten days thereafter, to return the License to the Office of the Clerk who issued the same, with an endorsement thereon of the face of such marriage, and of the time and place of celebrating the same.

MARRIAGE LICENSE.

VIRGINIA, King & Queen County, to wit:

To any Person Licensed to Celebrate Marriages:

You are hereby authorized to join together in the Holy State of Matrimony, according to the rites and ceremonies of your Church, or religious denomination, and the laws of the Commonwealth of Virginia, Mr. George W. Henderson and Miss Elizabeth Robinson,

Given under my hand, as Clerk of the _____ County, Court of King & Queen this 21st day of December 1871.

L. A. Tyler depty, CLERK.

CERTIFICATE TO OBTAIN A MARRIAGE LICENSE,
To be annexed to the License, required by Act passed 15th March, 1861.

Time of Marriage, 1871 Decr. 21st
Place of Marriage, King & Queen County
Full names of Parties Married, Geo. W. Henderson & Elizabeth Robinson
Age of Husband, 41 years
Age of Wife, 24 do
Condition of Husband (widowed or single), Widower
Condition of Wife (widowed or single), Single
Place of Husband's Birth, King & Queen County
Place of Wife's Birth, Do Do
Place of Husband's Residence, Do Do
Place of Wife's Residence, Do Do
Names of Husband's Parents, Peter Henderson & Elizabeth
Names of Wife's Parents, John Robinson & Mary
Occupation of Husband, Farmer & mechanic

Given under my hand this 21 day of December 1871.
L. A. Tyler depty, CLERK.

MINISTER'S RETURN OF MARRIAGE.

I CERTIFY, that on the 21 day of December 1871, at Gosges, I united in Marriage the above named and described parties, under authority of the annexed License. Lorenzo G. Robinson

The minister celebrating a marriage is required, within ten days thereafter, to return the License to the Office of the Clerk who issued the same, with an endorsement thereon of the fact of such marriage, and of the time and place of celebrating the same.

MARRIAGE LICENSE.

Virginia, King & Queen County to wit:

TO ANY PERSON LICENSED TO CELEBRATE MARRIAGES:

You are hereby authorized to join together in the Holy State of Matrimony, according to the rites and ceremonies of your Church, or religious denomination, and the laws of the Commonwealth of Virginia, Wiley Lockley and Phillis Ann Kaufman

Given under my hand, as Clerk of the County Court of King & Queen Co, this 17th day of December 1872
Mottewood Bird D. Clerk.

CERTIFICATE TO OBTAIN A MARRIAGE LICENSE.

To be annexed to the License, required by Act passed 13th March, 1861.

Time of Marriage, December 19° 1872
Place of Marriage, King & Queen Co
Full names of Parties Married, Wiley Lockley and Phillis Ann Kaufman
Colour, Colored
Age of Husband, Twenty five years
Age of Wife, Twenty three
Condition of Husband (widowed or single), Single
Condition of Wife (widowed or single), Single
Place of Husband's Birth, King & Queen Co
Place of Wife's Birth, do do
Place of Husband's Residence, do do
Place of Wife's Residence, do do
Names of Husband's Parents, John Gilmore & Fanny Lockley
Names of Wife's Parents, George Kaufman & Polly Robinson
Occupation of Husband, Farmer

Given under my hand this 17th day of December 1872
Mottewood Bird D. Clerk.

MINISTER'S RETURN OF MARRIAGE.

I certify that on the 19 day of December 1872, at _____ I united in Marriage the above named and described parties, under authority of the annexed License.

The minister celebrating a marriage is required, within ten days thereafter, to return the License to the Office of the Clerk who issued the same, with an endorsement thereon of the fact of such marriage, and of the time and PLACE of celebrating the same.

MARRIAGE LICENSE.

Virginia, King & Queen County to wit:

TO ANY PERSON LICENSED TO CELEBRATE MARRIAGES:
You are hereby authorized to join together in the Holy State of Matrimony, according to the rites and ceremonies of your Church, or religious denomination, and the laws of the Commonwealth of Virginia, Wiley Lockley and Phillis Ann Kaufman

Given under my hand, as Clerk of the County Court of King & Queen Co. this 17th day of December 1872.

Pottswood Bird D. Clerk.

CERTIFICATE TO OBTAIN A MARRIAGE LICENSE.

Time of Marriage, December 19, 1872
Place of Marriage, King & Queen Co.
Full names of Parties Married, Wiley Lockley and Phillis Ann Kaufman
Colour, Colored
Age of Husband, Twenty five years
Age of Wife, Twenty three "
Condition of Husband (widowed or single), Single
Condition of Wife (widowed or single), Single
Place of Husband's Birth, King & Queen Co.
Place of Wife's Birth, do do
Place of Husband's Residence, do do
Place of Wife's Residence, do do
Names of Husband's Parents, John Gilmore & Fanny Lockley
Names of Wife's Parents, George Kaufman & Patty Robinson
Occupation of Husband, Farmer

Given under my hand this 17th day of December 1872.

Pottswood Bird D. Clerk.

MINISTER'S RETURN OF MARRIAGE.

I certify, that on the 19 day of October 1872, at _____ I united in Marriage the above named and described parties, under authority of the annexed License.

Joseph Robinson

The minister celebrating a marriage is required, within ten days thereafter, to return the License to the Office of the Clerk who issued the same, with an endorsement thereon of the fact of such marriage, and of the time and place of celebrating the same.

MARRIAGE LICENSE.

Virginia, King & Queen County to wit:

TO ANY PERSON LICENSED TO CELEBRATE MARRIAGES:

You are hereby authorized to join together in the Holy State of Matrimony, according to the rites and ceremonies of your Church, or religious denomination, and the laws of the Commonwealth of Virginia, Curtis Robinson and Judy Carter

Given under my hand, as Clerk of the County Court of King & Queen Co. this 9th day of January 1873.

Spotswood Bird, Clerk.

CERTIFICATE TO OBTAIN A MARRIAGE LICENSE.
To be annexed to the License, required by Act passed 15th March, 1861.

Time of Marriage, January 20th 1873
Place of Marriage, King & Queen County
Full names of Parties Married, Curtis Robinson & Judy Carter
Colour, Black
Age of Husband, Fifty two years
Age of Wife, 45 "
Condition of Husband (widowed or single), widowed
Condition of Wife (widowed or single), Single
Place of Husband's Birth, King & Queen Co
Place of Wife's Birth, do
Place of Husband's Residence, King & Queen Co
Place of Wife's Residence, do
Names of Husband's Parents, Jim Robinson & Mary Gardner
Names of Wife's Parents, Gabriel Carter &
Occupation of Husband, Farmer

Given under my hand this 9th day of January 1873
Spotswood Bird, Clerk.

MINISTER'S RETURN OF MARRIAGE.

I certify, that on the 16 day of January 1873, at ____ I united in Marriage the above named and described parties, under authority of the annexed License.

The minister celebrating a marriage is required, within ten days thereafter, to return the License to the Office of the Clerk who issued the same, with an endorsement thereon of the FACT of such marriage, and of the TIME and PLACE of celebrating the same.

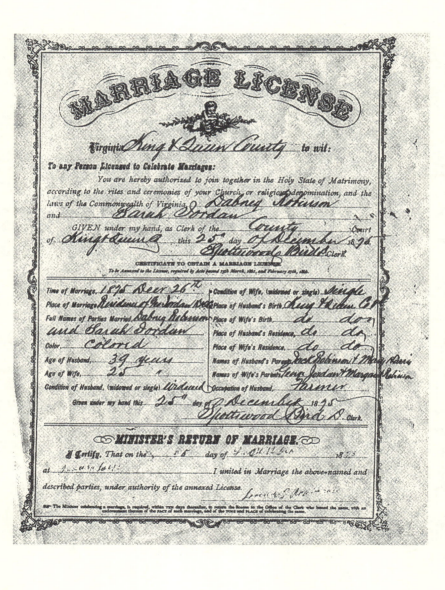

Printed in the United States
By Bookmasters